In SEARCH OF THE STONE OF DESTINY

Copyright © 2009. All rights reserved, including the right to reproduce this work or any portion thereof by any means whatsoever.

For bulk and special sales, please contact:
searchbook6228@gmail.com

For a copy of chapter reference Notes
please reply to the above email address.

Library of Congress Catolog Number: PAU 003427513

ISBN: 978-0-9996000-0-9

This is a work of fiction, and any names of characters or places mentioned, or incidents, are the product of the author's creative genius, and any likeness to actual persons, living or dead, except for actual historical figures is entirely coincidental.

CORONATION CHAIR IN WESTMINSTER ABBEY WITH STONE OF DESTINY THAT JACOB SLEPT UPON ACCORDING TO CELTIC LEGEND.

"And the Lord God shall give unto him [Jesus] the THRONE OF HIS FATHER DAVID: and he shall reign over the house of Jacob forever." (Luke 1: 32–33, (KJV)

Acknowledgments

I would like to thank Lujean Burak and Karla Bradshaw for reading my initial draft that encouraged me to go forward.

A special thanks to Allison at First Editing for providing suggestions and recommendations to enrich my characters and the flow of the story.

Lastly, I would like to thank Christine Horner from The Book Cover Whisperer who did such an amazing jacket design and provided guidance on the book formatting.

Contents

The Murder of the Curator	1
Dan, Bruce and Scotland	20
The Scarlet Thread	28
The Murder of Alidair Sinclair	33
The Murder of King Zedekiah	47
The Coronation of Queen Teia	59
The Second "Overturn"	78
Lecture on Early Celtic History	83
Secret Societies and Bloolines	91
Templars and the Inquisition	106
A Dinner Date with Sara	108
The Fifth Monarchy Men	115
The Oxford Murders	126
Genealogy Charts	116
The Missing Hearts	145
Finding the Ark	156
McNair turns Traitor	166
The Modern Druids	187
Creation prior to man	214
Dan a serpent	222
Invasion of the Body Snatchers	227
More invasions coming	231
Iron mixed with clay	235
In Search of the King	239

DNA clues to Kingly lineage	241
Sara provides clues	246
Sara meets her father's old Flame	250
A shocking past revealed	254
Simonides makes headlines	257
Simonides heals the sick	259
Simonides is worshipped	264
Father John is killed	271
A strange solution	276
Alex and Kelly reunite	280
Smithe provides the answer	286
The final battle	293

Introduction

The following explanation appeared in the official (*Westminster Abbey Official Guide,* 1994, pp. 46-47):

"Coronation Chair—the Coronation Chair was made for Edward I to enclose the famous Stone of Scone, which he seized in 1296 and brought from Scotland to the Abbey ... Legends abound concerning this mysterious object and tradition identifies this stone with the one upon which Jacob rested his head at Bethel—'And Jacob rose up early in the morning, and took the stone that he had put for his pillows, and set it up for a pillar, and poured oil on the top of it' (Genesis 28:18). Jacob's sons carried it to Egypt and from thence it passed to Spain with King Gathelus, son of Cecrops, the builder of Athens.

"About 700 BC it appears in Ireland, whither it was carried by the Spanish king's son Simon Brech, on his invasion of that island. There it was placed upon the sacred Hill of Tara, and called 'Lia-Fail,' the 'fatal' stone [i.e., stone of fate], or 'stone of destiny' ... Fergus Mor MacEirc (d. 501?), the founder of the Scottish monarchy, and one of the Blood Royal of Ireland, received it in [the area of Iona in southwest] Scotland, and Kenneth MacAlpin (d. 846) finally deposited it in the Monastery of Scone (846)"

Legend has it that when Irish kings sat upon the stone,' it groaned' if the king was a legitimate heir, but remained silent if he was a fake.

On December 25, 1950, the sacred stone was robbed from the Abbey by Scottish Nationalist, only to be found and returned shortly thereafter.

On July 3rd, 1996, Prime Minister John Major made a stunning announcement. The Stone of Scone was to be returned to Scotland, and brought back to England only for future coronations (The Coronation Chair, Westminster-Abbey, Faith at the heart of the Nation, Westminster-Abbey.org/our history/the coronation-chair)

Chapter One

It's a warm summer evening as Colin, Sean, and Maureen drive through the rough English countryside on their way to London in an old Morris Marina singing Scottish songs. They are on a journey that will shock the nation and prevent the coronation of the new King.

Scots shall flourish strong and free,
unless proved false the prophecy;
that where the Stone shall yet be found,
a Scot by princely right is crowned.

As the sun dips below the horizon, the sky is an array of pinks and purples, and soon night will be looming over them. After an eight-hour bumpy drive, they finally arrive in London England. Before they go to their hotel room where they have previously booked for three days at the Blackfriars Place, they take a ride around the city filled with tourists. Maureen, the ring-leader at twenty-five, tells twenty-year-olds Sean and Colin that she would like to eat dinner at Saint Martin's in the field.

"Let's eat at the café in the Crept where my mother took me to eat when I was here ten years ago. They have great salads there," she says.

"I'd like to see if the Fish & Chips tastes as good as back home," Colin says.

"I'm starving and could eat almost anything," says Sean, "let's do it!"

"How was your fish & Chips?" asks Maureen.

"Not as good as back home," says Colin.

After finishing their dinner, they ride around the city filled with tourists from all over the world who have come to see the pangenetic coronation of the new King. It has been years before any of them have been to London. They can't believe how the city's skyline has changed with so many new high-rise buildings, but there are still many of the old sites left for tourists to drink in of the old history that is so meaningful to them. Like the rest of the tourists, they are curious to see Big Ben, St. Paul's cathedral and Trafalgar Square, but that will have to wait until tomorrow as it is getting dark and they are very tired.

***

After a good night's sleep and a hearty breakfast, the troop head on out like all of the rest of the tourists.

"Look, the mousetrap is still playing," says Maureen. "My mother took me to see it when we were here. She said it was the longest play ever and it is still going on."

"I want to go on the London Eye," says Colin.

"Let's go to Trafalgar Square first," says Sean. The trio park their car and walk over to the crowded circle of tourists. People are walking about and sitting around the monuments listening to a musician singing, and watching artists doing face painting, and chalk sculpture drawings on the pavement.

The three of them sit down near a stone monument to watch the activities and to meditate upon what the world is about to experience. Sean thinks how much fun they are having and for a moment has forgotten why he was even there.

'Why can't these people understand what he understands about the monarchy?' He thinks. 'How could they have been so complacent about parliament?' But then again, they didn't have parents that helped him understand real history. How the present monarchy had nicked their families birthright to the throne.

Maureen enjoys the melody of the singer for a moment and then thinks about why she has come and what she must do to make things right for her family. She recounts how many times her father and grandfather have spoken of how their families' heritage had been usurped from them, and now she was going to make them proud of her. Her skills as a Veterinarian would prepare her for the atrocious job she must perform.

After an hour they tour Westminster Abby with many other tourists who can't wait for the coronation of the new King. It's been months since it was announced that the old monarch had died by the code words, 'London Bridge is down' and in a few days a new King would be crowned.

They have been waiting patiently for five years, thinking, planning this event on an unsuspecting country. Finally, the time had arrived, in a few days the new King would be crowned and the nation would be celebrating his coronation. Shawn, Colin and Maureen were having a celebration of their own as in a few days they would be the focus of one of the most incredible crimes in England's history.

There was one gigantic difference between them and the rest of the tourists! They were not there to see where Harry and Meghan got married and the new King crowned, but how to enter the building to carry out their sinister plot! As the trio walk through the Abby and view the coronation chair with the other visitors, Colin spots a window in the back that will help them gain access in the evening as the city sleeps. Sean, who is an electrician, observes there is no power to the window and that sirens will only go off in the morning as cleaning crews enter through the doors.

***

At two o'clock in the morning, at Westminster Abbey in London, one of the oldest churches in the world. Colin parks the car and he and his two friends, Sean and Maureen, head toward the back of the church with confidence.

After a brief moment, they crouch near a window. "Ready?" Sean said, and Colin and Maureen nod. Then, as quietly as he can, Sean smashes his crowbar into the basement window, shattering the glass. "Let's go," Sean says.

One by one, the trio crawl through the cellar window into the basement of the church. Quietly, they walk up the cement steps leading to the Abbey and head down the dark corridor, each holding a flashlight and a crowbar. The light throws shadows on the walls and in corners. The young twenty-year-olds have staked out the Abbey previously and know exactly where the curator's office is as well as what they have come for—the Stone of Destiny.

Two weeks ago, Dr. Alexander Flanders, head of Ancestry Institute in Wales, and internationally known author and lecturer on royal families through DNA analysis— had given a talk on his own Scottish kingly lineage to King Robert the Bruce. The three young radical nationalists were in attendance.

The oak coronation chair was built in the fourteenth century to house the Stone of Destiny, also known as the Coronation Stone, a block of sandstone that was used for centuries for the coronation of Scottish and English monarchs.

The renowned curator, Dr. Alexander Flanders, is sitting in his office looking at his computer when he hears a strange noise coming from down the hallway. *'That's odd,'* he thinks. He is six-eight, heavyset, in his seventies with a hooked nose resembling Charles de Gaulle. He gets up from his chair and enters the hallway, scanning his surroundings. It's eerily quiet. *'Maybe I'm just hearing things,'* he says with a chuckle. Just then, he's struck hard on his head and pain shoots down his spine. His knees begin to buckle and he hits the floor with a hard smack.

"You guys get the stone and I'll catch up," Maureen stammers. The old man has stopped breathing as a pool of blood oozes out of his head. Her hands shaking, she pulls out a knife. Then she rips the old man's shirt open to expose his wrinkled, sagging flesh. She looks around once more, then surgically removes the heart and places it in a plastic bag.

The two young men scamper down the hall and spot the coronation chair and immediately start to pry the stone loose from the wooden chair. There is a chain, which is connected to iron rings that are imbedded into the stone.

"The chain is catching the sides of the chair," Colin says. He's almost six feet, medium build, and has sandy-blond hair.

"I'll push and you pry," Sean yells. He's on his knees and examining the bottom of the stone.

Maureen has caught up and looks worried that an alarm will go off triggering Scotland yard and tells them, "Hurry up, you guys!"

Sean and Colin strain to free the chair. It makes a horrible scratching noise, but it is wriggling free.

"It's moving," Sean whispers. "Hurry, put the blanket down on the floor."

Just then, the stone slides out and slams into Maureen's shin, then slams onto the floor with a loud bang that echoes in the high-ceilinged building.

"Ouch! You stupid morons!" Maureen shouts. Pain shoots up and down her leg.

Colin looks around; he knows they are being too loud. "Shut up and let's get out of here."

Maureen has tears in her eyes, but she hasn't come all this way for nothing. She bites back the pain and before she leaves, she carves the initials *Dan* on the side of the chair.

"Hurry up," Sean says.

With all the strength they can muster, the trio drag the stone on top of the blanket down the corridor toward the escape window. Sean exists first and Colin and Maureen lift the stone on end so Sean can grasp it and slide it down a board they brought along to the ground. Maureen and Colin then exit and the three of them load the three-hundred-pound stone into the boot. The exhausted thieves get into their car and turn the corner and disappear.

***

DI Jonathon Smithe sits in his office and stares out the window. Sweat drips down his brow. The air conditioner broke early this morning and it's stifling. The dinky fan that's propped on the corner of his desk does nothing but blow the warm air around.

It's been a quiet few months. After twenty-seven years on the force, Smithe is getting ready to retire. His wife, Martha, has been prompting him to retire, as, in her words, he's too "tired and cranky." But the truth is that Smithe loves his job. He's in good shape for a man in his mid-sixties. But on days like today, when he's done nothing but push papers around on his desk and drink coffee, he wonders if Martha is right.

Just then, the alarms go off in the Abbey, triggering Scotland Yard. DI Smithe abruptly sits up when he hears the distant wailing. In all his years, he can only count on his hand the amount of times the sirens have gone off, and it can only mean one thing: Someone is trying to nick something at Westminster Abbey.

Smithe rushes out of his office and jumps into his car. With his car siren blaring and lights flashing, he drives to St. Edwards Chapel. When he arrives, he pulls his car up, then dashes toward the entrance. His partner, DC Humphrey, is standing there looking as pale as a ghost.

"What's going on here, Humphrey?"

"You're not gonna like what you see," Humphrey says, his blue eyes looking concerned.

When they head inside, Smithe is shocked. *'Humphrey wasn't kidding'*, he thinks. An elderly man is lying on his back as a pool of blood surrounds his head. His shirt is ripped open revealing a large tattoo, and his heart has been surgically removed. There are scratches in the floor, as if something heavy had been dragged down the corridor and then outside.

"Bloody hell, what a bloody mess" says Smithe as he looks at the curator's lifeless body and makes the sign of the cross! "What happened here?" Smithe asks. He kneels next to the man and observes the strange tattoo on his chest. The man's eyes are open, glazed over, but there is a peaceful look on his face. He searches for signs of a struggle. There are no bruises on the man's face, and there are no marks on his knuckles to indicate that he'd been struggling or trying to fight someone off. The top of his head is smashed in.

"What's that tattoo on his chest?" Smithe asks.

"It looks like a family crest of some sort," Humphrey replies.

Smithe orders Humphrey to have Sargent McGinty at Forensics to check it out.

"Will do," Humphrey says. "Find out from security if any videos will show anything as well," Smithe adds.

Smithe takes a moment to scan the scene for every detail. He has worked many crime scenes and has a certain routine.

He can't help noticing all of the wall charts in the curator's office which are quite unusual and remarks to Humphrey, "I wonder what the curator was into, and look at the Crest on the wall that looks exactly like the tattoo on the curator's chest. I wonder if there is a connection to why he was killed."

Smithe continues to look around the curator's office. It's small, cramped, and cluttered with paperwork and several books on end-time prophecy are on his desk. His computer is still left on indicating he was watching a website on several secret societies. Hanging on the walls are genealogy charts of the kings of Ireland, Scotland, and England that trace their royal bloodlines back to King David of Israel. There are also variations of the name 'Dan,' such as Dardanelles, Danude, Danniper, Dansmark, Danegal, Londonderry, Dunsmore, Dundee, Dunraven, etc.

Humphrey scans the wall charts and remarks, "Look at those biblical scriptures next to that picture of the Devil, I wonder what these verses mean?"

"The snorting of his horses was heard from Dan: the whole land trembled at the sound of the neighing of his strong ones; for they are come, and have devoured the land, and all that is in it; the city, and those that dwell therein. For, behold, I will send serpents, cockatrices, among you,

which will not be charmed, and they shall bite you, saith the LORD" Jer. 8:15-17.

"I'm familiar with the scripture under it as quoted by the apostle Paul," says Smithe.

"For we wrestle not against flesh and blood, but against principalities, against powers, against the rulers of the darkness of this world, against spiritual wickedness in high places" Eph. 6:12.

"Something very sinister and bizarre is going on here," replies Smithe.

Just then, one of the other detectives who has been examining the coronation chair, says, "Boss, you need to see what was carved into the coronation chair where the stone was nicked."

Smithe and Humphrey walk down the corridor and examine the chair where someone has carved the initials *Dan* in the side of the chair.

Smithe is intrigued. In all of his years on the force, he has never seen anything like this. He has been called one of the best police detectives in the business by his peers. If anyone can solve this case, he can. His methods may seem a bit unconventional and even a bit peculiar, but he always gets his man. "I wonder what all of this Dan stuff means. Humphrey, get the names of everyone who is connected to this museum and find out if there are any names with *Dan*."

"I'm on it!" Humphrey says.

***

Soon after the theft, instructions come from Scotland Yard to set up roadblocks on all roads that lead out of England. A press conference is given with Police Chief Jeff Stanton, who informs the public of the theft and asks that everyone be on the lookout for the famous stone.

Colin, Sean, and Maureen are silent. The stone is concealed in the boot with a coat covering. As they near the

Scottish border, Sean pulls into the gas station and parks next to the pump.

"I guess you've heard that the Coronation Stone was nicked from the Abbey?" The gas attendant says as he pumps the gas. "You guys ain't got it, do you?" he jokes.

Giggling, Colin says facetiously, "Aye, sure, it's in the boot," Maureen pales and swallows the lump in her throat.

The attendant chuckles. "Well now, I had to ask ya, for the reward is two thousand pounds for information leading to the recovery of the stone. The police have been around once asking me if I've seen anyone with the stone. If they come back, I'll tell them the stone went through this morning with three Scotsman."

They all have a hardy laugh as the three thieves drive out of town.

***

That night, long after his wife went to bed, Smithe sits in the study, his eyes blurry from staring at his computer and his notes. He is trying to figure out who would have the audacity to nick the Stone of Destiny and kill the curator from Westminster Abbey right under his nose. What is the motive? It doesn't appear that they were merely trying to nick the stone and the curator was killed by accident?

No, Dr. Flanders was into something very dark with all of those charts of Kings and bible verses on the wall next to a picture of the devil? And then there was that strange tattoo on his chest that was identical to the one on the wall. Why did the thieves want to cut out his heart? No, something told him that this was an occult act and very nefarious. His mind is getting dull from deep thought and he winds up falling asleep in his chair. He begins to dream of that horrific scene of Dr. Flanders laying on the floor in a pool of blood, bludgeoned to death with his heart ripped out! He is woken up at the crack of dawn by a nudge, and when he opens his eyes, he sees his wife Martha's smiling face. She notices that his brow is saturated with sweat and surmises he had a rough night.

"Here, love," she says, and hands him a cup of hot coffee.

Rubbing the sleep from his eyes, Smithe kisses his wife on the cheek. "Thank you love," he says, and sips the coffee. After a quick shower, he gathers his things and heads to the office.

***

Once there, he checks his messages—seventeen in total—and ignores all of them. Instead, he calls McGinty from the forensics labs to find out if he has any information regarding the death of the curator.

"The curator was hit on the head with a blunt instrument," McGinty says. "I'm still working out the details of what it could be. And the tattoo on his chest is a family crest of the Robert the Bruce family."

The name Robert the Bruce rings a bell, as Smithe is a history buff and wants to find out more about him.

"He was a famous king of Scotland in the Middle Ages," McGinty replies. "That's all I know."

"Thank you," Smithe replies.

Smithe types in "Robert the Bruce" into his search engine. According to his research, Robert the Bruce, King of Scotland, was invaded by King Edward 1 of England in 1296 when the King refused to annex Scotland to England. Bruce fled into hiding, and King Edward took the talisman back to England. DI Smithe is beginning to understand why someone, perhaps from Scotland might want to nick the stone and take it back to its origin— but why kill the curator who seemed to have an identity to Scotland and cut out his heart? Smithe will also view the CCTV video in the Abbey to see if any of the thieves can be identified.

***

A trying few days have gone by for Smithe, but unexpectedly he is informed that the stone has turned up in Edinburgh, Scotland and it is being returned to England for the Kings coronation.

Smithe is weaving through traffic as he heads toward Westminster Abbey to continue his investigation of the theft and to investigate any suspicious characters who might show up for the ceremonial of the stones return.

He quickly turns up the volume on the radio when he hears the "breaking news" music.

The radio announcer says, "We interrupt this program for a very important announcement. To the joy of all in Great Britain, the legendary Stone of Destiny, which had been nicked from the Coronation Chair in Westminster Abbey, has been returned from Scotland. The stone was discovered early this morning. Scotland Yard has begun urgent enquiries. As you recall, the stone is so important to our heritage ever since King Edward I conquered Scotland in 1296, and every king since then has been crowned upon it. Now our coronation of the new King can go on as scheduled. According to the legend, whoever possesses the stone has the power to rule the world! Now back to the music."

Smithe turns off the radio and sighs. This is his most high-profile case, and it is turning into a circus. When he arrives at the Abbey, he sighs again when he sees the press, photographers, and reporters already there. Smithe flashes his badge at an officer at a checkpoint and is waved through, where he then parks off to the side. The crowd rushes toward the grassy area where the stone has been returned and lies covered with the blue-and-white flag of Scotland.

Smithe meanders his way through the crowd, which is barricaded off by yellow roping. After showing his badge and is waved through, he makes his way to the stone. Clicks of cameras can be heard, but otherwise it is silent. He kneels next to the stone and pulls back the flag. He almost has an urge to touch it, but doesn't. It truly is magnificent.

"Well, I'll be! The little lady has returned!", he says out loud.

It didn't take long to locate the stone as only a few days have gone by as surveillance cameras showed pictures revealing certain clothing aspects of the thieves, but not their faces as they were wearing masks. An anonymous caller helped police to find the stone, but the thieves and the heart was still missing!

Smithe is mystified as to why someone would kill the curator, cut out his heart and nick the stone! Were they trying to send a message to England because of what King Edward had done to Robert the Bruce? But for the moment he is jubilant and shouts, "Long live the King!"

The crowd erupts into applause. Police officers then load the 300-pound stone onto a stretcher and carry it back into the Abbey while photographers take multiple pictures. Cameras flashing in every direction! It truly is a remarkable day.

***

After reminiscing about the crime scene, and thinking about the fact that Dr. Flanders's heart had been surgically removed, and reading the biblical scriptures next to a picture of the devil in the curator's office, Smithe arranges a meeting with Father Benedetti, his parish priest at All Saints Church. After Smithe picks up Humphrey, they are on their way to visit. He can't help but wonder if there is a demonic influence in the case.

"Good morning Father Benedetti," Smithe says as he greets him in the rectory and introduces Humphrey. They exchange handshakes.

Smithe informs him of the bizarre case he is investigating to see if Father Benedetti can provide him with any insight.

"It certainly sounds like something very satanic to me," says Father Benedetti. "There are many strange cases of demonic possession mentioned in the bible."

"That's something I am unfamiliar with and need your advice as to how to deal with this situation," replies Smithe.

"Do you really believe that there is a spiritual world out there, Father Benedetti?" Humphrey asks curiously.

"Indeed, my son, do you remember the story when Jesus cast out the devil in Luke 4:33, and Luke 8:27-33?"

"Sorry Father, I'm not a big fan of the bible," replies Humphrey.

Father Benedetti writes down Luke 8:2; 9:38-42; Mark 9:17-28; Matthew 10:1; 12:43:-45; 15:22-28; Acts 16:16-18; on a sheet of paper and hands it to Humphrey. "I suggest you read these scriptures my son and then tell me you are not a believer."

"Ok, I will," says Humphrey.

"Even if you don't believe the Bible accounts Detectives, do you remember the story of the *Three Faces of Eve* in which three distinct beings took over her body at different times?"

"I do recall that story," says Smithe.

"Believe me gentlemen, this stuff can be very dangerous. We have many documented cases in the Catholic Church of demon possession in which we have performed exorcisms. Adolf Hitler was known to dabble in black magic and occult, and there are many sources that believe he was possessed by the Devil," says Benedetti.

"Thank you for your candor Father," says Smithe. The two Detectives leave and drive home. That night they both had an eerie feeling in every room they went into.

***

The next morning, Smithe and Humphrey are on their way to visit with renowned Dr. Robert McNair, PhD, the distinguished Professor of Archaeology and Biblical History at the University of Glasgow. When they arrive on campus, Smithe and Humphrey exit the car. The campus is bustling with students rushing to class or just hanging out in the courtyard. After having to ask two separate students where the history building is located, they finally arrive at the main door, up a few steps, and step into the first-floor lobby. There's a woman sitting behind the information desk.

"Good morning, miss. I'm DI Smithe from Scotland Yard, and this is my partner DC Humphrey. We are here to see Dr. McNair. He is expecting us. Can you tell me where I can find the Professor?"

The woman shakes her head and her curly brown hair bounces. "Yes, detective, go down that corridor and make a right. His office is the second door."

"Thank you," Smithe says.

Dr. McNair is a very handsome, distinguished-looking man in his mid-forties. He is renowned in the field of archeology and religious history, and has won many awards, including the prestigious Howard Carter Award. Before coming to the University of Glasgow, he was Director of the National Museum of Wales and received the degree of doctor of science and is the author of many books on early Britain. His research appeared in many science journals, especially his discoveries of prehistoric and early Medieval Britain. He is very much an Indiana Jones-type of figure.

As they walk down the corridor, Humphrey says, "I really don't know what all this fuss is about a stone that everyone wants to possess."

When they reach Dr. McNair's classroom, Smithe knocks and then enters. "Good morning, Professor. I'm DI Smithe from Scotland Yard, and this is DC Humphrey."

"Good morning to you both," Dr. Robert McNair says. "Yes, come on in, detectives. I've been expecting you. What can I do for you?"

"Thank you for seeing us, Doctor. As I've said on the phone, we at Scotland Yard are trying to solve the outlandish murder of the curator and robbery of the Stone at Westminster Abbey. I understand that you are an expert on the stone's history, as you are a biblical history scholar, and I hope that you can help us solve this case."

***

"Surely, if I can be of assistance, detective, Dr. Flanders was a good friend of mine and I can't believe he is dead. We belonged to several Scottish societies together as we both have Scottish roots and I was just at a talk he gave a week ago. Please, have a seat." He gestures for the two men to sit in the front row of the classroom, and they comply.

"As you know, the stone has been returned to England," Smithe says. "Can you please explain why anyone would want to take the stone in the first place and why was it found in Scotland? It may help in our murder investigation."

McNair's eyes brighten. "Well, Detective, let me start by saying that every great king of Ireland, Scotland, and England has been crowned upon this stone, as well as Queen Victoria, King James who translated the Bible, King Henry VIII, Robert the Bruce, Richard the Lionhearted, and William the Conqueror. In 1296, King Edward I of England took the stone from Robert the Bruce, King of Scotland, when the king refused to annex Scotland to England."

"I know about Robert the Bruce as I did some research on him because Dr. Flanders had a tattoo of his family crest on his chest," says Smithe.

Humphrey furrows his brow. "But where did the stone originate from?" he asks.

"Aye! The story of the stone actually begins with the righteous patriarch Abraham of the Bible, who around 1900 BC was promised fantastic national materialistic blessings and that through his descendants the entire world would be blessed. You can read of this account in the book of Genesis. God further promised Abraham that kings would come from him and his wife Sarah, as well as culminating in the Jewish Messiah." McNair clasped his hands together in excitement. "If you are interested in reading further, the scripture references are Genesis 12:1–3, Genesis 22:16–18, and Genesis 17:6, 16."

"You mean the Christian Messiah?" Smithe asks.

"Depending upon your viewpoint, Detective," McNair responds.

Smithe continues his inquiry by stating that he is somewhat familiar with the biblical account, being a Catholic and all, and can see why this stone, if it is the same one of the Bible, would be of special interest for the coronation of the new King, and for anyone who did not want the new King to be crowned upon it. "But why would anyone kill someone over it?" he asks.

McNair sighs. "As part of our curriculum here at the university, we have a biblical drama class, and the students have put together some Bible stories and have acted them out in order for viewers to understand the Bible and historical events relating to it. I have helped in creating these biblical stories with the drama team, and we have a whole library of dramatizations throughout history."

Smithe looks at Humphrey, and they both shrug. McNair walks over to the library shelf that contains hundreds of dramatization videos the students have created over the years. "I have a video that shows stone's significance. Do you have time to watch it?" he asks.

"How long will it take?" Smithe asks.

"About forty-five minutes," McNair states. "The students have reenacted the story of Jacob's dream as told in Genesis 28:1–28."

Humphrey laughs. "I only have to get back to feed my dog."

Smithe wishes the man would just tell him, but he obliges. "Let's watch the video."

Dr. McNair finds the video, then inserts it into the DVD player. Then he rushes over to dim the lights. The three men sit back to watch the video.

After Jacob receives the blessing of the firstborn from his father Isaac, who received the same promise from his father Abraham, who received the promise from God, he comes to a place where he rests his head on a stone and then consecrates it after God appeared to him in a dream. Esau also wants the blessing from his father Isaac but does not receive it.

***

The sun has already set, so the patriarch Jacob picks up some stones, places them down, and lays down to sleep. He has a vision in a dream. He sees a ladder that reaches up toward heaven. He is bewildered, dismayed as to its meaning. He sees God's angels going up and down the ladder. Suddenly, he sees God standing over him.

In a booming, loud voice, God says, "I am God, Lord of Abraham your grandfather, and Lord of Isaac your father. I will give you and your descendants the land upon which you are lying. Your descendants will be like the dust of the earth and you shall spread out to the west and to the east, and to the north, and to the south.

"All the families of the earth will be blessed through you and your descendants; I am with you. I will protect you wherever you go and bring you back to this soil. I will not turn aside from you until I have fully kept this promise to you. Your name shall not be called Jacob any more but Israel and many nations shall come out of your seed. And kings shall come out of your loins. I am the God of your father Isaac and Abraham your grandfather."

***

Jacob wakes up out of his sleep, trembling, and proclaims, "God is truly in this place, but I did not know it. This place is so awe-inspiring. This must be God's Temple. This is the gate to heaven."

Jacob takes the heavy stone that he used as a pillow during the night and stands it upright. Then he anoints it as he pours oil on it and says,

"This place will be named Beth El—God's Temple—and if God will protect me on the journey I am taking, and feed and clothe me, and if I can return to my father's house, then I will dedicate myself totally to God. Let this stone that I have set up as a pillar become a temple to my God. Of all that you give me, I will set aside a tithe to you."

Jacob stands the stone up on end.

***

Dr. McNair stops the video and paces back and forth. "It is widely understood in some circles that a lineage of kings would spring from Abraham and Sarah's bloodline that would eventually culminate in the Messiah or Jesus Christ who would bring salvation and blessing to the entire world.

These promises were then repeated through Abraham's son Isaac and his son Jacob who had twelve children. One of the children was named Judah through whom Jesus Christ traces His lineage."

Smithe holds up his hands.

"Hold on there, Doctor. You're losing me with all this genealogy stuff! Are you telling me that the stone Jacob laid his head upon and used as a pillow is the same stone that was stolen from the abbey?"

Jacob standing up the Stone of Destiny,
A Biblical Case for Awesome Beards—RELEVANT Magazine. Relevantmagazine.com

McNair nods his head. "Yes, many people believe the stone that Jacob laid his head upon, known as 'Jacob's pillow stone' or 'Jacob's pillar stone,' is very likely the same stone taken from the Abbey. This reference can be found in Genesis 26:3–5 and Genesis 28:10–19."

Smithe chimes in, "I see now why it would be of significant value. Okay, let's say all of this is true thus far, but how do we know that the stone Jacob slept upon is the same stone that was taken from the Abbey?"

"Good question, Detective!" McNair says with a wide smile. "I had a feeling you were a detailed man. Well, to make a long story short, we don't really know. There are many in Scotland who believe that the current stone is fake, and the real stone was switched before King Edward I invaded Scotland in 1296.

"However, in 1935, a Palestinian government archaeological expedition under the direction of G.S. Blake found that the vicinity of Palestine where Jacob had laid his head had the same calcareous sandstone as the Stone of

Scone, and concluded that it might have come from Palestine since it was not indigenous to Scotland.

"But it's anyone's guess if the sandstone taken from the Abby is the same stone Professor Blake examined! Who knows if it hasn't been switched? It is also very interesting that the stone had a ring in it at each end indicative of the priests of Israel transporting it with poles. Are there any other questions, Detective?"

Smithe feels like his head is spinning from all of this information, but it is fascinating. "Thanks for the history lesson, Professor. And as you have stated, I am a detailed man, so I wonder if you could come with us to Dr. Flanders' office in London. You can see some of the very curious things he has in his office to perhaps give us a clue as to who would want to nick the stone and want it bad enough to kill Dr. Flanders. Of course, Scotland Yard will pay for all of your expenses."

McNair sat down. "That's kind of you, Detective, but I'd be glad to help in any way that I can. I have to be in London for a week-long conference meeting on Friday anyway. I'll meet you then and I'll bring some additional videos that I think will be of service to your investigation."

Smithe and Humphrey stand and shake Dr. McNair's hand and say their goodbyes. Smithe is looking forward to the upcoming meeting and hopes the Professor can provide him with some answers. If there's anything he can't stand, it's not being able to solve a case.

Chapter Two

After a seven hour journey back to England, DI Smithe is happy to be back in his comfortable home. Martha has prepared a delicious pot-roast meal. "How did your day go dear," She asks.

"It was a pleasant day spending it with Dr. Robert McNair who is head of the Religious Studies at the University of Glasgow. He knew Dr. Flanders, the curator of the Abbey who was killed and I wanted to see if he could contribute anything regarding the theft and killing." Smithe says.

"Did he provide any motives?" asks Martha. "Very possibly," says Smithe, "but I am not looking forward to interviewing Dr. Flanders's Widow tomorrow." After dinner, Smithe calls up Dr. Flanders's wife Mary to arrange a visit.

***

The next morning DI Smithe and his partner Humphrey drive to meet Mary. They pull up to the beautiful yellow brick Tudor house and knock on the door.

Mary answers the door and welcomes them in as she has been expecting them. They all sit down and the detectives offer their deep and sincere condolences.

"Thank you very much" says Mary, "Can I offer you a cup of tea and scones?" "No thank you" reply the detectives.

"I'm sorry to have to ask you some questions about Dr. Flanders's murder at a time like this," says Smithe.

"That's Ok, I'm only happy to answer any of your questions as I only want justice for my husband," replies Mary.

"Do you know if Dr. Flanders had any enemies or if he received any death threats on his life recently," asks Smithe.

"No, he never mentioned anything out of the ordinary and he seemed to be his normal self. Except, *'except, as she starts thinking more deeply,'* for a talk a week ago at the Scottish Heritage Center, and when he came home —he was very disturbed for some reason. He said there were three young people there that talked to him afterward and were very angry about something," says Mary.

"Well, thank you Mary, and again we apologize for disturbing you. We will keep you informed as to our investigation," says Smithe as he and Humphrey leave the house. "Is there anything we can do for you regarding Dr. Flanders's memorial service," asks Smithe politely.

"Thanks for asking Detective, but my daughter is handling that and has arranged for his organs to be donated to a DNA research organization called CCC," says Mary.

"Well, thanks again, and don't hesitate to call if you can think of anything that may be of significance," says Smithe as he and Humphrey depart.

***

It's a balmy day when doctor McNair arrives in London. When he arrives at Scotland Yard, he's shown to detective Smithe's office, and knocks on the door.

"Ah, Professor, good to see you," Smithe says. "Would you like anything to drink? A cup of coffee or tea?"

"No, thank you, and it's good to see you as well. I am much looking forward to seeing Dr. Flanders's office. But truth be told, I cannot wait to glimpse the Stone of Destiny," McNair says. He looks like a little boy excited for Christmas.

Smithe chuckles. *'He's a little strange, but I like the man,* he thinks.' "Right. Let's head on out."

And with that, Smithe and McNair jump into the car and head over to Westminster Abbey. Upon arriving, they meet up with Humphrey, then traverse the grounds and enter the building. When they reach Dr. Flanders's office, they find a pretty, young woman packing up some of his belongings. Smithe is shocked to see her as well as McNair, who knows she is Dr. Flanders's daughter from a previous relationship.

"Excuse me, young lady, I am DI Smithe from Scotland Yard investigating a murder that occurred here. This is a crime scene, so can you please tell me who you are and what are you doing in this office?"

The woman's eyes widen. "Yes, Detective," she stammers. "I am picking up my father's things."

McNair interjects, "Hello Sara, may I offer you my deepest condolences," as he walks over to her and gives her a hug and a kiss on the cheek.

"Thank you, Robert." Sara says.

"I see you two know each other," as Smithe softens. "Oh, Dr. Flanders was your father. My apologies and condolences as well."

Sara seems to relax a little. She is in her mid-thirties and has brown hair and blue eyes.

"Dr. Robert McNair of the University of Glasgow is helping me solve your father's case and helping me to understand why anyone would want to murder your father and take the Stone from the Abbey Coronation Chair. Perhaps you can be of assistance as well."

Sara stares at Dr. McNair and is in awe. They are very much attracted to each other and it is obvious they have had a previous relationship. She looks over at him shyly, blushes, and then looks away. The feeling seems mutual.

"I am truly sorry to hear about your father, Sara," McNair says. "We got to know each other famously as we have worked on several projects together over the years and were members of the same historical and archaeological society."

Smithe's eyes focus on the wall charts. "Do you see all these names on the wall charts, Doctor? They all include 'Dan.' And look at that family crest of Robert the Bruce. That's the tattoo Dr. Flanders had on his own chest. Can you tell me how all of these names of 'Dan' are connected to Dr. Flanders's death? Why would he have a tattoo of Robert the Bruce's family crest on his chest? And what are these

Dan, Bruce and Scotland

genealogy charts all about, not to mention those biblical scriptures next to that picture of the Devil?"

Smithe walks over to the wall and points to a large chart that's ripped in the corner. "Look, this one charts all of the kings of Ireland." He points to another. "And this one charts all of the kings of Scotland. And this one all of the kings of England going back to King David of Israel. What does it all mean, Doctor? And what about all of these flags and symbols?"

Sara steps forward and pipes in, "I can tell you what all of these names of 'Dan' mean, Detective. They are the places that the biblical tribe of 'Dan,' one of Jacob's twelve children, passed through on their journey from Jerusalem. The tribe of Dan left their mark or trail behind them with their name as was prophesied by their father Jacob in Genesis 49 when he was dying. My father studied this subject intently because he was very interested in our family ancestry."

McNair interrupts, "Yes! The scripture of Genesis 49:17, Joshua 19:47, and Judges 18:29. Of course!" His cheeks flush with excitement.

Smithe and Humphrey look over at McNair. His enthusiasm is through the roof, but he doesn't seem to care.

"I know all about Jacob's sons thanks to the history lesson the Professor gave me," Smithe says. "But why do some names have 'Dan' in them and some of them 'Dun' or 'Din?'

"Because there are no vowels in Hebrew as in the English language and therefore vowels were added by others," Sara says.

"You seem to be very knowledgeable about these things, Sara," Smithe inquires. "I assume that you've learned a lot from your father?"

"Well, linguistics has been my interest since I was very young and my father encouraged me to pursue my passion. I am a linguistics professor thanks to my father's guidance. I am also interested in our family ancestry thanks to my father's interest, as we go all the way back to a famous Queen in Ireland."

"Who was that?" asks Smithe.

"Her name was Teia," replies Sara.

McNair beams at her. He is impressed with her intellect. "She's right, Detective," he says. "Names like 'Dan,' 'Din,' 'Den,' 'Dun,' and 'Don' are all corruptions of the Hebrew name 'Dan.' "

Sara meets McNair's eyes and they smile at each other.

Smithe is still confused. He is a smart, intuitive man who always has a good read on people and a sense about things, but sometimes the academic types make him feel stupid. One thing, however, that Smithe doesn't have is pride, and he's never afraid to ask for help or admit that he's wrong. Martha seems to think that is why he's good at what he does, but he begs to differ.

"We also found the initials *Dan* carved into the side of the coronation chair by the thieves," replies Smithe.

"That's very interesting," remarks McNair.

"Do you think there is a connection to what Dr. Flanders was studying and the initials carved into the chair?" asks Smithe. "We noticed that he had on a website of secret societies on his computer and there were several books on end-time Bible prophecies. I wonder if all of this is connected?"

McNair responds by saying, "Yes indeed, I think there is a connection, as I was aware of his passion for biblical prophecy and I cautioned him to be very careful of these secret societies."

"But these names indicate they traveled all the way to places like Ireland, Scotland, and England from Jerusalem. Is that possible? That's a long way to travel on a donkey!" Smithe says.

"That's right, Detective, and that's what all these genealogies show, but they didn't get to Ireland on a donkey. The Danites were world travelers and placed their family name on rivers and territory they traveled through."

McNair walks over to a banner that displays the coats of arms and points to the bottom left corner. "Notice this harp in the British royal coat of arms and the flag of the Irish Republic. Most people would not associate these things with the ancient nation of Israel. But the six-pointed star is the star of David and the harp is King David's, as he loved to play the harp. It says in the Bible that he was known as the sweet psalmist of Israel. King David wrote many of the psalms of the Bible."

1. Israel flag. 2. Irish flag. 3. Scottish flag. 4. The British flag.

McNair points to another flag. "You see this Ulster flag?"

King David's Harp   Ulster Flag   Crest of Robert the Bruce

Smithe observes the six-pointed star with the red hand inside of it in the Ulster Flag with a crown above it. "Yes, but what does it mean?"

Ignoring him, McNair points to another flag. "Look at this picture of the crown worn by the kings of Ireland and Scotland during their coronation."

Smithe is getting somewhat annoyed. He just wants McNair to spit it out. "What does it signify?" he snaps. With a giant smile on his face, McNair says, "It signifies the twelve tribes of Israel who were the great grandchildren of Abraham. It goes back to the promise that God told Abraham that Kings would come out of his seed.

Feeling overwhelmed, Smithe responds, "I'll admit this is all unfamiliar, but what does the red hand have to do with the Stone of Destiny?"

Above the genealogy charts, Dr. Flanders had written several phrases. Between the chart of Judah and Ireland, he wrote, '**First Overturn.**' He drew another line between Ireland and Scotland and wrote, '**Second Overturn.**' He drew another line between Scotland and England and wrote, '**Third Overturn.**' With a scripture reference. Smithe doesn't know what any of it means.

__Thus saith the Lord GOD; Remove the diadem, and take off the crown: this shall not be the same: exalt him that is low, and abase him that is high. I will overturn, overturn, overturn, it: and it shall be no more, until he come whose right it is; and I will give it him. Ezekiel 21:26.__

Sara nods her head and says, "I think I know. My father explained this ancient history to me and why he had a tattoo of Robert the Bruce's family crest on his chest."

"I think I know as well, Sara," McNair chimes in. "I think it's time to see another history dramatization, detectives. Would you like to come along, Sara?"

Sara blushes and smiles. "You bet, I am a student of my father's and love history and genealogy."

McNair claps his hands. "Okay then, let's all meet tomorrow for breakfast at my hotel. They have a conference room with video set up and I can show you a very interesting dramatization that I brought along that will provide additional insight into your murder case."

"That's fine with me if it's okay with the detectives," Sara replies eagerly.

Smithe and Humphrey take a moment to discuss it privately. "I'm getting kind of frustrated," Smithe says. "But we don't have any answers as to why anyone who would want the stone so bad that they would kill for it."

Humphrey sighs. "To be honest, I've been lost in all of this. I don't know what they're talking about."

"Let's just agree to this tomorrow, but after that, we need to demand some concrete answers. Otherwise I will seek out another expert. Deal?" Smithe says, and Humphrey nods his head.

Smithe turns to McNair and Sara and says, "No problem. We'll see you tomorrow."

Smithe is bewildered and at the same time intrigued by all of this new historical information of the stone's ancient history and its connection to the biblical patriarch Jacob. Smithe's detective mind has been mulling over all of these facts of history, but he is puzzled by the mysterious clues contained in all of the variations of the name 'Dan' in the Dr. Flanders's office, not to mention the flags of Ireland, Scotland, and England and all of the genealogy charts. *Was the curator trying to tell someone about these clues and their relationship to the crest of Robert the Bruce on his chest?* He is confused about what the curator meant when he wrote "overturn" on the wall and hopes that this new video will provide him with more insight.

Chapter Three

Dr. McNair has invited Sara and the detectives to see another video as he explained he would provide more information about the royal bloodlines that may be helpful in their murder investigation. It is a dreary rainy morning as DC Humphrey drives to McNair's hotel with Smithe. He makes small talk, as he is curious about Smithe's family.

"So, how are your kids doing these days, Smithe? How old are your twins now, and are they withstanding the peer pressures of millennials?"

Smithe sighs. "You have no idea what it is like to raise impressionable boys these days, Humphrey. Most of their friends smoke pot and they don't think it's all that bad for them. They can get the stuff anywhere, as you are well aware. Bobby, my oldest, dropped out of college earlier this year, and we are very worried about his future. We are hoping that he will pursue a career in the armed forces like his twin brother."

"I know a little about that because my sister is going through a similar situation with her son," Humphrey says. "It sure is a different world from when we grew up."

"Ain't that the truth," Smithe says with a chuckle.

***

They finally arrive at the hotel. It's chilly and Smithe squints his eyes and pulls up his collar and he and Humphrey dash across the soggy grounds, forgetting to bring an umbrella. They are all eager to learn more about the history that McNair can provide that might help their case. A previous dramatization revealed that a kingly line would come out of the Patriarch Abraham's seed culminating in a kingly succession leading to Jesus Christ. This video would be significant as to which bloodline would inherit the throne and which one might claim the throne by having the Stone of Destiny in their possession.

When they enter the lobby, Dr. McNair and Sara greet them and they walk down to the breakfast area. After a hearty English breakfast of fried eggs, sausages, bacon, grilled tomato and mushrooms, toast and pastries—the entourage adjourn to the hotel's conference room to see a dramatization. McNair is ready to start the video on the birth of Judah's twin sons entitled, *The Scarlet Thread*.

"Here is another short video for you, Detectives. Its story is told in Genesis 38:28–30. I think you will enjoy this one and see the relevance of this history to solving your case. Have you ever seen a birth?"

Smithe laughs. "Have I ever! I have five kids."

"I'm not married," says Humphrey.

"Make yourselves comfortable," McNair says, as he turns on the video and shuts the light. The video begins.

The video begins with the midwife ready to deliver Judah's twin boys. They will be Jacob's grandsons, born from his daughter-in-law who deceived Judah as she played the harlot.

Humphrey jokes, "Do you have any popcorn?" Sara flashes him a dirty look. "Just kidding," he whispers.

The video continues . . .

The midwife is perplexed about the forthcoming delivery of Judah's twin sons. Astonished at what she is experiencing, she addresses the observant onlookers.

"What is this? The first baby has put out his hand but does not want to come out yet and has withdrawn his hand back into the womb. So, I will tie a scarlet ribbon upon its hand and call the baby Zarah. And here comes your brother; he is ready, so I will call him Pharez."

Tamar, the mother of Judah's twins and Jacob's daughter-in-law yells out to the midwife, "What's the matter with my babies?"

The midwife reassures her and says, "They are fine, but I tied a scarlet ribbon around the first baby's hand as it started to come out, but he withdrew his hand. According to our custom, he should be the firstborn and inheritor of his father's birthright. So, I called him Zarah, meaning 'scarlet,' to identify him. When his brother came out, I called him Pharez, which means 'breach' because this breach must be healed sometime in the future."

Tamar turns to Judah and says, "What did the midwife mean when she said the breach must be healed regarding our two sons?"

Judah responds, "The God of my fathers, Abraham and Isaac, has told us that kings will come out of our loins. And that someday this bloodline would be healed through their descendants."

***

The video ends. Dr. McNair says, "Well, DI Smithe, that is the end of our birth story. Did you learn anything from it?"

"Well, it did bring back some memories, that's for sure! I also have a set of twins. But I still don't know how this background relates to this case. It seems to indicate that this ancient bloodline from the Patriarch Abraham's great grandson Judah, would have a lineage continuing through one of his sons in particular that would be entitled to the throne, but I'm not sure."

"I agree" says Sara, my father told me the significance of the 'scarlet thread' to Bible prophecy and how there would be a rivalry as to who would inherit the throne of King David to this present day. He said there would be two overturns of the kingly lineage before it would be found in England. That's why there are lines drawn between Ireland, Scotland and England."

McNair smiles. "Fair enough everyone. I have another video that I would like to show you that will enhance your understanding of this subject."

Smithe says that he would like to at some other time because he has to get back to the office to fill out some paperwork. Sara says that she has to make funeral arrangements for her father's memorial service. She asks Dr. McNair if he will attend.

"Of course, as you know your father was a colleague and dear friend and I will definitely make it," says McNair.

***

Just then, Smithe's phone rings as he gets a very controversial phone call. "Hello, Smithe here," he says. He looks at the screen and sees that it's from Scotland Yard. What! You've got to be kidding!"

He turns pale and shakes his head and paces the room. After a minute or so, he hangs up. He rubs his hands through his hair, feeling frazzled.

"What's wrong?" Humphrey asks.

Smithe's facial expression is one of dismay as he looks at Sara and says, "Sit down, Sara. I have some very bad news."

Sara sits down on a chair and looks to be in shock. "Tell me what's wrong!" she screams.

"I'm sorry to tell you this, Sara, but I was just informed by the forensics team at Scotland Yard that when the coroner was about to cremate your father according to your instructions last evening, someone broke into the morgue during the night. They held a gun to the coroner on duty and made him give them some of your father's ashes after the cremation!"

"Why would anyone want some of his ashes?" asks Sara.

"There is more," replies Smithe. Since both of you are here and I think I can trust you, I am going to tell you something else that happened to your father that we are keeping from the press because only the killers would know."

Eager to hear what Smithe has to say, Sara asks, "What's that Detective?"

"When we found your father's body, someone cut out his heart."

"Father!" Sara shouts, as she crumbles to the floor, sobbing. "O my God, they did it again! They did it again!"

McNair walks over to Sara and puts his hand on her shoulder and comforts her as she cries uncontrollably. "I'm truly sorry this happened to your father, Sara," he says.

"I am very sorry also, Sara," Smithe says. "I don't mean to be insensitive at a time like this, but I must ask you some questions."

"Yes, I understand, Detective," Sara says in-between sobs. "I'm really OK", says Sara. "It was just a shock."

"Sara, you said 'they did it again.' Did what again? What did you mean by that statement? Who are 'they'?"

Sara stands up and says, "Robert and Detectives, I would like you all to come to my house tomorrow, because I have something very important to show you that I think will be of interest to you in solving this case."

"I'll be there," says Smithe.

"I'm scheduled to give a presentation at 10:00 but can come right afterword," replies McNair.

"Let's make it for Lunch, my treat," says Sara. Everyone agrees!

Chapter Four

The next day, Smithe drives to Sara's house. As he's sitting in traffic, he can't help but feel like they are not even close to blowing this thing wide open. Without any leads as to who killed Dr. Flanders, Smithe is desperate and willing to explore all avenues. Humphrey called an hour ago to tell him that he wasn't feeling well, so it was just Smithe today.

After winding through the city streets and spilling out into the countryside, Smithe finally reaches Sara's house, a cute one-story cottage with blue shingles. He parks the car, walks up the stone path, and knocks on the door. Sara answers and lets him in. McNair is sitting on the couch drinking tea.

"Please, make yourself comfortable," Sara says. "Can I get you anything . . . food, tea?"

"No, thank you," Smithe says as he sits down. "Humphrey couldn't make it today. He's feeling a bit under the weather."

"The reason I called you both here today is because I think you will find what I have of interest," Sara says. Then she walks over to a beautiful ornate harp sitting in the corner and starts to play the same song that her ancestor Teia Tephi played on the very harp of King David that was brought over from Jerusalem to Ireland. Sara plays and sings:

> *Unless the fates are faithless grown,*
> *And the prophets' voice be vain,*
> *Where ere is found the sacred stone,*
> *The wanderers race shall reign.*

When she had finished, Smithe says, "That was very beautiful, Sara, but what does this have to do with your father's case?"

Suddenly, it looks like a lightbulb has gone off in McNair's head and he jumps up from his seat and gazes at the harp. His hand shakes as he hovers over the ornately carved design. "I think I know. That's . . . that's the same harp that Queen Teia played, isn't it, Sara?" His heart is pounding.

Sara smiles and nods her head. "Yes, Teia was an ancestor on my mother's side, and this harp and that song has been in our family for generations. I was told it was King David's and that my ancestor Teia played it and it was passed on down through our family. My mother played it when I was a little girl and told me Queen Teia's story. It was almost like a nursery rhyme."

"Sara, I don't mean to pry, but it's my job and I am the detective on your father's case. What did you mean when you said, 'not again' when I informed you of your father's fate?"

Sara sighs. "I should have told you this when you told me about my father's missing heart, and I apologize that I didn't. I've just been emotional given the circumstances. A few years ago, a forty-seven-year-old man named Alisdair Sinclair was stopped by customs officials at Ben Gurion Airport on his way out of the country. After searching him, they found nine thousand Deutsche marks stashed in the bottom of his handbag and arrested him."

Smithe furrowed his brow. "I don't see the connection."

"After taking him to the police station, the police found him dead—he had been strangled by his own shoelaces. There was a gaping wound in his chest and the cell was covered in pools of blood. Now here's the interesting part and the connection to the ritualistic act of cutting out my father's heart, as well as Robert the Bruce. After the autopsy was performed, it was confirmed that his heart was missing."

"Did you say Robert the Bruce's heart was cut out as well?" asks Smithe.

"Yes, that is true," replies McNair.

"But why?" Smithe inquires.

He turns to McNair and says, "Is there anything else in any of this history that would give us a clue as to why this happened in connection to the stone?"

"Well, Detective, there might be, and also a connection to ancient Druid beliefs," McNair says. "You see, there are many families who claim they are descendants of the kingly bloodline of king David, including the Merovingian, Hapsburg, Lorraine, Plantard, Luxemburg, Stewarts, Devonshire, Montpezat, Buchhan, Flanders, and Monteith, to name a few. They would all love to claim the throne as their rightful inheritance and claim the Stewart lineage of the queen is a fake."

"Stop right there McNair," says Smithe. "You mentioned that some of these families want to claim Queen Elizabeth II's throne to be a fake lineage of the house of Stewart. But she is of the house of Windsor," Smithe says.

"You are absolutely correct Smithe," says McNair. "But as you know these royals tend to keep it in the family as they say, and many of them married into prestigious families of other countries. In fact, Queen Elizabeth II is the great-granddaughter of Edward VII in the male-line, whose mother was Queen Victoria.

"Edward VII's father was Albert of Saxe-Coburg, of the German House of Wettin. That is why some of these families believe they can trace the kingly lineage back to the house of Stuart, which originally was spelled Stewart in Gaelic. It is through Victoria's lineage that some of these families believe Elizabeth's male-line can be traced including the House of Stuart, to Queen Mary of Scotland, and Robert the Bruce."

"I see says Smithe. Ok then, continue with your theory as to why Dr. Flanders had his heart cut out."

"Fair enough," says McNair. "Here is where a very unusual event took place which might explain the cutting out of Sara's father's heart and the connection to Robert the Bruce, who was from one of Scotland's greatest kingly families. The most famous was Robert, and he stated that upon his death, he desired his heart be cut out and taken to Jerusalem to be buried in the church of the Holy Sepulcher where supposedly Jesus the future king of Israel was buried."

Smithe looks at McNair in anticipation, waiting for him to finish. When he doesn't say anything, Smithe presses him. "Well, did it happen?"

"Partly! The Knights Templar did cut out King Bruce's heart after he died, but his heart never reached the Holy Land because the Knight carrying it died in the battle of the Moors."

"So, we could have a copy-cat ritual here to fulfill the wishes of Robert the Bruce," he says.

"Maybe, but there's more!" McNair says. "If you recall your English history Smithe, King Edward I, also known as 'longshanks' because of his long legs being over six feet tall, appointed John Balliol, as king. But king John didn't last long as just after Edward annexed Scotland to England, he exiled Balliol— and demolished all of the Celtic organizations by claiming they were inspiring pagan ritualistic satanic beliefs which were heretical to the church at Rome."

"Well, did these ritualistic practices of the Celts offer hearts to be sacrificed?"

"Not that I know of, but then the Scots had a rebellion and Balliol's brother-in-law John Comyn struggled for control of Scotland with Robert the Bruce," McNair says. "You see, Bruce's family believed they had the right to the throne because they were descended from King David I of Scotland. John Comyn was the most powerful noble in Scotland and his family and the Bruce's had many disputes over rights to land. Comyn was much more determined in his opposition to England's rule than Bruce, who at first supported the English King.

"Robert felt betrayed by Comyn the red as they called him because of his red hair. In his anguish, Bruce killed John the red Comyn at Greyfriars Church in Dumfries with a dagger on the church's altar in what appeared to be a ritual killing. King Edward crushed the rebellion and hence was nicknamed 'Hammer of the Scots'. He also expelled the Jews from England."

"Why did Bruce kill Comyn in a church?" Smithe asks.

"Some believe it was a pagan Druid tradition that the victor emerge on sacred ground of the church," McNair answers.

"I'll bet that didn't go over very big with the church!" replies Smithe.

"You are absolutely right! The church excommunicated Bruce for this sacrilegious act and also started to come down hard on any of his associates, such as the Templars who went there as a safe-haven after being thrown out of France," McNair says.

"I remember a little about the Templars, now that we're on the subject, refresh my memory," says Smithe.

"That is another long story, Detective, so perhaps we should discuss it at another time."

"No, let's discuss it now," Smithe interjects. "It might be relevant to our case!"

Sara cries softly as she is thinking about what happened to her father. Smithe is feeling frustrated. He is running out of time and needs to head back to Scotland Yard.

Smithe paces the room, while Humphrey is on the phone. Sara quietly sobs and stares into space. Everyone is waiting for McNair to continue his story about the Knights Templar. Once Humphrey finishes his phone call, he walks back over to the group.

"What do you think is the connection to all of this ancient Irish and Scottish history and all of these secret societies including the Templars?" Smithe asks. His head is spinning with all of this information. "Why do you think there may be a connection to Dr. Flanders death and the Templars?"

McNair replies, "The Knights Templar were the supposed secret guardians of the Holy Grail. According to historical accounts, the group was founded around 1118 to protect Christian pilgrims visiting the Holy Land after the First Crusade."

"I knew that," Smithe says. "History was one of my favorite subjects, and I remember learning that. That's when Jerusalem was being taken over by Saladin, who led the Muslim military campaign and was defeated. Many of those who fought were cons who would get special dispensation if they defeated Saladin with the church's blessing."

"You do know your history, Smithe," McNair says with a smile. "After the First Crusade, the Knights were formed to protect sojourners who wanted to visit the Holy Land. Over the next two centuries, the Knights gained power and property and established a primitive banking system to finance their operations.

"Once the crusader kingdoms collapsed, however, the Knights' power and secretive ways aroused suspicions. King Philip IV of France, perhaps indebted to the Templars, arrested many of the leaders on allegations of heresy. Perhaps ten percent were killed, but many fled to Scotland where they were welcomed by Robert the Bruce."

"*Bruce, Bruce, Bruce* . . . that name keeps poppin' up!" Smithe says.

"Though absolved of the charges by Pope Clement V, as shown in a document recently published by the Vatican, the group reportedly disbanded in 1312," McNair says.

Smithe tries to understand. "Let me get this straight, Doctor. You're telling me that at least thirteen different families believe they have bloodlines going all the way back to King David of Israel and their descendants believe they are entitled to the kingly throne. Furthermore, these people are so convicted that they are willing to kill and offer up ritualistic sacrifice for it?"

"That's partly right, Detective. At least the part about their belief in their right to the throne."

"Okay, let me see if I understand you correctly," Smithe says. "According to tradition, there have been two overturns of King David's throne. The first was from Jerusalem to Ireland, and the second from Ireland to Scotland as Sara previously mentioned."

"That is what many people believe," McNair states.

Smithe runs his hands through his hair. "Now let me guess. The third overturn, and where we would find the current bloodline of the throne, would be from Scotland to England."

McNair smiles widely. "Boy, you're good, Detective."

"Now I suppose you going to tell me that the Queen of England is of the same bloodline as King David," Smithe says.

"That is precisely what many believe because she is of the Stewart lineage. In fact, the British Israel World Federation in London was where Dr. Flanders got his genealogy chart and a lot of history regarding this concept," McNair exclaims.

"That's what all these genealogy charts are about," Smithe says as the pieces of the puzzle start to fit together. He turns to Sara. She has stopped crying, but her eyes are puffy and red. "Sara, were you aware that your father was into all of this genealogy stuff?"

"Of course," she says. "My father talked to me about this constantly. It was his passion. He believed his family is also a part of this bloodline genealogy through the Bruce family. That's why he had the Bruce family crest on his chest. That's why he became the curator at the Abbey, to guard the Stone."

"Well, what else can you two genealogy experts tell me that will help us solve this case?" Smithe asks.

"I believe that my mother also has a bloodline that can be traced back to King David of Israel and we are of the Pharez lineage, as was Queen Teia Tephi," Sara explains.

"Okay, then maybe you can give me a clue as to who might have killed your father and whose initials are 'Dan,' as carved on the back of the coronation chair when the stone was nicked."

"Well, it is very possible from my father's wall charts he was trying to trace the family lineage of the tribe of Judah to the Stewart lineage of the Queen," Sara says. "Otherwise, why would he have a tattoo of Robert the Bruce?" She turns to McNair. "Robert, wasn't the tribe of Dan always at odds with the tribe of Judah in the Bible? And didn't they try to nick the rightful birthright promise from Judah?"

McNair nodded. "Sara has a valid point. You see, Samson was from the tribe of Dan and Dan was one of the twelve sons of Jacob whose name was changed to Israel. You might be familiar with some of the names of Jacob's other children, such as Levi, Judah, and Joseph."

"Of course I am familiar with some of these names from my catechism school," Smithe says.

"Well, then let me continue," McNair says as he sits down. "God made two promises to Abraham. The first was called the Scepter, or the promise of the Messiah to come out of his bloodline. The second was the promise of birthright, that Abraham's seed would inherit the land of Canaan, now present-day Jerusalem. Eventually, these promises were handed down to Abraham's son Isaac and Isaac's son Jacob who had twelve children.

"Usually the eldest son in the family inherited these promises, but the two promises were eventually divided among Jacob's sons, Judah and Joseph. Remember the Bible story of how Joseph was sold into slavery by his brothers to the Egyptians because they were jealous of him? Judah was to inherit the Scepter promise and Joseph the birthright promise. Dan was always jealous of his brother Judah."

"It's been a long time, but these stories are coming back to me," Smithe says. "Please refresh my memory about the tribes, especially the tribe of Dan, Doctor."

"First of all, we need to clarify a point that most people don't understand about these tribes. Two separate nations came out of the descendants of the twelve brothers known as Israel and Judah. Although they were all born from their father Jacob or Israel and therefore are Israelites, only the tribes of Benjamin, Judah, and some of the scattered Levites formed the nation of Judah. It's kind of like saying that all the people in London are British but not all British are Londoners. Do you get the point?".

"Yeah, I understand," Smithe says.

"Well, it seems that all throughout history there has been contention between God and the Devil over these promises. That is, of course, if you believe the Bible," McNair says.

"Let's say I do. How did people who believe the Bible, and who believe they are the rightful inheritors of these promises, ever believe in killing for their inheritance?" Smithe says, skeptical.

McNair clicks his tongue. "Let's start from the beginning, or at least after the flood. The Bible tells us that the Devil has worked through different people to deceive the world ever since the Garden of Eden. Deception continued to Noah's flood when humanity became so evil that God destroyed them.

"Then this deception soon started again after the flood as the Devil began working through an evil man named Nimrod who built the Tower of Babel. History tells us Nimrod was a powerful man who protected the people from the wild animals by building cities. As he began growing in power and popularity, he began exalting himself as a priest for the people to worship. Like the Israelites of old, the people wanted to worship something that they could see, not an invisible God."

"Where is the devil in all of this?" Humphrey asked.

"Aye, as they say, the devil is in the details," McNair laughed. "The serpent once again became an object of worship and so did the sun as it provided light and heat. Since the sun provided life, it was natural to associate the sun as God, replacing the true Creator God as the life bringer. This was how the Devil got man to unknowingly worship him instead of the true God.

"The Bible says Nimrod became a mighty hunter or as the Hebrew indicates 'a tyrant.' One of the most common symbols of ancient Druids was a sun god with a serpent encircling it. This was how sun worship became devil worship. Man changed the name to Baal, which means 'Lord.' People then began associating fire with the sun and even began sacrificing their children. Even the ancient Israelites got caught up in it and Moses strongly forbid it."

"I'm still confused," Smithe says. "How did all of this devil worship get passed down to the Druids in Ireland, and what do they have to do with the tribe of Dan?"

"That's a fair question Detective," McNair says. "After Nimrod died, he was deified through a form of worship that today we would call pagan. This system was known as the ancient 'mysteries' in which only those in the so-called elite knew that certain symbols represented these deities.

"There was a woman named Semiramis who was worshipped as well. In Egypt her name was Osiris. In Asia, she was known as Diana or Cybele and Deoius. In Rome, it was Fortuna and Jupiterpuer. And that is how it started, and many believe today these mysteries have continued through the Knights Templar into secret societies such as the freemasons and the Illuminati."

"I have read about these so-called secret societies," Smithe says. "What you are saying is that there are two groups of people who believe they are the true bloodline of King David and the coming Messiah, but one of them has been deceived by the Devil into thinking they are the true worshippers of God."

"That is a fair observation, Detective," McNair says.

"That's right Detective," says Sara as she recovers her composure and continues her thoughts. "Alisdair Sinclair was from one of the original families that formed the Knights Templar during the Crusades. They were in support of Robert the Bruce of Scotland who many believe tried to restore the

Druid Celtic religion which believed in sorcery, necromancy, and may even have had ritualistic overtures of human sacrifice. Isn't that right Robert."

"Sara is absolutely correct," says McNair. "The Bruce family held lands in the southwest of Scotland, their ancestry being Celtic, but their land grants and titles were under the Earl of Carrick following in the wake of the Norman Conquest. This provided them with lands in both Scotland and England and thereby producing hard choices for the Bruce's at the time when Scotland had no official King.

"Many believe the Templars were French aristocrats who journeyed to Jerusalem in the mid-1300s in search of the Temple artifacts of Herod's Temple— after it was destroyed by the Romans to bring them back to Scotland's hero, Robert the Bruce. Bruce welcomed the Templars after they were kicked out of France on trumped up charges of heresy. Did you ever see the movie *Braveheart*?"

"Yeah, I saw it, but I'm not fond of men wearing skirts," Smithe jokes. "But seriously, I still don't get the connection to these ritualistic acts."

"As I already said, Robert the Bruce wanted his heart to be buried in the Church of the Sepulcher in Jerusalem when he died?"

"Yeah, so?" Smithe answers. *It takes these people forever and a day to give an answer,* he observes.

McNair elaborates, "Well, there were three Knights who took Robert the Bruce's heart in a silver urn. Sir William Sinclair was one of the Knights who journeyed there. Sir James Douglas was the Knight who carried the heart in a silver urn around his neck and when the Moors attacked them, Sir James hurled the heart into the air and shouted:

Brave heart, that ever foremost led,
Forward! As thou wast wont
And I shall follow thee, or else shall die!

McNair joins in and starts chanting with Sara. Smithe is losing patience.

"Can we get on with it?" Smithe says.

"Alisdair was very proud of his heritage. His middle name, Rosslyn, was the name of the chapel in Scotland whose floor plan is said to be based upon Solomon's Temple. It was believed the chapel was built to protect the Templar artifacts and secrets, and was built by William Sinclair," says Sara.

"Yes, I'm familiar with Rosslyn, and that's all very interesting history, but once again I ask both of you, what does all this have to do with the murder of Dr. Flanders and the cutting out of his heart?"

"I'm not sure, I'm only informing you of historical facts that may be of interest to you," Says Sara as she continues the relationship of Alisdair Sinclair to the Templars and a most intriguing scenario.

"The Sinclair family was very prominent in Scotland as their name goes back several generations. Sir Henry St. Clair, 2nd Baron of Rosslyn, was one of the Knights who took back the city of Jerusalem during the first Crusade of 1099. Sir William, 3rd Baron of Rosslyn fought in the Battle of Bannockburn in 1314 along with his two sons.

"Sir Henry St Clair, the 6th Baron of Rosslyn, was one of the signers of the Declaration of Arbroath in 1320 that swore that Scotland's would never be ruled by England. Upon Robert Bruce's death, Sir Henry's son William, along with three other Scottish knights, took Bruce's heart to the Holy Land to be buried according to his wishes."

"I'm with you so far, but where is the connection to your father's murder?" asks DI Smithe.

"According to some historians, the Sinclairs were instrumental in starting the Templars along with their French relatives, the St. Clars. Their claim was that their founder Hugh de Payns married Catherine St. Clair, niece of his fellow crusader, the Duke of Champagne, Baron Henri St. Clari of Roslin in 1101. Baron Henri was a powerful broker, who supposedly had papal influence. They claimed their bloodline comes from the marriage of Jesus Christ and Mary Magdalene," Sara says.

Smithe laughs at the absurdity of it all. "That's absurd. This is *Da Vinci Code* stuff. Maybe 'Dan' stands for Dan Brown and he can solve this case."

"Well, maybe it is, but you must realize these people believe it," Sara says. "It pains me to think that my father got caught up in it. My father was well aware of his genealogy linked to the Pharez lineage, and was researching to see if his genealogy was connected to the Knights Templar as well."

"The way I see it there is a connection to the death of Robert the Bruce, Alisdair Sinclair, and your father. But I can't put my finger on it." Smithe is once again frustrated.

"How's that, Detective?" Sara says, confused.

"Let's say the ritual of cutting out the heart of royalty, is a practice of satanic groups to satisfy some ancient belief," Smithe speculates, "but I don't know why anyone would want to nick your father's ashes."

"I have known of these different bloodlines and secret societies and their strife for power and world domination ever since I was a little girl," says Sara. "My father told me that the tribe of Dan would one day try to destroy the bloodline of Judah in jealous revenge for God's judgment on their idolatry. They have always desired to nick the messianic birthright from the tribe of Judah and establish a false messianic kingdom in Israel. My father believed that one day the Antichrist would come from the tribe of Dan and he was about to expose their leader. That's why he attended all of those secret society meetings."

"Listen, it's been a pleasure, but I need to head back," Smithe says. He turns to Sara. "Thank you for opening your home to us, and for playing such a beautiful song on the harp."

Sara smiles. "You're quite welcome, Detective. I'm glad you enjoyed it. I just want to help in any way that I can. I love my father, and I want to see justice prevail for what has been done.

"I understand," Smithe says. "I am doing my best and promise that we will get justice for your father."

McNair chimes in and says he has to get back to prepare for his next seminar at the conference, but asks the group to meet again at his hotel for another video that he has brought along that will explain in more detail some of the concepts that Sara has just introduced. They all agree to meet on Sunday.

"Next time we meet, we will go back to a time when the nation of Ireland was founded and see how this famous bloodline of Jacob ended up there and the 'breach' of Judah's sons was healed through intermarriage. I think you will find this video very enlightening," McNair says.

After saying goodbye, Smithe heads outside into the rain, rushing to his car. As he pulls away from the curb, the windshield wipers swishing left and right, remind him of how he feels. He feels that his case is going back and forth and he feels as lost as ever. He can only hope that he will find justice for Alexander Flanders.

Chapter Five

It's Sunday morning and the rain has stopped as the group meet at McNair's hotel for another video presentation. DI Smithe has had another sleepless night thinking about all of the recent events. He can't seem to get the brutal murder scene out of his head. It is not like anything he has ever encountered in all of his years on the force. McNair starts the video presentation about the healing of the first overturn in Ireland.

It is a beautiful summer morning with the sun shining in Ireland 583 BC. King Heremon and Ethan, the king's closest friend and harper, are watching for the ship coming in with King Heremon's future bride, Princess Teia. Ethan is rugged looking and on the plump side and twenty-six years of age.

"There they are, Heremon!" Ethan shouted. "I see them. Look, Heremon over there! You can start getting nervous! Pretty soon you will be a married man!"

King Heremon is a handsome young man of twenty-seven. He watched as the ships came in to dock with his future bequeathed queen.

King Heremon responded, "Yes, I see the ships! Soon my future queen, who was promised me ever since I was a child, will soon be arriving. Indeed, I am getting nervous!"

Ethan, being facetious, replied, "I know, Heremon, I have heard this story of the healing of the Zarah–Pharez bloodlines a million times. I can hardly wait to see the beauty of the one they call Teia. Her beauty has spread from Egypt to Ireland. I hope for your sake she is as wise as she is beautiful and not a dragon! For my sake, I pray she has a beautiful friend!"

***

The ship finally docked and King Heremon spotted his beautiful maiden coming off the ship with her sister Scota. The patriarch Jeremiah was dressed in priestly garb, along with his scribe Simon Baruch 'Breg'. He and Ethan rushed out to meet Teia.

Heremon and Teia's eyes met. He bowed. "Princess Teia, I have heard so much about you and have been waiting for you for a long time, Heremon said."

Ethan rushed out to help Breg carry a huge chest that contained the Ark of the Covenant with a golden-colored banner wrapped around it with a face of a red lion. Inside the chest was King David's harp, Jacob's pillar stone, the sacred stones, *Urim* and *Thummin*, Aaron's rod that budded, and the Ten Commandments on stone, which were taken prior to King Nebuchadnezzar's siege of Jerusalem in 606 BC.

Ethan cried out, "I think I got the heavy load! We need you, King Heremon, and two others to carry this chest!"

Ethan looked with lustful eyes at the two beautiful Egyptian handmaidens who were still on the ship. "Nice day, eh, ladies?" he flirted.

The Egyptian handmaidens looked at each other and giggled!

King Heremon looked into Teia's beautiful brown eyes and introduced his friend Ethan from a distance. "That is my best friend, Ethan. We have been boyhood friends. He is a great companion but complains a lot! He is also my harper, and a good one at that!"

Princess Teia smiled. "Really? I love the harp as well. I brought my great-great-grandfather David's harp with me. Perhaps we can both play for the king someday!"

Ethan was getting anxious. "Are you coming, Heremon? We can't carry this heavy chest by ourselves!"

Heremon rolled his eyes. "I'm coming, impatient one!"

He picked up Teia and carried her out of the shallow water, then let her down gently on dry land. Heremon went out with two other men to help carry the huge chest to shore.

"Teia says she also plays the harp," Heremon told Ethan. "I think you will be good friends."

"Really, Heremon? I can't wait for the day when Teia and I play together for the king. Maybe we can both play for you some evening and put you to sleep."

Ethan gazed at one of the handmaidens and smiled. She returned the smile! As the men struggled to carry the huge chest, Ethan looked at the Egyptian handmaid and said, "Good heavens, is this chest heavy. Perhaps one of Teia's fair handmaids could give me a back massage afterwards?" The woman giggled.

***

Heremon caught up with Teia and they walked together along the beach. "How was your voyage, fair maiden? Were the seas kind to you?"

"It has been a very long voyage, from Egypt to Spain and from Spain to here," Teia explained. "At one point I didn't know if we were going to make it as the strong tempest tore at our sails and the water from the sea drenched us. But God had mercy upon us and I am so glad we are here on dry land. My stomach is still churning! I have learned so much about people along our journey. I have seen kindness as well as wickedness and treachery and deceit. Tell me, how long has your family been in this beautiful part of the world? The countryside is so beautiful. I have never seen anything quite like it!"

She glanced at the green rolling hills of Ireland.

Ireland coast, 2015, Ronald Wlodyga

King Heremon enlightened Teia regarding his family's history.

"Our family came here to Scota six hundred years ago just before the famine set in Jerusalem. We were very fortunate that we did not have to go through the wars with Babylon as did the rest of our Israelite brothers. We came with the tribe of Dan, or as we Irish call them, Tuatha De' Danaan, which means 'tribe' or 'people of Ireland.'

"They were famous for their shipbuilding, and so my great-grandparents came with the tribe of Dan when the famine started in Jerusalem. Our fellow Israelites have been scattered in many parts of the world. Many who first settled here are from the tribe of Dan, but my family is of the tribe of Judah, as are you!

"According to the prophets, our bloodlines must unite to heal this breach of our great-grandfather Jacob to fulfill the promise of Yeshua to his grandfather Abraham. You and I are destined to do so, and so we will be married soon and you will be my queen. I believe this marriage was arraigned in heaven!"

Teia expressed her concern. "I wish I was as confident as you and my counselor Jeremiah. He will demand a great diary. Time will tell."

"Yes, time will tell, fair maiden, but for now you and your entourage are my guests tonight at a party at Clothair, the court of our Irish Monarchs. It is a beautiful place and the royal residence of my ancestors."

***

Teia and her entourage arrived with their luggage to settle in and change their clothes. Heremon showed them the beautiful grounds of his palace with flowers and trees. Ethan flirted with the Egyptian handmaid. Heremon walked with Teia, Jeremiah, and Breg around the grounds. After the troop toured the grounds, Jeremiah sat on an outside porch and talked to Teia alone.

Meanwhile, Ethan flirted with the ladies and told a joke to the entourage. "Hey, did you hear the one when the patriarch Jacob asked his sons one day, 'Do you want to go to heaven'? His sons, Judah, Levi, Joseph, and Isachar, said, 'Yes, Father, we want to go to heaven.' So, Jacob said to them, 'Then stand over there against the wall.'

"Then Jacob asked his other sons, 'Do you want to go to heaven'? Simeon, Dan, Gad, Asshur and Zebulon said, 'Certainly we do.' So, Jacob said, 'Then stand over there against the wall with your brothers.'

"Then Jacob said to his youngest son Benjamin, who had not yet responded, 'Do you want to go to heaven, Benjamin'? And Benjamin said to his father, 'No, I don't Father.' And Jacob said to his remaining sons, 'I don't believe this. You mean to tell me, Benjamin, that when you die you don't want to go to heaven'? And Benjamin said to his father, 'Oh, when I die, yes. I thought you were getting a group together to go right now!' "

***

The group had a hardy laugh! After walking around the grounds, Jeremiah the Prophet spoke to Teia about his concerns, he said,

"This is a beautiful place, Teia, but I feel the spirit of so many false gods that have come here over the years, as one can tell from these wooden and stone objects of Baal. It seems that Baal has followed us everywhere! While most of our fellow Israelites had to suffer the pain and anguish of famine in Jerusalem and the slavery in Egypt, these Zarites were most fortunate to come here with the ships of Dan.

"Look, Teia, see the flag of Zarah with the red hand and King David's harp? It still flies here! I almost feel like we are back in Jerusalem when I warned your father, Zedekiah, about the wrath of God for putting idols in the land and not trusting in Him."

Jeremiah pointed at a huge stone obelisk and says to Teia, "That obelisk has to go! Oh, if your father had only listened to me as God revealed his fate to me. Oh, if he had only listened to me your brothers would still be alive!"

***

After the long walk, Jeremiah returned home and being exhausted he sat in a rocking chair and began to dream. He was taken back to a time his beloved Jerusalem was destroyed in 568 BC as he rebuked Zedekiah, the last King of Judah, in King Zedekiah's palace in Jerusalem before its fall to the Babylonian king Nebuchadnezzar. Jeremiah 1:38.

King Zedekiah was getting a back massage from one of his servants after bathing in a whirlpool. The king had a towel wrapped around him.

Jeremiah came up to him and said, "You know King Zedekiah, God has called me to be a prophet to this nation before I was even formed in my mother's belly. He appeared to me when I was a child and ordained me and told me then that I must speak to whoever he commands me and to not be afraid even though I was a child."

King Zedekiah said, "Yes, I know this to be true, Jeremiah, God's Prophet!"

Jeremiah admonished him. "So, you understand that the words that I speak are not mine but the Lord's!"

King Zedekiah nodded. "Yes, I know this also, Jeremiah the Lord's prophet!" He turned his head and said, "Servant, bring me a cold drink and one for Jeremiah!"

Jeremiah continued the Lord's warning. "Then hear these words of the Lord, King Zedekiah. He has told me that because this wicked nation has forsaken the Lord their God and has burned incense to other gods, committed adultery, and worshipped and followed Baal, the sun god instead, He is going to bring utter destruction upon it.

"The Eternal is angered that His chosen nation has forgotten how He brought them out of the land of Egypt when they were in bondage and fed them and protected them forty years in the desert. Yahweh sent many prophets over these years to warn this rebellious nation of what He would do if it did not change its ways. Now I am its last prophet and the Eternal has told me this nation is doomed to destruction!"

King Zedekiah's eyes widened. "You have told me these things before, Jeremiah, and I hear the words of the Lord! But what can I do?"

Jeremiah declared, "The Lord said this nation has turned their back on Him and not looked upon Him with their face! Now they will see that their gods of wood and stone will not save them. Only God can save them! You plead with Him, but He will not listen anymore. How quick this nation, which was a bride unto Him, has forsaken her attire. She has played the harlot instead by pursuing other gods! Gods that our fathers did not know!"

***

Just as Jeremiah had predicted, the invading armies of Babylon brought God's wrath upon the rebellious nation. Jeremiah stayed in the court of the prison and watched the invading armies of Nebuchadnezzar ransack, pillage, and burn the city of Jerusalem. Zedekiah fled the city by way of the king's garden, by the gate between the two walls, and ran out to a field as Nebuchadnezzar's armies chased him and his sons.

They caught Zedekiah and his sons in the plains of Jericho and brought him up to Nebuchadnezzar king of Babylon, where he gave judgment upon him. King Nebuchadnezzar of Babylon took out his sword and killed the sons of Zedekiah before his very eyes, then he put out the eyes of Zedekiah! Jeremiah 52:10-11.

The captain of the guard gave Jeremiah food and released him. His friend Azariah said, "Jeremiah, you speak falsely. The Lord our God has not sent you to say, Go not into Egypt to sojourn there: But Baruch your scribe, the son of Neriah set you against us, for to deliver us into the hand of the Chaldeans, that they might put us to death, and carry us away captives into Babylon."

Johanan the captain of the Babylonian forces told the people, "Get all of the people moving. We are leaving this land of famine and going to Egypt where there is food and water."

All the remnant of Judah including men, women, children, and king Zedekiah's daughters, and Jeremiah the prophet, and his scribe Baruch headed out to the land of Egypt: for they obeyed not the voice of the LORD. Jeremiah chapters 42- 43.

***

Jeremiah's reminiscence of his journey has ended and he returns back to the reality of Ireland where he is known by his Irish name, Ollam. He tells Teia of his dream and how he had warned her father of the impending invasion if he would not change his heart.

"I know, Ollam," Teia said to comfort him. "Even though I was very young at the time, I still remember it well! I also remember our grueling trip to Egypt on those stinky camels. But we were treated so well there and our time there was very enjoyable in the Kings palace!"

Ollam responded, "Yes, I, too, remember that bumpy ride on camels, and at my age it was not much fun! But we were very blessed that King Hophra of Egypt took us in and adopted you and your sister as his very own daughters. But now I am frightful of what God may do to this place as He did in Israel and to the Egyptians if they did'nt stop worshipping these idols. Heremon's father was like Zedekiah who has been so influenced by other nations that they have forgotten and forsaken the God of our fathers Abraham, Isaac, and Jacob. I must tell Heremon, as I have told all leaders before him, that these idols of Baal are not pleasing to our great God, for He is a jealous God."

***

King Heremon entered the room. "Teia, shall we entertain with the harp?"

"Yes!" she exclaimed.

They each sat down on a stool in front of beautiful, ornate harps.

They both played as Teia sang,

Unless the fates are faithless grown,
And the prophets' voice be vain,
Where 'ere is found the sacred stone,
The wanderers race shall reign.

After the song was over, Teia said, "Now you sing one, Heremon."

Heremon complied.

And you, Tower of the Flock,
You fair maiden of Zion!
Produce your adornments, and come forth the queen,
The princess of kingdoms, Jerusalem's daughter!

After they had finished the song, the people clapped. Teia and King Heremon took a bow, then mingled among the crowd. King Heremon approached Ollam to inform him of his intentions to marry Teia.

"The prophecies say that the breach to heal the Zarah and Pharez bloodlines must be fulfilled and I would like to marry Teia. I pray that you, as her guardian, would give me her hand in marriage, he said."

Ollam smiled. "Yes, I know the prophecies very well, King Heremon, for that is part of the commission Yeshua gave me. But first, before I agree to this marriage, you must rid this place of all of the idols of the Druids and start worshipping God the way He desires. You are king, and like all the kings of Israel, including Teia's father who went astray, our God will not bless your marriage. You must rid this land of all its idols and reinstitute the Torah before I will agree to your marriage to Teia."

King Heremon was relieved. "I know the Druid priests believe they have the true religion but are deceived, and I have argued with them about their pagan practices on many occasions. I am glad you are here to give me strength to confront them!"

Ollam pated the king on the back. "King Heremon, together we will confront these pagan priests of Baal, and like Elijah, we will kill them and rid this land of them, and with God's help we will restore God's true ways!" 1 Kings 18:40. A few months passed and the kingdom was bustling with excitement for the royal wedding in Ireland between King Heremon and Teia. On the morning before the wedding, Teia was playing a harp when Ollam entered the room.

"You play such beautiful music, Teia," Ollam said. "I could listen to you all day long. It reminds me of the good old days in Jerusalem and all the wonderful times we had there. If only your father and all the kings before him had listened to me, we would still be there. Instead, they threw me in prison. I tried to warn them for many years of what would happen if they did not repent before the Lord.

"If only they had listened! But that was then, and now we are getting ready for you to marry the king of Ireland and heal this breach between the Zarah and Pharez bloodlines. God had planned that you would marry this Israelite prince of the Zarah bloodline long before we arrived here, just as He planned my commission before I was even born. God has indeed kept His promise to your great-great-grandfather Jacob and his grandfather Abraham before him." Jeremiah 1:4–7; 21:1–14; 34–37.

***

Teia acknowledged her prophetic destiny. "Yes, the Lord is good and you have been a father to me through it all. I know I am about to marry Heremon of the Zarah bloodline, the high king of Ireland. I can hardly believe it. What a wonderful God we worship. Do you like this dress that Heremon has picked out for me to wear on this glorious occasion?" She said.

Ollam smiled with pride. "Yes, the dress is beautiful and you are beautiful as your Hebrew name Tephi implies. You were also named Tara after your great-grandmother of the scarlet thread which in Hebrew means 'palm.' This is a name given to many of the woman of our heritage of royal blood.

Here they call you Teia. Your beauty goes beyond your radiant skin, and as long as you keep your heart pure, our God will be with you and your children." 1 Chron. 3:9; 2 Sam. 14:27.

Teia went back to her harp and sang a song of one of the Hebrew psalmist's hymns:

It is a good thing to give thanks unto the LORD, and to sing praises unto thy name, O most High
To show forth your loving-kindness in the morning, and your faithfulness every night,
Upon an instrument of ten strings, and upon the psaltery; upon the harp with a solemn sound.
For you, LORD, has made me glad through your work: I will triumph in the works of your hands. Psalm 92:1–4.

***

Ollam reminisced once again about the good old days. "That was just beautiful, Teia, and it reminds me of the happy days in Jerusalem when your father Zedekiah was king before Nebuchadnezzar of Babylon invaded us and plucked his eyes out and killed all of your brothers. Nebuchadnezzar was God's instrument for Judah's disobedience, but God made sure that his promise to King David would also be fulfilled.

"That the kingly line of King David would always be preserved. And when a child is born of you and Heremon, the kingly bloodline will continue and God's promise to your great-grandfather Jacob will be fulfilled. King David would be happy that we took his harp with us so you could play his psalms to music. And tomorrow you will be coroneted as queen over the very stone that we brought with us that your grandfather Jacob slept upon that all of the kings of Israel have been crowned upon."

"Yes, Ollam, it will be a happy day," Teia said. "We have come such a long way to fulfill God's promises. I love to play my great-grandfather David's harp to remind me of the happy days we spent in Jerusalem before its fall. I remember at that time I called you by your Hebrew name Jeremiah. Here in Ireland, they call you Ollam Fodhla because you are a wise teacher.

"I often think of the journey that we took to Egypt and the happy times we had there as well with my father Hapti, who adopted us and how he arranged for us to sail in ships with our Danite brothers to Spain. God said we would be a special people to Him and that we are a chosen people. Without them we wouldn't have made it to Spain and then to Ireland. Ollam, tell me more of the promise God gave to my great-grandfather and of the commission he gave to you concerning my destiny."

"Teia, God told me to pull down, to destroy, and then to build and to plant or to take you and your sister out of Jerusalem so that the promise He made to King David in the scriptures would be fulfilled. God told David that he would always have a descendant of his bloodline on the throne until the Messiah would return and restore our nation to prominence in the world. They called the Messiah Shiloh, meaning 'peace'."

Jeremiah 1:9–10; 35–36; 33:17; 38:1–4; 41:10–17; 43:6; Ezek. 21:25–27; Gen. 17:4, 6; 1 Kings 2:4; 9:1–5; Isa. 54:17; 2 Chron. 7:17–18; Psa. 89:3–4; 132:10–12.

Teia was confused about her role and asked, "What did Yeshua mean when He told you to pull down, destroy, build and plant?" Teia inquired of Ollam.

"This I do not know, my child, just as I did not know that we would wind up here in Ireland until it was revealed. Perhaps your seed will someday be joined with someone in another country and this will be part of the meaning! Perhaps it will then be turned over in two other countries before it is given to its rightful owner. The Prophet Ezekiel indicated that the crown would have 'three overturns' before it would be given to its rightful owner—our Messiah." Ezek. 21:26–27.

Chapter Six

The video ends and Dr. McNair turns on the lights.
"Well, that is the end of this video, and before I start the next one, let me explain its importance to the murder investigation."

Smithe perks his ears. He found the video interesting, but still doesn't know how it all relates and waits for Dr. McNair to elaborate.

"Thus far we have clues from Dr. Flanders that the stone appears to be connected to the monarchies of England, Ireland, and Scotland, which most people understand," McNair says. "But I believe he was also showing us a connection to the bloodline of Robert the Bruce by showing us the family crest.

"He demonstrated this by the genealogy charts on his wall, as well as providing a clue of his family crest of King Robert the Bruce of Scotland. He especially seemed interested in the tribe of Dan in their travels, which brought us to Ireland in the last video.

"Some researchers believe the Prophet Jeremiah brought the daughter of King Zedekiah, Tei Tephi, to Ireland to heal the breach of the Zarah–Pharez bloodlines. This was called the first 'overturn' of the royal crown, that is, until He comes whose right it is, which is Jesus. We will now continue our story of what was going on in Ireland as paganism became rampant and may be connected to the renegade tribe of Dan."

***

Dr. McNair had just given Smithe, Humphrey, and Sara more historical insight as to the connection to the Stone of Destiny and how it ended up in Ireland to heal the Zarah–

Pharez breach of the royal bloodline, fulfilling the promise God gave to the Patriarch Jacob. Ezekiel 21:26–27.

Smithe is feeling somewhat impatient. He appreciates the Doctor's knowledge, even if he is a bit eccentric. But still, after all this time, he doesn't have any concrete answers. This isn't a shut-and-close case, but he thought he would be further along in the investigation by now.

"My father told me of the three 'overturns' written in the book of Ezekiel and that the first one occurred in Ireland. He believed the coronation of Queen Teia of our ancient ancestry and King Heremon took place over the Stone of Destiny, thus healing the breach of the first 'overturn' of royal bloodlines from Jacob's son Judah of kingly lineage," Sara says.

"Sara is spot on, and the first video explained this ancient history," McNair says, "I hope you found it fascinating. Now I will play part two that will show some of the ancient beliefs of these people that have filtered into today's world and the possible reason for the cutting out of Dr. Flanders's heart."

***

Once again, the video begins as Queen Teia and King Heremon are about to take their marriage vows. They are dressed in royal garb and they give their pledges of faithfulness to each other and then stand on the Lia Fáil Stone, as it was also called, with the golden banner waving over them.

Heremon states his vows to Teia. Ollam is presiding over them. Heremon is handsome; he's clean shaven except for a shadow of a beard. He is wearing a blue velvet suit with a red velvet bonnet with a cock feather and a red ruby brooch around his neck with a gold chain. He speaks to a gathered crowd.

"From this time onward, this hill shall be called Tara, meaning 'Torah,' as I have reinstituted the Torah law of the Lord and His ways according to Ollam Fodhla's instructions. No longer will our people worship the false gods of Baal in this place! We shall keep the Lord's Sabbaths and circumcise our children according to our customs. No longer will we eat the swine and allow the pagan customs of the Druids in our land. The impure gods and goddesses of Zidon, Tyre, and Phillistia that have influenced our lands for generations will be abolished!"

Heremon walked over to Teia who was seated on the coronation stone, draped with a purple velvet cloth dressed in a white gown with flowers in her hair. He sat down beside her and clasped her hand, looked in her eyes, and smiled. A crown was placed upon his head and the mantle upon his shoulders.

The crowd cheered and shouted, 'Long live the king!'

King Heremon gave Queen Teia a gentle kiss on the lips, then said, "As long as we both shall live, we shall rule this land together making sure that the laws and customs of our forefathers are preserved for the benefit of God's people!"

"Yes, my lord, we shall!" Queen Teia shouted.

Heremon looked into Teia's eyes and prognosticates,

Except old seers do feign and wizard wits be blind, the royals in place must reign where they this stone shall find! He who is crowned upon this stone is destined to be the true king of the people and rule all the lands.

The Marriage of Queen Teia and King Heremon.

It is not long after their marriage that trouble began to stir. The home of Queen Teia Tephi was thirty miles west of

Newgrange, Ireland. Bressail 'Bres', a handsome and tall man of six-five, was the king of the nearby town of Ulster and a favorite of the people, especially the women. He was popular because of his good looks and tall stature, but he began to take advantage of the people by taxing them, which caused the people to become poverty-stricken.

***

After hearing the voices and concerns of the townspeople, Ethan arrived on horseback to tell Queen Teia of what is happening and what the people were saying of Bres. "Teia, where is the king? I have something very important to tell him?"

"King Heremon is away on important business," Queen Teia replied. "Is there a problem?"

Ethan informed her of what had just happened in town. "I have just heard the people of Ulster complaining about the high taxes and hoarding of the people's money by King Bres. He is becoming very wealthy while their lives are miserable, and they hate him but don't know what to do about him. He is ambitious and wants to extend his territory toward Tara. I thought you should know, my queen!"

Queen Teia appreciated Ethan's loyalty. "Thank you, my faithful servant, Ethan, for keeping me informed as to that scoundrel Bres's intentions. Ollam, what should we do about this tyrant?" She said.

Ollam, who was listening, provided his insight. "Bres has indeed been wrongfully misguided by his Druid advisors and their false magic and sorcery. He is just like his great-grandfather Nimrod who built that high tower and wanted the people to worship him instead of the God of our fathers in Noah's day. Now Bres is building a tower to himself to be worshipped!"

Breg, who was better known as Ollam's scribe Baruch, jumped into the conversation. "Ah, Nimrod was Satan's instrument to deceive the entire world into worshipping the Devil instead of the true God just after the flood. The Druids have carried on his false teachings and magical practices in their priesthood to this very day and we must stop them! They worship the serpent and the sun, and it is your responsibility as God's chosen to stop them, Queen Teia."

"Breg is right, Teia, we must stop these shemesh worshippers from influencing God's people by their sorceries and mysteries, just like Shem stopped Nimrod," Ollam shouted. "We must rid this land of these priests of Baal and the offering of innocent children to Moloch just like Elijah! Their drunken orgies and pleasing of the flesh with their woman and their wild music are abominations to our great God just as they were when God destroyed them by the great flood!"

Teia nodded her head in agreement. "Yes, we must be prepared to rid them of our land before they try to enforce their ways upon us just like Nimrod."

***

Heremon had just returned home and overheard the dilemma. In a stern voice, he exclaimed, "Ethan, prepare the men for a fight!"

Ethan nods his head. "I'll ring the warning bell to summon the men in the village," he said.

"How many men do we have?" Heremon inquired.

"Although Bres has thousands, we only have two hundred and fifty, but we can muster up the most dedicated fighters he will ever see!" Ethan said, "Besides, our God is stronger than his!"

Filled with rage, Heremon turned to his men and yelled, "Get our horses ready and let's prepare a battle plan. I think I know of where we can ambush him as his men approach Tara!"

Ethan rang the bell to summon the men in the village. Heremon and Ethan mounted their horses to assemble the men in the nearby villages. They charged into the village, shouting at the top of their lungs for the men to unite, and for as many men as they can find to join their army.

***

In another village, Bres prepared his men for battle. Bres was dressed in a white robe and sandals. He was wearing a white mitered hat, which is symbolic of the chief temple Druid priest, with a gold chain around his neck and a medallion with a black snake on it. Several temple Druid priests were putting on their headdresses that resemble the faces of eagles with long beaks and costumes filled with yellow feathers.

A prophetess named Ashua was involved in temple rituals. She was getting ready for a human sacrifice in preparation for the battle against the queen of Tara. The sacrifice was a young twelve-year-old virgin, who was crying hysterically along with her mother.

The priests were also bathing their sick in white milk as a herd of white cows were grazing nearby. Bres asked them if their power was more powerful than the god of Abraham. The temple was well lit as flaming torches gave off a reddish-yellow light. They lit candles upon the altar and there was a noticeable stench in the air from the blood of animals sacrificed on the altar, camouflaged by the aroma of the scents of aloe, frankincense, and myrrh.

Bres addressed his Druid prophetess Ashura. She was an old woman with long gray scraggly hair in tattered clothes. She was sitting by the altar with a bowl of ashes mixed with oil and spices and herbs. She had a bowl ready to be mixed with blood and handed it to Bres. She read from an occult book and chanted something in a mixed Gaelic-Hebrew to the god of Baal to help them in battle.

"Ashura, what can you tell me regarding the visions and the power we wield over Queen Teia of Tara?" Bres inquired.

"The visions have come to me, my lord, and our god Baal will be with you if the sacrifice is prepared to satisfy him. He says you will defeat this evil queen and Tara will be yours!" Ashura responded with a cackle.

Bres asked if the sacrifice was a virgin. "Is she pure?"

Ashura declared, "She is a pure virgin, my lord!"

Bres then told her to bring the virgin to the temple. Ashura grabbed the young virgin and pulled her from her mother as both were screaming and crying, knowing her fate. She was led up to the temple, and two of the temple priests grabbed her arms so she was not able to get free. She was naked. Accompanied by other temple priests, Bres walked over to the girl and said a prayer to the god Baal to accept the offering. Then he took his knife and slit the girl's throat.

"Catch every drop of blood!" Bres said to Ashura.

"Yes, my lord, and I will mix the virgin's blood with my brew for your men to drink to give them strength. Mix it with the fruit of the vine!"

Ashura poured a little blood into a bowl of a powder mixture of herbs, then handed it to Bres who poured wine into it. He held up the wine mixture, then took a sip. He passed it around to the others.

Bres turned to Amhergin, his Druid metal forger, and said, "Here, drink of this alchemy. Tell me, Amhergin, what power do you wield over this queen of Tara?"

Amhergin drank the brew. He said, "It is not hard to tell, my lord. For every spear that is made by me or sword that has been forged by my hand shall no skin which they pierce taste life afterwards."

Bres smiled evilly. Then he turned to Lug, his healer. "Here, drink of this alchemy, Lug. Tell me, what power do you wield over this queen of Tara?"

Lug took a sip of the brew and said, "It is not hard to tell, my lord. For every man that is wounded in battle, unless his head has been severed, I will bathe in the anointed white milk and make him whole again."

Bres then inquired of Ogam, his armor maker. "Here, drink of this alchemy, Ogam. Tell me, what power do you wield over this queen of Tara?"

Ogam took a sip of the brew. "It is not hard to tell, my lord. I will supply all of the armor for battle."

Bres turned to Feir, his spear maker. "Here, drink of this alchemy, Feir. Tell me, what power do you wield over this queen of Tara?"

After taking a sip of the brew, Feir said, "It is not hard to tell, my lord. I will provide all of the javelins and shafts and shields."

Bres finally turned to Gisors, his sorcerer. "Here, drink of this alchemy, Gisors. Tell me, what power do you wield over this queen of Tara?"

Gisors took the last sip of the drink and said. "It is not hard to tell, my lord. I will provide the power of my sorcerers and cast a spell upon them that they will be filled with fear."

Bres was pleased with his men and the power they would yield. "So, let it be!" he shouted. "For tomorrow we shall rule not only Ulster, but Tara as well and all her treasuries! Then let us feast and dance tonight before we engage in battle. For if we die tomorrow, then we shall be in glory tonight!"

The men cheered and the festivities began. They drank wine, toasted to one another and ate like pigs, ripping off bread and the legs of quail and geese that had been roasting on spits and drank out of bowls. The army made love to their women and danced and sang and frolicked! It was a night filled with drunkenness and debauchery.

***

The next morning, Bres arose and called out his men to prepare for battle. They were armed and ready.

Prior to the battle, Ollam was dressed in priestly garb and praying at an altar that he made. He was wearing the breastplate of Aaron that had been stored in the large trunk that accompanied him and Teia on their journey from the Holy Land to Egypt, then on to Spain and finally Ireland. The breastplate that he brought with him from Jerusalem that the high priest Aaron wore contained twelve precious stones engraved with the names of the twelve tribes of Israel and pouches in the back that contained the onyx stones of enlightenment and perfection called *Urim* and *Thummin*.

Heremon observed the two stones of enlightenment and perfection on the breastplate that Ollam was wearing as he prayed to the Eternal for wisdom.

"Tell me, Ollam, what do the two enlightener stones, *Urim* and *Thummin,* upon your breastplate say concerning this war with Bres?"

Ollam said, "As you know, Heremon, when the high priest of Israel was consulted concerning the will of God, he prayed and waited to see Yeshua's answer through these precious stones. If a cloud appeared around the *Thummin* stone on the left side of the priest's breastplate, it meant that it was not the Lord's will. And when the *Urim* stone on the right side of the priest's breastplate had a glow around it, it meant that God was giving his blessing or approval.

"What then is Yeshua's will concerning this war with Bres?" Heremon asked.

Ollam reached into the pocket on the back of the breastplate containing the *Urim stone*. "As you can see, the *Urim* is glowing, which means the Eternal has spoken to me through these precious stones as He did Moses's brother Aaron, the High Priest of Israel. The stones of light and truth have told me that we will be successful against these enemies of darkness. God will once again triumph over evil as in the days of Moses! These magicians and sorcerers will come to nothing like they did in Egypt. Their lust for money and power will come to an end. For greed always breeds hatred like bees on a honeycomb."

Heremon shook his head. He had some doubt and lacked faith. "But, Ollam, how can a measly two hundred and fifty men with little armor defeat six thousand trained and well-armored men?" he inquired.

Ollam encouraged God's will. "You forget one important thing, Heremon. God is on our side and that tips the balances. Remember how our great God has intervened in the course and affairs of our people over the years to save us despite the odds? Remember how He smote the Egyptians to take us out of slavery when our people had to make bricks with straw for the Pharaoh? And how the Eternal destroyed the mighty army of the Assyrians who outnumbered us one hundred to one.

"Remember how he defeated the Ammonites and Moabites who came against Judah with a vast army in the days of Jehoshaphat. 2 Chron. 20. Like Jehoshaphat, I will petition Yeshua for mercy and ask the people to pray and sing and have faith. Recall how the walls of Jericho came tumbling down as the priest circled the city with the Ark! With God on our side, who can be against us?" Heb. 11:30.

Heremon understood what Ollam had said, but he still had doubts. "But we don't have the Ark, Ollam!"

Ollam clasped his hands together. "You know not of what you speak, Heremon my king! Remember that heavy chest that your friend Ethan and you carried from the ship when we landed?"

"Do I ever, it was so heavy! My back still aches! You mean it was the . . . the Ark?"

"The same one our forefathers carried all the way from the wilderness to Jerusalem! Aside from the Ark, there are two other objects inside the Ark that can give us power from above!" Ollam said.

"What are these two objects you speak of, Ollam?"

"Because the light of perfection has lit up, it indicates that our merciful God has spoken to us and He will be with us!" Ollam explained. "Inside the Ark is the Stone of Destiny and Aaron's rod that budded! As you know the story of the rebels of Israel Heremon, how God separated them from God's chosen leader Aaron—when the princes of Israel, including Aaron placed their 12 rods before the tabernacle of witness and only Aaron's budded with almonds. These three give evidence of our great God and each has power within. There is only one more holy vessel that is more powerful than all of these and can nullify their power." Numbers 17:5–10.

Confused, Heremon said, "What vessel is that?"

"The king that God has made holy by sitting on the coronation stone as King of Israel," Ollam replied. "If God delights in that king, he is granted God's power from above. If God does not delight in him, God will not be with him even if these holy vessels are in his possession. It is the King that can influence the people to repent, just as Jehoshaphat encouraged the people to have faith and sing praises of his holiness."

"Who does God grant this power to today?" Heremon questioned. "And how did you bring the Ark here from the Holy Land?"

Ollam chuckled. "You ask a lot of questions, my son. When the armies of Nebuchadnezzar were invading and burning our Temple, I went into the Temple along with the High Priest Eleazor, to recover the Holy artifacts. At the same time, Eleazor went into the Holy of Holies where the Ark was, who alone could enter it. Eleazar dragged the Ark to the other side of the curtain where I was waiting with some of the other priests, and together we carried it out of the Temple. It was very heavy and I felt my back crack!"

Heremon's eyes widened. "Well then, what happened to it?"

"The flames were shooting out of the Temple like a dragon's breath coming out of his nostrils on a cold winter's night! It was hotter than the fiery furnace where Daniel and the three lads were imprisoned by King Darius. The priests dug a deep hole on the north side of the Temple where it was not burning and buried the Ark there. I left for Egypt with Teia and many others, and then years later when I was allowed to return to Jerusalem, I dug up the Ark and sailed to Spain with Teia on the Ships of Tarshish!" Daniel 3:11–30.

"So, if the stone did not light up, Yeshua would not be with us?" Heremon asked.

"So, it would be, but it did light up and our God will be with us as He was in the days of Moses!" Ollam reaffirmed God's will.

Heremon was still confused. "But, Ollam, what if you had not taken the Ark and temple artifacts? What if Nebuchadnezzar's army had confiscated them and they came into the possession of the Druids? Would they have received this power?"

"No, my son. You see, these are holy artifacts and can only be used by those whom Yeshua considers holy. Remember when Uzza died when he tried to help steady the Ark when it was falling? 2 Sam. 6:6-7. And when fifty thousand men of Bethshemesh looked into the Ark and died instantly? This only proves that not just anyone can handle or carry the Ark! Our great God has shown us that only those chosen by Him for special purpose will be blessed.

"I had hands laid upon me by the High Priest before Jerusalem's fall as Eleazer was dying and transferring his power to me. He had hands laid upon him by his father and so on all the way back to Aaron. When I married you and Teia, I anointed you and pronounced you as king upon the Stone of Destiny. God has accepted you as King of Israel!" 1 Chron. 13:9–10; Numbers 27:18–24; 1 Sam. 14:36–46.

Heremon finally understood God's will for him. "Praise be to our great God! I will serve Him and try to glorify Him with all of my heart and soul as did King David!"

"Remember, Heremon, how God delivered our people out of the hands of the Egyptians and how He delivered Solomon from the Philistines? So shall it be with us! Yeshua will be with us. As long as we have the Stone, Aaron's Rod that budded, the Ark, and a righteous king, we have power!"

***

Heremon felt protected by God's love and power and was ready for battle as Bres's army approached several days later.

King Heremon was dressed in his kingly outfit, quite different than his men who were wearing ordinary leather garb. He was riding a gray-and-white Meyer. Most of the men did not have any armor. King Heremon was wearing a dyed red deerskin fur cap with white fur trim. His boots were shiny black leather as were his gloves. Heremon looked more like a king than a warrior. He had on a red ruby necklace with a gold chain. He was clean-shaven and quite a contrast to the grubby, bearded Bres, who had exchanged his priestly garb for ordinary battle clothes.

Bres was speaking to his warlords marching forward mostly on foot with hundreds on huge warhorses. "We must defeat King Heremon and his army because he wants to take our gold and silver and our land away from us and give it back to the people. He wants to teach them the Torah. We cannot let this happen, for we shall lose everything. We must show him and his new queen that our god Baal is more powerful than theirs!"

Meanwhile, Ethan and Heremon were talking about their battle plan among the assembled army of 250 men. Half of them were on horseback and the others were sharpening their spears, flexing their bows and strapping on their leather and chain armor suits. Like king Jehoshaphat, Heremon had summoned singers in the vanguard before the army, singing:

Give thanks to the Lord
For his love enures forever

Like Jehoshaphat's example, Heremon and Ethan planned an ambush. Ethan pointed to a very large hill that his men could hide behind. "See that steep hill over there, Heremon? I will take fifty of our best men on horses and fifty long-bowman and hide behind it. You and your fifty men on horses will stand out in the open for Bres and his army to see. They will think you are easy prey.

"We have also dug trenches that are covered with leaves that Bres's men's horses will fall into when they ride like the blazes toward you. Stand your ground! When you see them coming within fifty feet, start riding with your men to meet them with your swords and lances high in the air, but stop short of the trenches. We have fifty men hiding in the pits under the leaves, and when they have fallen into the pit like apples from a tree and are out in the open with their men on foot, we will attack from behind!"

Heremon concurred. "May the God of our fathers be with us to smite the sorceries of this evil man!"

The battle began as warriors clashed their shields, lances, and swords. Javelins were thrown and arrows flew.

Heremon rode his horse to Teia who was on her white Arabian horse under a tree in a safe place. She would watch the battle along with Ollam and Breg from afar.

"Our plan is ready, my love," Heremon said to Teia. "If I should die in battle, I know I will see you again in heaven's kingdom." Then he reached over to give her a final kiss.

Heremon then raced out to his men, and Teia yelled as he left, "May our God be with you, my love!"

***

In the distance were five hundred horses of Bres's army with lances galloping toward them. Heremon's men were mostly on foot advancing with spears and axes in hand. The ground below the horses' hooves shot up in the air and the noise of their hooves sounded like a drummer. As both armies advanced, the thunder of pounding hooves became louder and louder.

One of Bres's men was holding a pole with a green flag that had a serpent on it. Bres spotted Heremon's men out in the open and immediately started galloping faster toward them while Heremon held his position. One of Heremon's men had a lance in his hand with a red flag with a gold Lion on it.

As Bres's army neared the trenches, Heremon rode with his men faster and faster until they were five feet from the trenches. They stopped their horses dead in their tracks, while Bres and his riders, unaware of the pits covered with leaves, fell into them. Men were flying off their horses and being crushed underneath them.

Heremon's men got off their horses and the battle began in the pits. Wounded horses laid everywhere, and Heremon's men arose from beneath the leaves to cut the throats and stab the fallen men. The clash of steel against steel could be heard, as well as horses whinnying and screeching in pain echoing in the air. Crushing, thumping noises bellowing out could be heard for miles! Horses and the men of Bres's army laid dead on the ground.

Arrows were protruding from the bodies, as Ethan's bowmen were shooting arrows into the sky. The sky was thick with arrows and looked like a flock of black crows. Ethan advanced with his men, who were clad with metal helmets, lances, crossbows, and axes from the rear to do battle with Bres's men on foot. Swords were clanging and sparks were flying from the axes.

Heremon spotted Bres coming out of the pit with a sword in hand. Their eyes met and their anger for one another was apparent.

With venom in his mouth, Heremon shouted, "Come on, Bres! Let us finish this thing! Let's see how much sorcery you have now!"

"You royal arse, come and get your due!" Bres shouted.

***

From a distance, it appeared that Bres's army was winning the battle. Ollam was on top of a hill in the distance, raising his arms to the sky with the rod of Aaron in his hand just as Moses did in the battle with Amalek, and it appeared that Heremon's army had increased tenfold! This could only be explained as miraculous! Exodus 17:10–16.

The fight between Heremon and Bres continued. The two men did battle with swords. Bres cut Heremon's arm, and Heremon's sword went flying into the air. Bres was ready to run Heremon through with his sword.

"Now we'll see whose god is more powerful, you royal arse!" Bres sneerd.

Bres thrust his sword through Heremon and blood gushed out of his side. Heremon moaned in pain. He fell to the ground and the world seemed to be moving in slow motion. His eyelids felt heavy, his body cold, and the pain seemed to vanish. He was ready to go home to his Father.

Ethan spotted him and dove upon Bres with knife in hand ready to cut his throat. Teia, who was observing the entire scene, rode furiously toward Ethan to stop him from killing Bres.

Teia, thinking her husband was dead and the battle over, admonished Ethan. "Wait, Ethan, there has been enough violence this day!"

Ethan pulled Bres by his hair and pressed the knife to his throat. Bres's head was cocked back and his eyes looked as though they were ready to pop out of their sockets.

Ethan shouted to Teia, "Do you want to spare this heathen's life, my queen? He has just killed your husband and our king! What about an eye for an eye, a tooth for a tooth, and a life for a life?"

Teia got off her horse and ran over to Heremon. She held him in her arms as he had blood all over his lifeless body. She wept and held him tight.

"Oh, Heremon, the love of my life! Please, God, let it not be so!" she wailed.

Overseeing everything from afar, Ollam came running to the scene and gently took Teia's arm and moved her aside to pray over Heremon. He looked up to the sky as he held the stones *Urim* and *Thummin* in his hands.

"Yaveh Rofeca, our great healer God, I call upon you to perform a miracle this day and heal this king you have set over your people to guide and teach your laws," Ollam said. "I pray that you will heal him even as you did raise up King Hezekiah and granted him an additional fifteen years of life. I pray that you will raise him up from the dead even as Elijah raised a young boy. I call upon you to perform a miracle this day even as you delivered our people from Egyptian bondage and fed our people in the wilderness for forty years!" Isaiah 38.

Ollam placed the stones of light and perfection on Heremon's side where the sword wound had entered. Suddenly, the *Urim* stone started to glow and then a halo appeared around Heremon's lifeless body. His fingers started to pulsate and then his legs started to move. Then a bright glow emerged from his body as though re-energized by a supernatural force! Everyone was silent and in disbelief.

Teia was surprised and bewildered. "Look, the *Urim* stone is getting dimmer and Heremon's body is starting to glow. It's as though the power is leaving the stone and entering Heremon's body," she said.

Heremon's eyes slowly opened, and he started coughing and spitting out blood. When he stoped coughing, he looked around, confused.

"Why is everyone looking at me?" he said. "Let's get on with the fight!"

Laughter and tears of joy could be heard from the crowd of people watching this miracle take place before their very eyes.

***

Teia looked into Heremon's eyes with tears of gratitude and praise to God and said, "Heremon, my love, the battle is over and our God has been with us!"

Then Teia looked over at Ethan, who was still holding a knife to Bres's throat. "Ethan, release Bres, the battle is over," she said.

Ethan complied and Bres was set free. He walked over to Queen Teia, and got on his knees, and looked up to her and said with sincerity.

"Oh, fair maiden of Tara, I have witnessed many miracles here this day and I have sat in the seat of folly and sowed seeds of destruction and I beg your forgiveness. I have entertained the brazen serpent instead of the God of Abraham and lost. Your God is truly more powerful than Baal. I have lost my sons and friends in battle today and I am a defeated man. If you spare my life, my life will be yours in service forever."

Teia scanned the battlefield in horror to see so many men bleeding and dying.

"Much innocent blood has been spilled here today," she said. "Many brave men have died, and for what? Pride and greed have brought this about and it must end! Do you agree, Bres?"

Bres nodded his head in agreement. "I agree, my lady, it must end! War is hell!"

Ethan gently taped Heremon on the shoulder. "Heremon, where did all of those men come from? It seemed like we had ten thousand men fighting for us today!"

"We did, Ethan!" Heremon responded. "They were the army of the Lord! He has been as gracious to us as He was with our forefathers!"

The men tended to their wounded. It was a sad scene. Approximately six thousand of Bres's men died in the battle, and only a few of Teia's army died headed by King Heremon. But everyone knew that the battle was truly the Lords.

***

The next day, Queen Teia instituted the Teltown games at Tara as crowds of people were gathered around her. There was a parade of floats in honor of the day depicting biblical scenes such as Adam and Eve in the garden, Jonah and the Whale, Samson and Delilah, Noah and the Ark, Cain and Abel, among others. Ethan depicted Adam on the float with Teia's beautiful Egyptian handmaid depicting Eve. Ethan had on little clothing except for a few leaves between his legs. There were two small trees on the float, as well as an imitation black snake that was ten feet long.

Queen Teia addressed the crowd. "I have seen enough bloodshed in my lifetime, and before I die I want to institute the Eternal God's Torah law. We will have a fair to demonstrate the fairness to both rich and poor of God's timeless laws. We will show God's love to everyone through these games. There will be no more taxes on the people for selfish reasons which only endorse bribery and corruption. In God's eyes, everyone has been created equally. Your lands have been returned to you in honor of the Lord's jubilee, so take good care of them! Treat them like the Garden of Eden!" Leviticus 25.

The crowd erupted into applause. Heremon concurred God's blessings. "Hail, hail! These games will show that God is a fair and just God and they will be known as the funeral games to commemorate Teia's death when that time happens, but I hope it won't be for a long, long time. That way she will be remembered for generations to come! The rules of the games will be according to the Torah. There will be no taking of anything by force and no wounding of any man. There will be no contention or gambling."

***

A week later, the town prepared for the fair. Tents were set up at the Teltown fair in honor of Teia Tephi. Arts and crafts were exhibited with weaving and spinning. Children were having their face painted. Lots of local produce was being sold. There were rewards for the best behaved children at the fair. There were pony and donkey rides for the kids. Woman were wearing traditional fancy dresses. There was traditional music and dancing. There were wood and leather work demonstrations. There was a traditional plowing match. There was an archery and fishing competition. Couples were river kayaking. Everyone was having fun and laughing.

Eventually, Heremon and Teia had four children and the firstborn, Aedh, died as a teenager and was buried at Tara, as well as Teia who later died. Her third son Aengus succeeded his older brother Aedh to the throne and became high king of Ireland after his parents' death. Gen. 49:24; Josh. 24:27; 1 Sam. 7:12.

Chapter Seven

The video ends, and McNair turns on the lights and says, "Thus, the first 'overturn' of the genealogy bloodlines was completed as prophesied by Jacob's handmaiden. But two more 'overturns' prophesized are still to come."

Smithe scratches his head. Things are starting to fall into place.

Smithe sits there long after the video finished and wonders what it all means. Things are starting to make sense, but he still doesn't know how it all connects to the bizarre murder of Dr. Flanders. He contemplates, *'Ok, so now I understand how the story of the scarlet thread is part of the three overturns of a kingly bloodline, that eventually ends up in Ireland with ancient Druid rituals including sacrifice. But then there must be two more overturns in other countries, one of which must be Scotland,'* he thinks.

"That was the first 'overturn' that you saw on the genealogy chart on my father's wall," Sara says. "It was the transfer of the royal bloodline of King David of Israel's seed through King Zedekiah of David's Pharez line that brought his daughter Teia to Ireland to marry King Heremon of the Zarah bloodline, thus healing the breach between Judah's twin sons as the midwife said in the biblical account."

"Sara is correct," McNair reiterates.

Smithe chimes in, "But then there must be two other overturns of bloodlines according to what the midwife said and what your father believed as demonstrated by his genealogy chart. What happened then?"

McNair answers Smithe by providing more history. "The second overturn is about to occur in Scotland, as the clans of

The Second "Overturn"

Leslie, Stewart, Monteith, Robertson, and Bruce get together to claim the right to the monarchy. They write the Declaration of Arbroath to the Pope, claiming that, '*as long as a hundred of us remain alive, never will we on any condition be brought under English rule.*' It is their belief that the Lia Fáil stone, as it was called in Scotland, found in their possession, gives them the right of heaven.

"These families believed they had the right to the throne and not the Stewart lineage of Queen Victoria. Following the extinction of the royal line of the House of Dunkeld, no clear successor existed to the throne of Scotland. King Edward I appointed John Balliol to be his puppet king instead of Robert the Bruce.

"In 1296, King John Balliol was humiliated and forced to abdicate by King Edward I, and there followed a period when there was no king in Scotland for ten years. But more intrigue followed and in 1304, Bruce made a deal with John Balliol's nephew, John Comyn the Red as he was nicknamed— about the succession to Scotland's throne. But Comyn didn't keep his end of the bargain and deceitfully informed King Edward of Bruce's plans. Bruce was nearly captured by the English King but escaped by the seat of his pants. Robert the Bruce felt so betrayed, in a fit of outrage, in retribution, killed Comyn with a dagger on the altar of the church in Dumfries in what appeared to be a ritual killing."

Smithe is interested in this ancient history as it may be connected to what appears to be a ritualistic killing of Dr. Flanders. "By the way, I know that was just a dramatization in the video, but do you believe all of this history and genealogy stuff, Professor? And what about those miracles that Jeremiah or Ollam performed? It almost seems like a lot of Irish myth and foolery to me!"

Humphrey, who has been quiet, decides to chime in. "Yeah, I don't believe in miracles!"

"Well, I can understand your skepticism, Detectives, and why you might think that this history, like other histories, is just another fable," McNair says. "But usually stories don't come from hearsay. You know what they say, 'Where there is smoke there is fire!' As far as the miracles that were performed in the video are concerned, remember this was done by our drama class and they based it upon tradition. But many people believe these artifacts do indeed have exceptional powers within them, and that's why I think the stone was taken.

"But why kill Dr. Flanders, cut out his heart and nick his ashes? Do you think it was because of an ancient religious ritual like Bruce killed Comyn, or do you think they hated him as much as they hated England?" inquires Smithe.

"If I think I understand your question Detective, you are wondering if the motive for killing Dr. Flanders was because some Scottish nationals hated the English for when King Edward usurped the Stone from Scotland, and they took it out on Dr. Flanders. This is anyone's guess."

"Since we don't have any leads thus far as to who nicked the stone and killed Dr. Flanders, I'll let you continue with your theory McNair," says Smithe.

"By the way Detectives, I know you are skeptical concerning miracles, but have you ever heard of St. Bernadette? Being a Catholic, I'm sure you have Smithe."

"Well, I have heard that millions of people go to see St. Bernadette every year in Lourdes France, as her body has been miraculously preserved and many think that is a miracle."

"Thank you, Detective, you've just proved my point why people believe in miracles."

"Okay, maybe I should view this history in an impartial way," Smithe says. While he doesn't believe in miracles, per se, Smithe does believe in the power of God. But after years on the job and working numerous cases, he always found the answers. Every question, every inconsistency, was always answered because of facts, of something tangible he could trace back to the original source.

The Second "Overturn"

"Trust me, Detective. I have done a lot of research on this subject and I do believe there is something to all of this ancient history—that people believe in just as miracles. Many ancient family bloodlines believe they are God's kingly lineage and use this ancient history to validate their claims. There seems to be just too much coincidence to all of these Hebrew words, such as 'Lia Fáil,' which derives from the Hebrew Isle of Destiny, and the name 'Tara' from the Hebrew Torah or law.

"And Tamar or Teamair, the king's daughter, and the standard of Judah, being a lion. Not only a golden lion for the Pharez lineage, but a red lion for the Zarah lineage of the scarlet thread. Not to mention the red hand with thread in the Ulster flag.

"And then the names 'Ollam Folla' all indicating an entire Hebrew system arriving sometime in Ireland. What is the meaning of all of these strange names, symbols, institutions, and nomenclature? There must have been an overwhelmingly Hebrew influence in ancient Ireland by some Hebrew innovator. Why else would the people submit to this kind of system? I think all of these legends of Ireland and names including 'Dan', are more than just baseless myths! Let me show you some quotations from early historians concerning this 'so-called myth,' as you call it, Detective."

"Okay, Doctor. I'm interested. But I just want to make it clear. In my line of work, I deal with tangible evidence and facts. So, please don't take offense at my questioning a miracle or myth, per se," Smithe says.

"Yes, of course," says McNair. "No offense taken. Perhaps you would like to attend my lecture tomorrow at the Scottish Heritage center where I will be explaining some of this ancient history and how it is connected to the Hebrews."

"I do love history and you've got me interested. What time is it?" asks Smithe.

"Seven O'clock."

"I'll be there," says Smithe.

"Your invited to Sara," says McNair with a smile.

"Yes, I can make it as this has been a passion of mine as well."

That night, DI Smithe sits in his chair and falls asleep. Once again, he dreams of the bizarre murder scene and the three apparent ritualistic hearts that have been cut out and tries to make a connection.

Chapter Eight

Dr. McNair has just greeted the 132 people who are in attendance, and begins his lecture on the early Celtic history of Ireland and its settlers. DI Smithe and Sara are in attendance.

"I'm sure you are all familiar with the Macedonian general and Egypt historian Ptolemy who was one of Alexander the Great's generals and appointed to be ruler of Egypt after it was conquered. The Ptolemy world map is a map of the world known to Hellenistic society in the second century. It is based on the description contained in Ptolemy's book *Geography*, written in 150 B.C. based on an inscription in several of the earliest surviving manuscripts. Let me show you."

McNair walks over to a table that sits along the far wall under a large window. He moves some things aside, then carefully picks up a large glass frame. He walks over to the front desk and places it down. Inside the glass frame is an old, yellowed map. There is still some coloring—yellows and blues—and the writing is faint, but it can still be made out in some spots. It is obvious that it is very old.

Ptolemy map Detail of East and Southeast Asia in Ptolemy's world map. European library. Wikipedia article.

'Wow! This is really an old map,' Smithe says to himself. He is very impressed. "It dates back to 300 BC." McNair then points to sections on the map. "Many historical records point to Israel's presence, particularly Dan and Judah, in Ireland at a very early date. Notice on Ptolemy's ancient map of Ireland, we find in the northeastern corner of the Island such names as 'Dan-Sowar,' meaning 'Dan's Resting Place,' and 'Dan-Sobairse, meaning 'Dan's habitation.' Gladstone's *Juventus Mundi* and the *Old Psalter of Cashel* both state that some of the Grecian Danai left Greece and invaded Ireland. Writers such as Pentanius and Hecatoeus of Abdera in the sixth century speak of Danai as being Hebrew people, originally from Egypt, who colonized Ireland.

"The *History of Ireland* by Professor Moore states that the ancient Irish, called the 'Danai' or 'Danes,' separated from Israel around the time of the Exodus from Egypt, crossed to Greece, and then invaded Ireland. The 'Tuatha De Danaan,' means the 'Tribe of Dan.' The *'Leabha Gabhala,'* or *'Blood of Conquests of Ireland,'* give their earlier name as 'Tuatha De,' meaning, 'People of God.'"

Smithe is truly amazed at McNair's knowledge of ancient history. He wishes he was taught this in school! He is beginning to see the relevance of knowing this ancient history to understanding the mindset of these murderers.

McNair continues his lecture as he quotes from another book.

"The great Irish historiographer, Eugene O'Curry, says,

'The De Danann were a people remarkable for their knowledge of the domestic, if not the higher, arts of civilized life.' The ships of the Tuatha De Danann are accredited with bringing Jeremiah and Jacob's pillar to Ireland. Among the names in the genealogy of Gallam are several that are specifically mentioned as belonging to the 'red' or 'scarlet' branch of Judah. Many historians today erroneously refer to these people as 'Celts' and 'Gaels' whereas in fact they were only forerunners of the Celtic tribes that wound their several ways across Europe from the east.'"

McNair then pulls out a few books out of his briefcase, and places them on the table. "Now, here is a book titled, *Jacob's Pillar*, by Professor Cap. You can get it at the library, but on page twenty-seven he says that Zarah's hand bound with a 'scarlet thread' probably accounts for the origin of the heraldic sign employed today in Ulster, northern Ireland, consisting of a red hand cuped at the wrist with a scarlet thread."

McNair continues, 'The Celts were a European cultural group first evident in the seventh or eighth century BC. The Romans called them 'Galli' and the Greeks called them 'Keltoi,' both meaning barbarians. Their maximum expansion was in the third to fifth century BC, when they occupied much of Europe north of the Alps. The Celts arrived in Britain by the fourth or fifth century BC and Ireland by the second and third century BC and possibly earlier, displacing an earlier people who were already on the islands.

'Tuatha de Danaan' was a mythical race inhabiting Ireland before the Gaels or Celts came. They were descendants of Danu and were later defeated by the Gaels.'

"I'm sure many you have heard of the book of 1 Maccabees. Here is a quote from the *Duaway version* regarding this history.

'At that particular time Arcadia was ruled by Spartans . . There appears to have been a relationship between the Spartans and the Jews. It has been found in writing concerning the Spartans and the Jews that they are brethren and are of the family of Abraham' (*Maccabees* I 12:21). "

'I never knew there was a correlation between ancient Israel and the Spartans', Smithe thinks to himself. Being a Catholic, he has a *Duaway version and* is going to read this history when he gets home. He is finding all of this history very informative and almost forgot about his case.

McNair pulls out another book,

"According to Elizabeth Van Buren's book, *The Sign of the Dove,* she identifies the Spartans as Jews, and states that the Jewish historian Josephus, who wrote in the first century

AD, makes references to the blood ties between the people of Sparta and the Jews of Israel during the Maccabean period.

"Elizabeth Van Buren is a respected expert on the occult, and the great-great-granddaughter of US President, Martin Van Buren, whose ancestors emigrated from Scotland in the 1700s.

"According to Van Buren, the Tuatha de Danaan were demi-gods, the descendants of Danaus, the son of Belus, and founders of the Druidic priesthood. The Old Irish word *tuath* 'plural *Tuatha*' means 'people, tribe, nation,' and Van Buren's book, The *Sign of the Dove*, presents fascinating details revealing the Hebrew roots of the Celtic Druids."

'Elizabeth Van Buren, yes, she is very reputable, being the granddaughter of the former president,' Smithe thinks!

"I think you would agree she is upright as well as other reputable historians putting together this fascinating history. Van Buren further states on pages 141-143:

'The Tuatha de Danaan ruled in Ireland for about two centuries and were highly skilled in architecture and other arts from their long residence in Greece. Along with Belus, they came with his fifty daughters to Argos, the home of his ancestor Io. They were said to have possessed a grail-like vessel. In pre-Christian Briton, the Celts were the Druids, descendants of the tribe of Dan which had been driven from their territory in northern Israel by the Assyrians. Some historians believe the 'Hebrew-Celtic connection' presents compelling evidence that the heathen customs of the Celtic Druids were replications of the pagan traditions adopted by the tribe of Dan.'

'This is all so fascinating history, and I can see why your trying to enlighten me personally, so I may see the connection to the ritualistic murder of Dr. Flanders,' Smithe thinks.

McNair picks up another book. "Yes, but there is more, much more. Of course, I believe the best source of this history is the Bible, and I'm glad many of you are reading it. But let me continue with more historical evidence to show

how a person's ancient roots can affect their current behavior. The respected Dr. Thomas Moore's, *History of Ireland,* states on page 40:

'That most common of all Celtic monuments, the Cromlech, is to be found not only in most parts of Europe, but also in Asia, including Palestine. Not less ancient and general among the Celtic nations was the circle of upright stones, with either an altar or tall pillar in the centre, and, like its prototype at Gilgal or ancient Israel, serving sometimes as a temple of worship, sometimes as a place of national council or inauguration . . . The rough, unhewn stone . . . used in their circular temples by the Druids, was the true, orthodox observance of the divine command delivered to Noah, *If thou wilt make me an altar of stone, thou shalt not build it of hewn stone. Ex. 20:25.*'

Smithe is flabbergasted. *'Unbelievable! I've been to Ireland and have seen these stones, but now it has much more meaning!'* he thinks.

McNair reads from another book. "Dr. Beauford in *Druidism Revived* says on page 42:

'It is remarkable that all the ancient altars found in Ireland, and now distinguished by the name of Cromlechs or sloping stones, were originally called Bothal, or the House of God, and they seem to be of the same species as those mentioned in the Book of Genesis, called by the Hebrews, Bethel, which has the same signification as the Irish Bothal.'

'The Bible in Judges 9:6; 2 Kings 11:12–14, and 2 Chronicles 23:13; indicates that Hebrew kings were crowned either standing upon or next to a pillar of stone. The practice of seating the new king upon a stone, at his initiation, was the practice in many of the countries of Europe. The monarchs of Sweden sat upon a stone placed in the center of twelve lesser ones, and in a similar kind of circle the Kings of Denmark were crowned. Note also the significant Bible number, 'twelve' which was common to both European Celts and the Hebrews.'

McNair quickly finds another book, flips through it, and says, "The book, *Identity of the Religious Druidical and Hebrew*, adds, 'Circular temples . . . abound in England and other parts of Europe. The most ancient account of them is to be found in the book of Exodus 24:4: 'And Moses . . . builded an altar under the hill and twelve pillars according to the twelve tribes.' In Europe, Stonehenge, Avebury, and many other early Celtic sites were designed in a circular pattern.' "

Smithe is intrigued. He thinks to himself, '*I always wondered about all the circles in ancient societies! I know some people think they were put there by aliens, but I never bought it.*'

"Dr. Moore also writes of the similarities between the ancient Israelites and the Druids," says McNair as he continues his lecture:

'Since early times, the Israelites sinned against God by adopting many of the pagan practices of their neighbours, and so we find evidence of both Hebrew and Canaanite culture among their descendants in Europe. The ancient Baal pillar is one of many such religious monuments which have been found from the Middle East to Ireland.'

"There are many other examples, however, of customs linking the Celtic Druids specifically with Israel. English historian, Williain Borlase, in his *Antiquities of Cornwall* written in 1754, presented many pages of such evidence. Druids worshipped but one God and allowed no graven images, identical to the Hebrews, and in contrast with almost all other ancient religions."

'*I'm beginning to get the picture,*' Smithe thinks to himself. He is starting to see how the ancient customs and civilizations are all connected to people in modern-day nations— who are descendants of these people and still have the same desires to rule and lay claim to the throne of David with support of modern-day historians.

McNair provides the connection to Druidism and the Old Testament Hebrew worship of the tribe of Dan that became a renegade tribe as he continues reading from the *Welsh Question and Druidism*:

'Consecration was by sprinkling with blood, as in the Old Testament Hebrew worship. Druid priests were clothed in white, similar to the Hebrew priest's white ephod; sacrificial victims were bled to death, and the blood was collected in basins which served to sprinkle the altars; bulls were sacrificed, and the image of a bull 'the heraldic sign of the Hebrew tribe of Ephraim' was carried into war. While they performed their horrid rites of human sacrifice, the drums and trumpets sounded without intermission, that the cries of the miserable victims might not be heard. (Compare Jer. 7:31-32, the Hebrew/Phoenician place of human sacrifice was called Tophet, meaning 'the drum').

'They prayed with uplifted, hands, examined entrails for necromancy, and held the oak in veneration. The Druids used the magic wand in imitation of Moses's rod, poured libations, sacrificed upon the tops of rocks, investigated truth by lots, anointed rock pillars with oil, and marked out boundaries with stones. (pp. 104–132, 161). In these and so many other distinctive ways, the religious customs of the Celts and Hebrews bear an unmistakable resemblance!

'From the uttermost part of the earth (*Hyperboreans—Britons)*, have we heard songs (of the Bards and Druids), even glory to the righteous... HYPERBOREANS. We are perfectly satisfied that the Hyperboreans of the ancients were the Ancient Britons. They had but a confused conception as to where these remarkable and peculiar people lived, because, as we have before explained, Dan and the kindred tribes kept their colonies a deep secret, hence their name CELTAE.'

'Amazing, but I see the possible connection to Dr. Flanders's murder' Smithe thinks to himself.'

"Now the biblical connection to the tribe of Dan, and the connection to the Druids. Jacob's prophecy in the Bible foretold that the tribe of Dan would be the seed of the serpent, which was more subtle or cunning than any beast of the field in Genesis. 3:1. Like the serpent, the tribe of Dan would infiltrate and conceal its presence wherever they lived, lying in wait and plotting the destruction of their host. Notice what the Bible says the tribe of Dan would be like in the last days: *'Dan shall be a serpent by the way, an adder in the path, that biteth the horse heels, so that his rider shall fall backward.'* That's in Genesis 49:16.

"In Gaul and in Briton, the Druids worshipped the serpent, Lucifer, who required human sacrifice. Their religion was a continuation of the Baal-Molech worship in the Canaanite territory inhabited by the tribe of Dan. According to Elizabeth Griffith, the Druids justified their human sacrifices by using Scripture, falsely interpreted. For example, 'Glorify ye the Lord in the fires' in Isaiah 24:15 was claimed to mean that the Druid fire festivals and ritual sacrifices at Stonehenge and Avebury glorified God!

"That ends this lecture for this evening. Thanks for coming and we will continue this series next month," says Dr. McNair.

After the lecture, DI Smithe and Sara surround him as well as others who are asking many questions. The onslaught of questions continues for 45 minutes as DI Smithe and Sara sit down and wait patiently an opportunity to talk to Dr. McNair privately.

Chapter Nine

Finally Smithe and Sara get a chance to talk with Dr. McNair after everyone has left. "I've enjoyed all of this fascinating ancient history Doctor, and I appreciate this background as it will help me in my murder investigation as to a possible motive," says Smithe.

McNair continues to enlighten the detective as to motive,

"Despite their profession of worshiping the Lord God of Israel, the Celtic Druids did not worship the God of their Hebrew forefathers, just as the ancient Israelites committed spiritual whoredom against the Lord God. Many preachers on prophecy believe the future false Messiah or the Antichrist will come from the tribe of Dan. Scripture says, In the last days '. . . a beast will rise up out of the sea' and will not worship the God of his fathers. That's in Daniel 11:37. Do you see the connection of the ancient Druids to certain customs and beliefs of some religious radicals?"

"Very possibly," says Smithe. "But I'm still confused to the relevance to this case. I see your point Dr, and all of this history is very interesting. But I'm still not completely convinced it is pertinent to the brutal murder of Dr. Flanders and the Stone of Destiny being nicked. Speaking of ancient artifacts Doctor, what did happen to the Ark and the Temple artifacts? I saw the movie *Raiders of the Lost Ark* and it stirred my interest."

McNair chuckled. "I saw that movie too, but remember it was only fiction. As far as the real history of the Ark is concerned, it's anyone's guess, but perhaps when you have more time, we can discuss it and I will give you my opinion."

"I'd like that," Smithe says. "Okay, Doctor, let's talk about Scottish history a little more and the second 'overturn' of the supposed bloodline transfer of King David of Israel. What can you tell me of these families and how it relates to this case and why anyone would want to kill Dr. Flanders for the Stone of Destiny."

Sara sighs. "That has been a very bitter subject in our household for many years, as my father was influenced by his father into believing what the Templars, Robert the Bruce, and these secret societies believed."

"What do you think about all of this Doctor?" asks Smithe.

"Well, Detective, as we have been discussing, there have been many families that have claimed bloodlines to the Scottish throne and claim to be descendants of King David. As I said earlier, the families that signed the most important document in Scottish history called the Declaration of Arbroath were the clans of Leslie, Stewart, Monteith, Robertson, and Bruce. They got together and wrote a declaration to the pope for dispassionate intervention in the bloody quarrel between the Scots and the English. It set the wishes of the people above the monarchy," McNair says.

He pulls out his cell phone and types in 'the Declaration of Arbroath' and he hands the phone to Smithe.

Smithe reads the declaration:

> **"For as long as but a hundred of us remain alive, never will we on any conditions be brought under English rule. It is not for glory, nor riches, nor honors that we are fighting, but for freedom—for that alone, which no honest man gives up but with his life itself."**

"Wow," Smithe says. "These people were sincere and passionate about freedom and their right to the throne, weren't they? I'm beginning to see why a member of one of these ancient families who signed the Declaration would feel they have the right to the throne —and would nick the stone. But I don't know why they would kill Dr. Flanders and cut out his heart in what appeared to be a ritualistic vengeful attack."

Just then, McNair starts singing a peculiar Scottish song:

Cinnidh Scuit saor am fine,
Mar breug am faistine:
Far am faig hear an lia fail
Dlighe flaitheas do ghab hail.

"What's that Gaelic? What does it mean?" Smithe asks.

"It is a saying that all free Scots believe. That wherever the Stone of Destiny is found, they shall prevail by the right of Heaven. Indeed, these people are sincere in their beliefs Smithe. I believe many would die and kill for it because they believe so strongly that their descendants should occupy the very throne of the bloodline of King David. They even believe that very throne is in England today! Some even believe this bloodline culminated in the eventual marriage of Jesus Christ as Sara has just mentioned and produced offspring entitled to the throne in Jerusalem until their Savior returns."

"You seem to know a lot about what these people think," Smithe says. "Do you know any of these families personally?"

McNair appears to be a bit nervous. "Well, one of my ancestors was one of the signers of the Declaration of Arbroath and this history has always kept my interest," he stutters. "I have gone to some of the secret meetings of these organizations with Dr. Flanders just to see what they are up to and hear what they believe."

Smithe's eyes widen. 'Ah, now I'm getting somewhere,' he thinks.

"You mean that the families that wrote the Declaration of Arbroath thought they were the legal inheritors of the throne and that's why they weren't going to be ruled by the English," Smithe says, trying to clarify everything in his head.

"That's right," Sara says. "That's why I believe my father's heart was cut out."

"But by whom?" McNair says. "These sacrificial ceremonies go back to the ancient Celtic customs of the Druids, but our challenge is to find the family that has been influenced the most."

"I wish I knew the answer to that," says Sara. And I wish my father hadn't gotten involved with those weird people he used to get together with and go to their meetings. He would always tell me, 'Someday things will be different, Sara. Someday things will be better in this world.' " Sara fights back tears as she thinks of her father.

"As I see it," says Smithe, "there is a plot to take over the throne of King David by divine inheritance and to rule the world. At least thirteen families believe they are entitled to it based upon their bloodline. Then we have three missing hearts that have been cut out because of a ritualistic belief and a stone that these same people believe will be used as the corner stone in a rebuilt temple in Jerusalem. To conclude, we have a being called the Antichrist who will rule there someday because they believe he will be the true descendant of King David and the rightful inheritor of the throne. Is that about it?"

"I think you have a motive for this case, Detective," McNair says.

"What else can you tell me about this global conspiracy?" Smithe asks.

"Are you sure you want to hear this?" McNair responds.

Smithe is getting a bit testy. "On with it, Doctor."

"Okay, okay. Have you ever heard of the Illuminati, the Bilderbergs, the Freemasons, the Jacobites, the Fifth Monarchy Men, or the Merovingians?" Says McNair.

"I believe they are all secret societies, and that is what Dr. Flanders had on his computer the night he was killed, but I haven't studied them in great detail as you and Dr. Flanders have. Enlighten me," says Smithe.

"Indeed, the Merovingians trace their roots back to the tribe of Dan and later their bloodline supposedly is found in many of the Kings of Europe," says McNair.

"What about the Illuminati?" asks Smithe. "I have herd of them, but I don't know much about them."

"Most people are not familiar with the Merovingian history and the connection to the Illuminati. The real-world origins of the group trace back to Bavarian law professor Adam Weishaupt, who in 1776 established a group to free the world from the control of the Catholic Church and, perhaps, establish a New World Order. That group is thought to have disbanded by 1790, though some theories suggest that the Illuminati continue to operate today," McNair says.

"Well, I didn't know all of those facts, but I have seen several documentaries on these so-called secret societies. I have also read an article or two about the secret societies that are trying to take over the world, supposedly through economic means to promote their hidden agenda of world domination, but frankly I don't buy it," says Smithe.

"Me neither," echoes Sara. "I think there is something more sinister in these family bloodlines that believe they are the rightful inheritors of God's promise to King David."

"Have you heard of the Seven Noahide Laws?" McNair says, throwing a wrench into the conversation.

"Can't say that I have," Smithe confessed.

McNair is energized once again. He gets up and paces around the room. "Well, they are a set of faith-based moral values that many world leaders feel need to be imposed upon all societies to maintain peace in the world."

"Can you give an example?" Smithe says.

"Civil justice, prohibition of blasphemy, the abandonment of idolatry, the prohibition of incest, murder, theft, and cruelty . . . to name a few." McNair claps his hands together.

"Well, those don't sound so bad. In fact, I can see where they might bring about a lot of good if every society were to practice them," Smithe says.

"So, you agree. I mean, that all sounds logical, doesn't it? But there is more. The breaking of these laws is capital punishment. These laws do not apply to Hebrews but only to Gentiles or non-Jews. You see, there are Bible prophecies that seem to indicate that a being called the 'Antichrist' or 'beast' will someday rule the world from Jerusalem and want to impose these laws on the Gentile world," says McNair.

Smithe shakes his head. He loves a good conspiracy theory, but at the end of the day, his job supports facts. But what McNair is saying has his interest piqued. "Tell me more," he says.

"Are you ready for this, Detective?" McNair says with a grin.

This guy really likes to drag things out, Smithe thinks. "Yes, get on with it." "Here is the connection to the Knights Templar and the Catholic Church and this Hebrew elite. I'm sorry to say, but history tells us that it was the Catholic Church that organized the First Crusade in 1095 to secure the Holy Land from the Turks who were invading. At this same time, the Knights Templar were formed, which were an order of warrior-monks drawn from the ranks of the European nobility for the express purpose of protecting the pilgrims to the Holy Land.

"They became very powerful and wealthy throughout the next two centuries to where the power of the papacy was beginning to be questioned. The Knights had acquired a very large portion of wealth and controlled trade along with the Jews from the Eastern Mediterranean to Italy and across Western Europe as far as the British Isles. Something had to be done."

"Be careful McNair, I'm a good Catholic and you're standing on holy ground."

McNair nods in understanding. "I understand your concern Detective, but facts are facts. After the First Crusade, the surviving Jews were kept on as tax collectors, banking associates, and middlemen for converting the confiscated bounty the Templars had acquired into money. The Jews were good at this and the Knights Templar became intertwined with them. Becoming partners with them, if you will. The Templars were also learning the ways and customs of the Jews they associated with and were very intrigued by their esoteric knowledge, or *Kabbala,* that unlocked the secrets of the Hebrew prophecies as written in the apocryphal books."

"What are these apocryphal books that you speak of?" Smithe asks, intrigued.

"These were books that were branded heretical by the papacy and not inspired by God. The Knights Templar were becoming the 'bad boys' of Christendom according to the Catholic Church. The papacy was trying to draw the center of power from Paris to Rome. The campaign against heresy began by the papacy, and the Templars were forced to leave Jerusalem."

"Wow, I never knew that. You have my attention, Doctor, go on."

"Heresy was so prevalent throughout Europe, especially in France and England, that King Edward I expelled the Jews from England in 1301 and then commenced his war against Scotland's Robert the Bruce."

"There you go again with Robert the Bruce. What did he do? asked Smithe"

McNair continues, "Well, it depends upon which version of history you want to believe. According to some theories regarding the motives of the Catholic Church, Bruce wanted to restore the Celtic monarchy, which included teachings of the Templars who brought these heretical *Kabbala* teachings of mystical powers with them from certain Jews in the Holy Land. These Jews believed they followed the true teachings of the church and were followers of the apostle John who was the last of the apostles to die and headed the churches in the East at Antioch. They often clashed with the church at Rome over specific doctrines."

"I do remember that John the Revelator was in prison when he wrote the book of Revelation," Smithe says.

"That's right" says McNair. He was on the island of Patmos, and the churches in the East believed the church was being infiltrated in the West by wolves in sheep's clothing. They believed the church at Rome was the real heretics substituting Easter for Passover, Sunday for Saturday, and the like. Remember, the early church was composed mainly of Jewish believers, but the conservative Jews were always trying to make the new Christians do things out of the Old Testament, such as being circumcised. Polycarp was one of the leaders in the Eastern Church and claimed to be loyal to the apostle John. He sent several letters to the pope at Rome giving his concerns."

"I do recall that the Old Testament was supposedly done away with or something," says Smithe as he comments.

"On the other hand, the Catholic Church believed they were following the apostle Peter and were the true church headed in Rome. Throughout the course of time, many apocryphal books circulated during the first few centuries of the church and that's why we have all of the confusion today. There were texts written that indicated Joseph of Armethea was the natural father of Jesus instead of Joseph. Furthermore, it was circulated that Mary Magdalene and Jesus were married and sired children, eventually of the Merovingian lineage. All kinds of heresy was spreading. It was hard to tell who was telling the truth." Says Dr. McNair.

These concepts are all very new to Smithe, and he is hesitant to ask more questions without showing his ignorance, as he has a lot of pride. But he decides to ask anyway, "So what happened to the Templars?" Smithe asks.

Chapter Ten

Sensing DI Smithe is a Catholic and this is such a sensitive subject, McNair ponders how best to explain the Merovingian connection to the Templars and the Merovingian belief to the bloodline of Christ.

He thinks, *'should I start with the Roman Emperor Constantine who divided the Empire into Rome and Constantinople, back in 324 A.D. when the controversy began after Constantine's death—and, the Empire split between East and West. I don't want to offend him, but this is when a division in Christianity began, as the Eastern Orthodox Church grew in power and influence, while the Roman church faltered.'*

'Will he believe that this is when an astonishing legend was being promoted that Jesus Christ did not die and was taken from the cross, stolen from tomb, and married Mary Magdalene, even producing children. That, when the Romans destroyed the Temple at Jerusalem in 70 AD, Mary Magdalene fled with her sacred children by boat across the Mediterranean to France.'

McNair thinks how absurd all of this sounds even to him but proceeds to explain the theory. Would DI Smithe believe that Mary found refuge there in a Jewish community. Would he believe that future generations of her offspring were said to have married into the royal Frankish family, and by the fifth century produced a king whose name was Merovee. Would he believe Merovee was the first in a series of kings called the Merovingian bloodline?

Smithe can't believe his ears, "I've never heard of this," He says.

"Well, it's not something they preach about at Sunday Mass," McNair replies, then he continues his story. "It is said that the offspring of Merovee were noted by a birthmark above their heart in the shape of a red cross. In 496 A.D., the Bishop of Rome made a pact with Clovis, the grandson of Merovee and king of the Franks, calling him the 'New Constantine,' giving him authority to preside over a 'Christianized' Roman Empire. The pope did so to consolidate the power of the faltering church at Rome.

"From the Merovingian bloodline has come most of ruling families of Europe and, believe it or not, has even included some of the popes of the Roman Catholic Church.

"Many of the Crusaders were French who went to Palestine to liberate the Holy Land from the Moslems. By 1061 AD, the Catholic Crusaders had conquered the city of Jerusalem and established Godfroi de Bouillon of the Merovingian bloodline on throne of Jerusalem. A great rivalry developed.

"On Friday, the thirteenth of October, Phillip the Fair of France arrested all of the Knights Templar that he could round up, tortured them, to extract confessions of heresy from them and then handed them over to the Inquisition

Jacques de Molay. Encyclopedia Britannica. An Illustration of Templar grand master Jacques de Molay being led to the stake. Hutton Archive/ Getty Images

Pope Clement V, who had them burned at the stake."

McNair searches for the execution of DeMolay on his cell and hands a picture of his execution, to Smithe.

"The Inquisition period was a dark period for the church," Smithe says.

McNair gives a grim history: "It was said that such a barbaric massacre remained unequaled until the fourteenth century when the Roman Church launched the Inquisition, destroying the Knights Templar and other dissident groups as some sixty thousand men, women, and children were slaughtered in a single day. Unfortunately, many other groups of people, who called themselves various names depending upon where they lived and who they followed, such as Waldenses, Bogomils, Cathari, Albigenses, and Anabaptists, were also persecuted. Anyone who disagreed with the Catholic Church was suspect. Eventually, many false beliefs filtered into the Celtic church."

Smithe sighs, appalled. "Sometimes I'm ashamed to be called Catholic.".

"Those were different times," Sara chimes in. "Yes, I can understand your feelings, Smithe. That's how much truth and error has gotten into the various churches throughout the ages, but the bottom line is that every group believes they have the absolute truth."

"Are there any families of these Knights in existence today?" Smithe asks.

"The last Grand Master of the Knights Templar was Jacques de Molay, and to this very day their successors still swear to avenge his death. Some of the surviving Knights escaped to Scotland where Robert the Bruce received them and protected them. It was said that de Molay was crucified, and one of the reasons was that he knew the secret of the true history of Jesus and Mary. This was the basis for the Merovingian family's belief that they have a bloodline from Jesus and Mary and why the Catholic Church proclaimed them heretics. It has been written that in his dying breath de Molay summoned the King of France and Pope Clement to join him before God's court of justice within the year. It is believed, Justice came as both men did die within a year," replies McNair.

"So, was de Molay a good guy or bad guy?" Smithe asks.

Again, McNair replies, "That's anyone's guess and only time will tell. But we may never know since he might have had all the Templar documents destroyed. It is thought that he started the order known as Scottish Masonry or the Occult, and that's the problem. These families formed secret societies that believe, like de Molay, that they have the truth about Jesus' true bloodline and are the rightful heirs to the throne—the same throne Jesus will inherit upon his return."

Quietly listening, Sara sits up in her chair and says, "Everything Robert has said is true, for my father told me of this history and this power struggle of the Knights and Jewish elite against the church. In France, there were families that became Roman Catholic by name, but inwardly they embraced this spirit of nationalism. Today it is spearheaded by such groups calling themselves various names, but their desire to change the world and enforce the Noahide Laws has not changed."

"This is unbelievable. I can't believe what I'm hearing. My head is exploding," Smithe says.

"This may seem so, but because the world seems to be getting out of control, there are many in the world today who desire to reinstitute the Mosaic Law of an eye for an eye and a tooth for a tooth," Sara says. "But first, they need to restore the royal dynasty to the descendants of King David. My father told me that the modern-day descendants of some of these families would shake hands with the devil if they could regain the authority and power that they seek. My father also had made some startling discoveries of his own and told me that if anything should ever happen to him, and when strange things seem to be happening in the world, that I should open his deposit box. He gave me the key."

"That's scary," Smithe acknowledges.

"Indeed. In fact, some believe the hidden objective of the Knights was to restore the Temple of King Solomon in Jerusalem and proclaim the Patriarch of Constantinople the true leader of the Christian world. Then he would prevail over the church at Rome," McNair says.

"Some believe they were the forerunners of the Masons whose signature was the sword and trowel, the same symbols of the Freemasons, which is a corrupt version of the French name of the Templars, *Freres Macons*. Throughout history, their names have changed, such as the Johannites who claim succession from Saint John but their objective has not changed.

"This was the basis of the Celtic Church, which was an infusion of both pagan pre-Christian and Christian beliefs. The origins of the Freemasons may go back to groups of independent stonemasons who banded together as they built churches for the Knights Templar. But the Freemasons are perhaps best known in the United States for their hand in building the country," adds Sara.

"Wasn't George Washington a Freemason?" asks Smithe.

"Yes, and Benjamin Franklin, John Hancock, and Paul Revere, to name just a few. The society, more a patchwork of independent lodges, remains active today. Some conspiracy theorists claim the true intent of the Freemasons is world domination and see signs of their influence everywhere, including the Great Seal of the United States. Did you see Dan Brown's thriller, *The Lost Symbol?*" Says McNair.

"Not yet," Smithe replies.

"Well, there is a lot of Masonic lore figured in it. In fact, the 33rd degree, which is a very important part of Freemasonry, has its fingerprints all over the Knights Templar and the French Merovingian Dynasty. Believe it or not, many of these families trace their bloodlines back to the tribe of Dan. Did you ever hear of the Protocols of the Learned Elders of Sion?"

"No, I haven't, what is it," asks DI Smithe.

"No one knows for sure who wrote it, but it was a booklet that circulated in Russia during the twentieth century that exposed a Jewish conspiracy to take over the world."

"Really!" says Smithe.

"Yes, but here's the interesting part. The booklet was signed by the representatives of Sion of the 33rd Degree," says McNair.

"That definitely sounds like there is a connection," says Smithe.

"It sounds like the Celts had a lot of truth mixed in with a lot of myth because of all of the outside influences. I guess I had better do some more research instead of accepting everyone's version of the truth."

"That's not a bad idea, DI Smithe. We probably all should. Instead, most of us just take for granted the conclusions of trusted and impressive persons without checking things out for ourselves. People tend to make judgments about things they know nothing about."

"You are absolutely right, Doctor."

"But getting back to the subject at hand. One more thing, according to the Catholic Church, the Knights Templar were essentially non-believers and heretics who they eventually had put to death," McNair says.

"Sara, if McNair is right, then we have another motive for killing your father," Smithe says.

"That may be true Detective, because some of these families believe they are direct descendants of Jesus Christ and their ancestors were unjustly persecuted for crimes they did not commit," Sara says. "The Templars and their families felt that the very church they swore to protect made them feel betrayed."

McNair chimes in, "Not to mention the money and artifacts they may have found as treasure while in Jerusalem."

"What money and artifacts?" Smithe asks.

"Well, Sara has already mentioned, the Rosslyn Chapel in Scotland was designed like the Temple in Jerusalem. And when the Templars were persecuted by the Catholic Church, many found asylum in Scotland. Archaeologists have found many tunnels and Templar artifacts underneath Rosslyn, believing the Templars hid Solomon's gold and the Temple artifacts there."

"It's all true, but unfortunately we will never know what the Templars were up to, as all of their documents were destroyed either by their leader or by the church," Sara says.

"But why?" Smithe questions.

"If it was their leader who destroyed the documents, he might not have wanted the church to use this evidence against them as they were being persecuted. If it was the church, they might not have wanted anyone to know of incriminating evidence of Jesus' marriage and bloodline," Sara says.

"Then where did your father stand in all of this controversy?" Smithe asks. "Did he take the side of the Templars or the Church?"

Smithe looks at his watch—it's getting late, and he wants to get back to the office before heading home.

"What do you say if we continue this conversation when we can all get together at your convenience," says Smithe. They all agree and he tells them he will be in touch.

Chapter Eleven

A week later, after the memorial service for Dr. Flanders, Dr. McNair invites Sara out for dinner to share his experiences with Sara's father. She complies and they exchange phone numbers. Another week passes until Sara receives a phone call from McNair.

"Hello, Sara, this is Robert, and I was wondering if you would like to go out to dinner tomorrow as I am in town for a conference and would like to tell you more of some of the adventures your father and I shared."

Sara is honored. She misses her father so much, and she would love to hear stories about him. "I'd like that very much."

"I was thinking of going to McFarland's for some Irish stew?" McNair says.

"I always liked that place, and you know that is one of my favorites," Sara replies.

***

It is a beautiful summer evening but fall seems to be around the corner as the leaves are turning red, orange, yellow, and brown. The air is crisp and smells like winter is on the horizon. McNair picks up Sara in his 1997 stylish Bentley. He and Sara walk out to his car and he opens the door for Sara. They smile at each other. She can't help but notice how huge a man he is and with hands the size of tennis rackets as he opens her door in gentlemen-like fashion. She remembers what attracted her to him in the first place and wonders why they ever broke up. They arrive at an elegant Irish restaurant and are seated at a cozy table in the back.

They place their order. McNair also orders a bottle of Pinot red. He and Sara raise their glasses and click them together.

"Here's a toast to your father, one of the finest men I have ever known," McNair says.

"Did you go on many expeditions with my father?" Sara asks.

"Yes, I went on several, including a most memorable one to Israel where we met Prime Minister Rabin. We had a delightful time. Your father was so informative and knowledgeable regarding history as you well know."

Sara nods her head and fights back her tears. She misses her father. "He was always talking about history, and if he wasn't talking about it, he was reading about it. Anyway, tell me about yourself Robert. It's been years since we dated," says Sara.

McNair takes a sip of his wine. "Well, I have two teenage sons who live with their mother and I get to visit them as much as I can. They love history as well and I have taken them on several trips visiting various countries. Soon they will be off to college and hopefully get jobs in their field."

"I'm sure they will follow in your footsteps," Sara replies. "So are you divorced or separated," inquires Sara.

"Divorced," replies McNair, "How about you."

"Me too, but no kids" says Sara.

***

After a wonderful evening, the two leave the restaurant and McNair drives Sara home. McNair is nervous—he doesn't want to be too forward—so he holds out his hands to shake hers as they say goodnight, but then Sara leans in and gives him a kiss on the cheek.

"Thank you for a delightful evening Robert," she says.

"I had a wonderful evening as well. I hope we can do it again soon." McNair responds as he walks back to his car — and as he drives to his hotel he can't stop smiling the whole way home.

Chapter Twelve

Several weeks have gone by and DI Smithe is still pondering all of the thoughts he has had during his discussions with Dr. McNair and Sara. His mind is swirling with bloodlines, overturns of monarchy, secret societies, and now what appears to be a ritualistic phenomenon of missing hearts. It seems he wakes up almost daily from a cold sweat. He drives frantically up to the University of Glasgow on a rainy morning to meet Dr. McNair to ask more questions concerning the murder of the Sara's father.

"Good morning, Dr. McNair," Smithe says as he enters the classroom and shakes his hand. There are books and papers piled everywhere; it looks like a tornado has ripped through the room.

"I see you're studying, Doctor, and at your suggestion, I have been doing some research on my own regarding the connection to Dr. Flanders death. At our last meeting, you mentioned there were a lot of different religious beliefs going on during the time period of the Templars which led to the beliefs of the Fifth Monarchy Men. I would like to know more about them, as it may be relevant to our investigation of Dr. Flanders murder, as we may have a religious motive as well."

"Yes, indeed. The Fifth Monarchy Men were a religious group during the seventeenth century who wanted to make England a theocracy," says McNair.

The Fifth Monarchy Men

"I'd like to know more about them, as we are investigating all angles in our investigation of the murder of Dr. Flanders," Smithe responds.

McNair motions for Smithe to take a seat, in which he complies. The two men are sitting opposite each other.

"The Fifth Monarchists, or the Fifth Monarchy Men as they were called, were active from 1649 to 1660 following the English Civil Wars of the seventeenth century. They took their name from a prophecy in the book of Daniel that four ancient monarchies—the Babylonian, Persian, Macedonian, and Roman—would precede the kingdom of which Jesus would return and rule. The year 1666 was significant to them as it seemed to relate to the biblical Number of the Beast as mentioned in the book of Revelation. They were one of a number of nonconformist dissenting groups that emerged around this time," McNair says.

"So far they sound harmless," Smithe says, "But I wonder if any of these royal bloodlines could be tied to them and that is why they may have nicked the stone from the Abbey. I have a hard time thinking they would have killed Dr. Flanders being a religious group. I wouldn't think they would be violent."

"Well, here is where it gets more interesting." McNair says. "The Fifth Monarchists believed that the timing of the events when England didn't have a normal government between successive reigns, was significant because the calendar year 1666 loomed large on the near horizon. The apostle John mentioned the number 666 in the Book of Revelation in connection with the Beast or human despot who would one day rule the world before the second coming of Jesus, the Messiah. Upon His return to the earth, Jesus would destroy him.

"These scriptures supported the belief that the Fifth Monarchy was about to begin. A number of Fifth Monarchists took a leading part in the events of the time. General Thomas Harrison and John Carew were commissioners at the trial of King Charles I and signed his death warrant. Following

Charles's death, Oliver Cromwell, Lord Protector of the Commonwealth of England, Scotland, and Ireland, set up the Commonwealth as a more pure form of government to replace the existing monarchy."

"Refresh my memory Dr. McNair, what was the reason King Charles was executed," asks Smithe.

"King Charles 1 was beheaded in London in 1649 for treason. Charles 1, was the son of King James VI of Scotland, and King of England and Ireland as James 1. James 1 was of course the son of Catholic Mary, Queen of Scots who clashed with her cousin, Queen Elizabeth 1 of England who was Protestant, and was persuaded to finally execute Mary. Thus, like his father, Charles 1, was King of three countries.

"Obviously, he was born of the Stuart lineage. He was beheaded for several reasons. He offended many Protestants by marrying the Catholic princess Henrietta Maria. This did not bode well with many Reformed groups such as Puritans and Scottish Presbyterians known as Covenanters. He quarreled constantly with Parliament because of his belief of the divine right of Kings. Many in Parliament opposed his policies on taxes without the consent of Parliament who thought he was becoming a tyrant," replies McNair.

"So, one of these royal bloodlines could have caused King Charles I to be put to death so they could take over the throne. I heard that Cromwell wasn't a nice guy," Smithe says.

"Cromwell had not intended it, but not long after establishing the Commonwealth, he dismissed the Parliament and became, in effect, a military dictator. Cromwell was not fulfilling what the Fifth Monarchists perceived to be—that is to turn England into a more 'godly' nation."

"What happened next as it might be relevant to our case?" Smithe asked.

"Well, Major-General Thomas Harrison, who had commanded the troop that aided Oliver Cromwell in

The Fifth Monarchy Men

dissolving the old corrupt Parliament, suggested that there be a ruling body based upon the Old Testament Sanhedrin of seventy selected 'saints.' This was based on his beliefs, as a Fifth Monarchist, that the rule of the saints would usher in the reign of Jesus Christ on earth.

"A modified version of this proposal was accepted by Cromwell and the Council of Officers. Soon after the dissolution of the Parliament, Congregational churches in every county in England were asked to nominate those they considered fit to take part in the new government. The total number of nominees was one hundred and forty: one hundred and twenty-nine from England, five from Scotland, and six from Ireland."

"I'm with you thus far, Dr. McNair, but I'm waiting to see a reason for hatred of the execution of King Charles I, and a possible motive for nicking the stone as some sort of vindictive proof of monarchy right," Smithe says.

"Okay, here's where it gets interesting," says McNair. "After the restoration of the Parliament, Major-General Thomas Harrison was the first person to be found responsible for the deliberate killing of King Charles I. He had been the seventeenth of fifty-nine commissioners to sign the death warrant of the king in 1649. He was the first of them to be hanged, drawn, and quartered because he was considered by the new government to represent a continued threat to the re-established order."

"Those people were ruthless," Smithe says, shaking his head.

"Yes, they were because they thought the new movement would convert England and perhaps all of Europe into believing in Jesus Christ and His soon return. It was kind of like why the Pharisees rejected Jesus. The Fifth Monarchists movement consisted of two divergent beliefs. There were those who genuinely believed in the transformation of a morally corrupt England and Europe and the world through prayer and example —and a second group who was more militant and wanted change by political action and through the force of arms. At first, both of these groups were more moderate in their viewpoints. Many Baptist laymen and ministers became involved in the movement as the kingdom of God message became the message of the Fifth Monarchist."

"Were Catholics a part in this spiritual revolution," asks Smithe.

"No Smithe they weren't. At first these two groups got along as they had a common enemy in the government of Cromwell. Some of the more prominent Fifth Monarchy Men were London preachers including Christopher Feake, of Christ Church; John Rogers from Dublin; John Canne of the Robert Overton Regiment at Hull; John Simpson and Vavasor Powell. These men were all powerful preachers and new Bible prophesy. They preached on the second coming based upon the scriptures in chapter seven in the Book of Daniel. Although these preachers believed the return of Christ was imminent, their focus was on Christian living, especially loving one's neighbor and helping the poor."

"Those all sound like noble gestures." Smithe nods his head.

"True", says McNair. At first the two groups were all on board, but then things got out of control. The Fifth Monarchists were early advocates of Oliver Cromwell, and even believed God was using him to change abhorrent things in English society. They believed he would make it a more godly kingdom in preparation for the returning kingdom of God, ushered in by Jesus Christ."

"So, what happened?" Smithe asks.

"Cromwell appeared to have betrayed the Fifth Monarchy men for his own personal and political ambitions when the Loyalists regained power. He did not support General Harrison who was later executed by the restored Parliament for the death of King Charles 1, and tried to save his own skin," says McNair.

Smithe is dismayed. "What a terrible fate."

"Well, you asked if any of these so-called religious people were ever violent," says McNair. "As I said, there were two different groups of Fifth Monarchy men. One group was headed by a radical preacher named Thomas Venner who wanted to topple the Cromwell government and establish a theocracy.

"The other group, headed by General Thomas Harrison, was set against Venner's plan of a violent overthrow. When General Harrison was put to death, and the horror of a return of the monarchy and a new popish Church of England— the Fifth Monarchy men of Venner took things into their own hands and attacked the centers of power around the greater city of London. Their war cry was 'King Jesus and the heads upon the gates.'

"The uprising was quickly put down, Venner and many of his men were captured and sentenced to die. Many of the rebels who were captured were executed and Venner was hanged, drawn, and quartered outside of his own church doors. Eventually, many of the wealthy power brokers of England formed a peace treaty with King Charles 1's son, King Charles II of Scotland after Cromwell's government was dissolved.

"Once again, the Stuart lineage prevailed. Approximately one hundred Fifth Monarchy Men were arrested and put in prison by King Charles II's new government. Some of these men were Quakers, who did not take part in the actual fighting, but none the less were labeled as rebels in support of those opposed to the new government."

"So, there is a connection to Scotland?" says Smithe, and he wants to know the conclusion of their fate. "What happened then?"

"There was another leader in the Fifth Monarchy movement that was also charged with treason and his name was John James." James had little formal education and came from a poor family. After his health declined from manual labor, he became interested in religion and became a London preacher. He became interested in the Fifth Monarchy movement and was arrested along with his congregation on charges of high treason against Charles II. Although he was not involved in Venner's actual uprising, he said he supported Venner at his trial. He was found guilty for his embrace of Venner and his rebels and was hanged, disemboweled, and quartered at Tyburn."

"There definitely could be a religious motive here," says Smithe.

DI Smithe is bewildered with this new information and calls up DC Humphrey and asks him to do further investigation on these families of interest.

"Humphrey, your assignment is to go to the library and dig up anything on past ritual killings, as well as information about the Templars and Fifth Monarchy Men that might have motive to our case," says DI Smithe.

"Will do," Humphrey complies.

And just like that, Smithe feels as if he is one step closer to finding out what happened on that fateful day when the Stone of Destiny was nicked from the Abbey and Dr. Flanders lay dying protecting what he loved— for he loved his country and what the Stone of Destiny symbolized —including God and country.

Chapter Thirteen

Detective Humphrey is rummaging through old newspaper clippings of past ritualistic murders at the local library at the request of DI Smithe. Suddenly, his eyes focus on a possible link to murders of the occult as he reads the newspaper headline: Two students hanged at Oxford, school closes.

> **The hanging of the clerks in 1209**
>
> By Simon Bailey BBC Oxford contributor
>
> Oxford's papal legate: It was a violent episode that caused a rift between the 'Town' and 'Gown' for centuries. It led to scholars leaving the University of Oxford and forming a new institution in Cambridge. The most detailed source for the events, which took place in 1209, is a passage written in the 1220s. It is in a chronicle history of England: the Flores Historiarum of Roger of Wendover, a monk of St Albans who died in 1236. The particular passage relating to Oxford reads as follows:
>
> "About this time, a certain clerk engaged in the liberal arts at Oxford killed a certain woman by accident and when he found that she was dead he decided to flee." But when the mayor of the city and many others who had gathered found the dead woman they began to search for the killer in his house which he had rented together with three of his fellow clerks. "Not finding the man accused of the deed they seized his three fellow clerks who said they were wholly ignorant of the murder and threw them into prison; then a few days later they were, by order of the King of the English [King John], in contempt of the rights of the church, taken outside the city and hanged. "When the deed had been done, both masters and pupils, to the number of three thousand clerks, left Oxford so that not one remained out of the whole university; they left Oxford empty, some engaging in liberal studies at Cambridge and some at Reading."... It was not the case that every clerk left Oxford as some who remained were subsequently

> punished. The involvement of King John is quite plausible as he was at this time in dispute with the Pope over the appointment of the Archbishop of Canterbury. John was hostile to the Church and had been personally excommunicated; the country had been laid under a papal interdict by which all functions of the Church were suspended. Most of the ecclesiastical hierarchy had gone abroad…. All those who had been involved in the hanging of the clerks were to go to their graves barefoot and unbelted, without caps or cloaks, followed by the rest of the citizens, and to bear their bodies with honour and respect to a reburial elsewhere.
>
> Simon Bailey is Keeper of the Archives at the Bodleian Library, University of Oxford

A jubilant Humphrey immediately calls detective Smithe with some very interesting news he has just discovered that may be pertinent to the case.

"I think I found something very interesting in the library archives!" says DC Humphrey.

Smithe is eager to know what it is Humphrey has found. "I'll be right over." Smithe rushes down the steps from his second-floor office, jumps in his car and drives frantically to the library. Humphrey is looking out for his arrival and motions to him as Smithe enters the library. The two detectives walk down a hall, with Humphrey leading the way to the library archives. He shows Smithe the Oxford commentary. Smithe's eyes bulge as he reads the article and he says to Humphrey, "You're right, Humphrey! I think we need to have a talk with Dr. McNair!"

Smithe calls up McNair and asks him if he will be in London any time soon.

"I won't have another lecture for two weeks," McNair informs him.

"This is extremely urgent," Smithe tells him. "Detective Humphrey and I would like to get together with you at your university office ASAP." McNair agrees to a time, and Smithe and Humphrey bid each other goodbye and leave for the day.

***

The next morning, the detectives head on out to visit Dr. McNair at his office. It is a long drive, but the detectives believe they are on to something that might crack this case wide open. Anxious as to what they have discovered, Smithe and Humphrey arrive at the university, and because they have been there before, they head up to McNair's office.

McNair hears the knock on the door and says politely, "Good morning, detectives, come in. How can I help you?"

Smithe informs him, "Detective Humphrey has just discovered an interesting article about a bizarre murder that took place in 1209 at Oxford, in which a young woman was murdered and several monks were hung as a result. Do you know anything about this rather dark story, and could it have ritual overtones that could be relevant to solving our case?"

Aware of the strange story, and to Smithe's surprise, McNair declares, "Yes, I do recall that unusual incident and the uproar it had when Oxford became a university. You see, Oxford University, the oldest university in Britain, had its origins in informal groups of masters and students who gathered in Oxford in the twelfth century, and as a result of these unfortunate murders, was shut down. That is how, in the year 1167, Oxford University was born!

"At the same time, the University of Paris was closed to Englishmen, and this accelerated Oxford's development into a university college in 1249.

"Now here is where the link to those murders and the foundation of the university had a reputation for the occult. In the early thirteenth century, the Ancient Order of Druids was supposedly formed at Mount Haemus Grove. They met at the site now occupied by Oxford University, and the order is still in existence. At that time, a secret society appears to have developed as Druids appeared together with Rosicrucians and Freemasons, which were a blend of mystical-occult societies of eighteenth-century London."

Smithe, hanging on the Doctor's every word, wants to know more about the beliefs of these mystics. "So, what you're telling me is that this ancient Druid custom of some weird beliefs, and even ritual killings, somehow permeated into Oxford University? Do you have any proof of this?"

McNair justifies his observation and gets out some books on the subject. "Here in *A History of Pagan Europe* it states that the Ancient Order of Druids of Oxford was revived and established in London in 1781—he mumbled incoherently, while his finger ran across the line of text, then stopped—"This book also confirms that the Ancient Order of Druids of Oxford descended from the Mount Haemus Grove Order, which originally met in Oxford."

Smithe's mind begins to connect the dots. "Very interesting!"

McNair gets out the *Ancient Order of Druids* book and reads a quote.

"Now where is it? Ah yes, here, on page 211. This according to authors Pennick and Jones: 'In 1781 ... the Ancient Order of Druids was set up in London by Henry Hurle, as an esoteric society patterned on Masonic lines. In 1833, a split between the mystics and those who wanted a friendly society led to the majority forming the United Ancient Order of Druids. The mystical side continued as the Albion Lodge of the Ancient Order of Druids of Oxford, claiming descent from the Mount Haemus Grove.' "

Smithe is becoming a believer and says, "So there appears to be a connection to the occult."

McNair confirms, "Most definitely, there appears to be. I'll look into this matter in more detail, DI Smithe. I'll be in London in two weeks for a meeting, and I'll give you an update then."

Smithe appreciates McNair's help and says, "Thanks again, Doctor. Let me know what you uncover!"

Humphrey adds, "Yea, I will be very interested in what you have found out Dr. McNair."

McNair is agreeable and says, "Will do, see you then!"

The two detectives get into their car and begin their long drive home. They are both curious as to what McNair might find that will help solve this case. "I can't believe some of the things that happened at Oxford. I'm beginning to wonder about this supernatural stuff!" says Humphrey.

"Something very macab occurred there," says Smithe.

***

A week later, McNair arrives in London and walks up to Smithe's office at Scotland Yard. As he enters the building, he is greeted by the security guard who then calls up Smithe to inform him of McNair's arrival. Smithe comes down to greet him and the two shake hands. Smithe then takes McNair to his office and McNair shows Smithe an interesting article he has discovered.

"Look at some of these interesting discoveries at the University of Oxford," he says excitedly. "The November/December 2013 issue of *Archaeology Magazine* reveals that a mass grave of human remains dating back to around the year 1000 AD was found under the site of St. John's College, one of Oxford University's oldest colleges!"

Ecstatic, Smithe says, "Unbelievable!"

McNair provides additional substance. "Yes, and there is more. Much more! He reaches into his briefcase and brings out a book, and flips to a page. "Notice this on page 48 of *Vengeance on the Vikings*," as he begins reading:

'The research team first found the previously unknown remains of one of Britain's largest Neolithic henges, almost 500 feet in diameter. The find immediately changed the perception of prehistoric Oxford from a rather insignificant ford across the Thames to potentially one of the most important ritual sites in southern England. The henge's eight-foot-deep ditch had become, by the medieval period, a dump for waste, including broken pottery and food scraps.

'It was there, in the garbage-filled ditch, that the team found the remains of 37 people. All the bodies in the grave appear to have been male, and most were between 16 and 25 years old. As a group, they were tall, taller than the average Anglo-Saxon at the time, and strong, judging by the large muscle-attachment areas of their bones. Despite their physical advantages, all these men appear to have met violent ends. One had been decapitated, and attempts at decapitation had seemingly been made on five others.

Twenty-seven suffered broken or cracked skulls. The back and pelvic bones of 20 bodies bore stab marks, as did the ribs of a dozen others. A number of the skeletons had evidence of charring, indicating that they were burned prior to burial.'

Startled, Smithe states, "There was definitely something sinister going on here. Just as there appears to be with Dr. Flanders's missing heart and Alisdair Sinclars. I wonder if these rituals go back to these Druid beliefs that even influenced Robert the Bruce."

McNair gives his opinion as to what happened. "I agree, and even though the archaeology article doesn't mention any connection to Druid history in Oxford, I don't think we can rule it out. It appears that the men were not killed in battle, as they didn't find any weapons. Because some of them were dismembered in some sort of bloodbath, and because the University of Oxford sits upon an ancient Druid henge dedicated to some sort of sacred ritual of human sacrifice—we must consider this a possibility. What other logical reason is there for what they uncovered?"

DI Smithe is starting to get the wheels turning in his head as to the possible connection to a Druid custom and Dr. Flanders's missing heart.

"Now here is another interesting fact that came to light in 1994, of an unusual finding near Oxford and Stonehenge, this time in 1921. The remains of large numbers of human babies were found," says McNair as he begins reading from volume 84 of *The Journal of Roman Studies*. "Right at the beginning of this article, 'Child Exposure in the Roman Empire,' William V. Harris writes:

'A previous excavation of Hambleden in 1921 determined that the site has 97 infant burials, the largest number of such burials for any Roman location in Britain. The excavator at the time suspected infanticide 'with surreptitious disposal of the bodies.'

Smithe is mystified, "Pardon my ignorance, Doctor, but this sounds like the Middle Ages!"

Disgusted as to what may have occurred, McNair replies, "Indeed, infanticide is the intentional killing of children under the age of 12 months. Naturally it has no place in today's world."

Sympathetic, Smithe responds, "I love my kids. Who would do such a thing?"

Appalled by the ignorance of these ancient societies, McNair observes, "Unfortunately, the practice of infanticide has taken many forms over time. Child sacrifice to the god Molech was performed by the Israelites, and may have been influential in Druid rituals. Infanticide has been practiced on every continent. A frequent method of infanticide in ancient Europe and Asia was simply to abandon the infant, leaving it to die by natural causes, such as hypothermia, dehydration, or animal attack."

Smithe exclaims, "How cruel!" and inquires further, "How do we know that those murders occurred because of some ancient ritualistic offering to the gods, and not just because the parents didn't want the child or because it wasn't the right gender?"

"When the Romans were invaded by barbarian tribes in the first century, it was discovered that many of the tribes offered up the sacrifice of newborns to appease their gods," explained McNair. "This was done in an endeavor to win over their gods to help them in their resistance to the invading Romans. The Romans believed that the Druids were involved in this practice, and believed that human sacrifice was repugnant. Did you ever hear of the Wicker Man, Inspector?"

Smithe declares, "Of course, who hasn't!"

McNair says, "Well, then you know it is a custom from the ancient Druids."

Smithe, on defense, replies, "Well, I guess I thought it was just a harmless custom that a bunch of college kids did for the fun of it."

McNair enlightens Smithe, "That may be so, and I'm sure the majority of students and masters at Oxford are not involved in any of this, but there are always some people who are easily influenced into doing the bizarre. In pre-Christian Britain, the Ancient Order of Druids were teachers of esoteric, or mystic, schools, with dictatorial authority in religious and political matters. The Romans, who introduced Christianity to the British Isles, tried to obliterate Druidry, but failed in their attempt. Researcher Manly P. Hall believes the traditions of the Druids influenced Freemasonry.

"During the Rosicrucian Enlightenment, Druidism was revived in Great Britain. According to Jean Pierre Bayard, the Scottish Rite of the 'Golden and Rosy Cross' was first practiced in France, called Knight of the Rose Croix, deriving its name from oral tradition of the Knights Templar. The association of the cross and rose was found in Portugal in the Order of Christ, home of the Knights Templar, in 1530."

"Druidism, Knights Templar, Fifth Monarchy Men, Rosicrucians, Scottish Rites, Illuminati, Freemasons . . . all of these so-called 'secret societies' keep popping up," observes Smithe. "Sometimes I feel like a blind man touching an elephant trying to figure out what they are. I wonder if there is any connection to any of them. And even though I'm not sure any of them have relevance to the killing of Dr. Flanders, I'm hooked into knowing more about them."

"I can understand your interest in knowing more about them, because it is fascinating history," says McNair. "And yes, I believe there is a connection to all of them; as they all started out for good reasons. But like a lot of history, there are always those who will change their intended purposes into evil."

"How's that?" asks DI Smithe.

McNair gives a brief history. "Undoubtedly, one cannot argue that Masonry does have certain forms of Masonic Templarism, and the Scottish Rite contains a degree revolving around the Templars. Freemasonry, like all of those societies you mentioned, was meant to improve humanity's nature and moral and spiritual development. 'Know thyself,' in Freemasonry, is similar to the Scottish Rite initiation ceremony. Just like the Christian faith, Freemasonry has many emblems and symbols that relate to higher principles in allegorical form.

"For example, it is thought that the Rose Croix ritual is understood to represent the Passion of Christ in some circles. Thus, we have the connection of Rosicrucianism and Freemasonry. Early Rosicrucian manifestos proclaim that the first thing needed to transform the world is to transform the spirit in man. Clearly, there appears to be a closely woven bond between these organizations. Why the red color of the rose chosen to represent the body of Christ in their symbolic ceremonies is anyone's guess.

"Even King Henry VIII wanted to find out how Masonry gained a foothold in England. He appointed John Leyland to find any books or manuscripts from various religious groups to be brought to him. To his amazement, the King found a document written by King Henry VI that answered that question."

"What did he find out?" asks Smithe.

"Speculations abound, and are as different as those who have provided them," McNair points out. "A theory arose in the early 1700s that the Freemasons began in the medieval deserts with the Knights Templar. But many Freemasons reject this theory."

"You mentioned the Illuminati as also having moral ground. How was that?" inquires Smithe.

"Yes, like the other so-called secret societies, the original purpose was to reach man's highest human potential of morality. It was thought that once man could reach this goal of high standards of morality and virtue, he could change the world and, by example, he would change the world of evil men," says McNair.

"That sounds a lot like Christianity—and a lot of religions that practice the golden rule" says Smithe.

"Spot on!" replies McNair, happily pointing a finger at Smithe.

Smithe replies, "This history is all very interesting! It seems I read somewhere that even Benjamin Franklin was a

Rosicrucian! I guess they were secret, but had moral values originally."

McNair concurs, "I believe you are right, Smithe, and the book *The Ancient Druid Order: British Circle of the Universal Bond* confirms that the Rosicrucians, Freemasons, and Druids, often had members in common."

"If these groups started out with good intentions, how did some of them go astray?" inquires Smithe, thinking back to the reason for this meeting.

"Like a lot of organizations, there are always individuals with twisted minds that will turn a good thing into something evil. The Bible has a whole history of good people that turned evil. When Christianity became the preferred religion of the Roman Empire, the Druids took their dark practices of sacrificing—even humans—underground," says McNair.

Smithe is very disturbed by this ancient history and repeats his concerns, "This is scary stuff, Doctor, and I thank you for enlightening me."

"One more thing Smithe, before you get to overwhelmed with bodies being found in Oxford. Bodies are being discovered all over England and for many reasons. The bubonic plague wiped out a lot of people in 17th century Britain. In London alone, it is estimated that 100,000 people died from 1665-1666."

"I know a lot of people died from the plague, and that they were buried all over England in massive graves called 'plague pits.' Do you think the bodies could be from the black death?" inquires Smithe.

"No, I don't," says McNair emphatically. I have spoken with many archaeologists concerning the stories of these so-called 'plague pits' and most of them believe they are simply lore. There is no historical basis for these claims and most people were buried in church cemeteries.

"How then did these rumors get started? I heard people were buried in these pits from the plague in Green Park and that's why the Piccadilly underground is winding," says Smithe.

"Pure legend, once a rumor starts in print it becomes real in people's minds. Don't forget there are bodies scattered all over England from ancient sacrifices to burning at the stake from religious persecution," says McNair.

McNair appreciates Smithe's interest. "You're entirely welcome. By the way, Smithe, I will be giving a series of lectures at the Historical Heritage Center on biblical history that you might find of interest to your case, and you are more than welcome to attend."

"I appreciate the invitation, and I'll be there. Just let me know where and when."

Just as McNair is about to leave Smithe's office, his cell rings. "Hello Sara, what? When? How? Oh, I'm so sorry to hear that Darling. I will be right over."

"What's wrong McNair?" asks Smithe.

"Sara's mother has just died."

"I'm sorry to hear that. I only met her briefly when Dr. Flanders died and she seemed like such a nice person."

"Yes, she was very nice but Sara told me that when Dr. Flanders died she died inside as well and was never the same."

Chapter Fourteen

After six months of investigation, and many sleepless nights, DI Smithe has once again summoned Professor McNair to his office at Scotland Yard to summarize his findings regarding the murder mystery of Dr. Flanders. McNair walks up the steps to Smithe's office and knocks on the door and without waiting for an answer, says as he opens the door, "Are you in there, DI Smithe?"

Smithe answers brightly, "Come in, Professor!"

Startled as to what he sees on Smithe's walls, the expression on McNair's face tells what he is feeling. He exclaims as he looks with amazement at the genealogy charts on the walls, "What in the world is all this, Smithe?"

Pointing to the wall charts, Smithe replies, "Well, at your suggestion, Doctor, and after hearing your lectures, I've been doing my homework and studying a lot of history and religious beliefs. I'm trying to zero in on the possible murder suspect of Dr. Flanders, and why they may have nicked the Stone of Destiny. The first thing I decided was that there is definitely a Scottish connection, because the stone was wrapped in a Scottish flag. After thinking of all the families connected to Scotland with possible motive, I put together some charts."

"I'm impressed!" admits McNair.

Smithe gets out a yardstick and points to a wall chart and says, "First, we begin with the 'first overturn' of the transfer of the stone from Ireland to Scotland. We then have the kingly connection of Scotland through Robert the Bruce."

Smithe points to the next chart. "We have the Bruce connection to the Templars. Then we have the Arbroath connection to Scotland. And this is the history that I find most interesting, and is a direct link to everything we have been discussing. I got to thinking about that very first video you showed me, where Jacob had the dream in which God told him that kings would come out of him, and then he slept on that stone that has represented the rightful kingship to Ireland, Scotland, and England. In essence, we have a game of thrones!"

"I'm with you so far, Detective," says McNair.

"The Bruce was loyal to England at first—until King Edward I appointed Balliol to be his puppet king. That was a slap in the face for Robert the Bruce, and he then hooked up with William Wallace's rebellion. After Robert killed his rival, John Comyn—Balliol's nephew—in what appeared to be a ritualistic killing, Robert was excommunicated by Pope Clement V. This began the most famous document in Scottish history, from which you already showed me a quote. But after reading the document in its entirety, things began to click," says Smithe.

"How's that?" asks an enthralled McNair.

"I could see that the many families that signed it really believed they were descendants of Israel and had God-given rights to the throne. Look." Smithe points to a chart that has some direct quotations from the Declaration.

> *They journeyed from Greater Scythia by way of the Tyrrhenian Sea and the Pillars of Hercules, and dwelt for a long course of time in Spain among the most savage tribes, but nowhere could they be subdued by any race, however barbarous...The Britons they first drove out, the Picts they utterly destroyed, and, even though very often assailed by the Norwegians, the Danes and the English, they took possession of that home with many victories and untold efforts; and, as the historians of old time bear witness, they have held it free of all bondage ever since...In their kingdom there have reigned one hundred and thirteen kings of their own royal stock, the line unbroken a single foreigner...The high qualities and deserts of these people, were they not otherwise manifest, gain glory enough from this: that the King of kings and Lord of lords, our Lord Jesus Christ, after His Passion and Resurrection, called them, even though settled in the uttermost parts of the earth, almost the first to His most holy faith...The Most Holy Fathers your predecessors gave careful heed to these things and bestowed many favours and numerous privileges on this same kingdom and people, as being the*

> *special charge of the Blessed Peter's brother...**'It is in truth not for glory, nor riches, nor honours that we are fighting, but for freedom - for that alone, which no honest man gives up but with life itself.'**...Thus our nation under their protection did indeed live in freedom and peace up to the time when that mighty prince the King of the English, Edward, the father of the one who reigns today, when our kingdom had no head and our people harboured no malice or treachery and were then unused to wars or invasions, came in the guise of a friend and ally to harass them as an enemy...The deeds of cruelty, massacre, violence, pillage, arson, imprisoning prelates, burning down monasteries, robbing and killing monks and nuns, and yet other outrages without number which he committed against our people, sparing neither age nor sex, religion nor rank, no one could describe nor fully imagine unless he had seen them with his own eyes...But from these countless evils we have been set free, by the help of Him Who though He afflicts yet heals and restores, by our most tireless Prince, King and Lord, the Lord Robert...He, that his people and his heritage might be delivered...Yet if he should give up what he has begun, and agree to make us or our kingdom subject to the King of England or the English, we should exert ourselves at once to drive him out as our enemy and a subverter of his own rights and ours, and make some other man who was well able to defend us our King; **for, as long as but a hundred of us remain alive, never will we on any conditions be brought under English rule.**

"It does indeed look like you have made a connection for motive to the Scots, DI Smithe. There seems to be a lot of bad blood between them and the English. It also appears that there was even a warning to Robert the Bruce; that if he didn't live up to his intentions, he could be deposed as well," surmises McNair.

"Yes, the words in this document tell a lot about what these people thought, and how far they would go to ensure their sovereignty," says Smithe.

"You have a valid point," declares McNair.

"I sure could use your input on this." Smithe scratches his head and points to another wall chart. "Now over here is the bloodline that came out of Jacob's son Judah, culminating in the twins Pharez and Zarah of the scarlet thread, as you said. Not that I necessarily believe this stuff, but as you have said, as long as these people believe it, they are all suspects. I'm trying to understand this genealogy to see possible suspects to Dr. Flanders's murder. You know, perhaps some radical zealot with a twisted mind from one of these secret societies. Someone who wanted to possess the stone as historical proof that they are the true bloodline to King David may have committed this crime."

McNair is amazed with the detective's work, as well as being curious about his conclusion. Smithe then shows him the chart of the Pharez lineage.

"Correct me if I'm wrong, Doctor, but over here is the

> **CHART OF PHAREZ LINEAGE**
>
> Abraham
> Isaac
> Jacob
> Judah
> Pharez
> David
> Zedekiah
> Queen Teia Tephi
> Queen Teia

blood lineage from Jacob to Pharez to King David, to all of the kings of Israel. This chart shows the last king of Israel, Zedekiah, who was Queen Tephi's father. Queen Teia Tephi, who married King Heremon of Ireland, was in Sara's bloodline. Am I right thus far, Doctor?"

"Spot on" replies McNair. "Yes, Inspector, I'm impressed. You have been a good student!"

Smithe then points to the Zarah chart and garners McNair's attention. "Now over here is the bloodline of the Zarah line of the scarlet thread. Here we begin with Queen's Tephi's marriage to King Heremon of Ireland, and show all of the kings of Ireland. This began what Jeremiah the prophet said was the 'first overturn.' Am I right so far, Doctor?"

"Spot on! Right again, Smithe. Perhaps you should give

> **CHART OF ZARAH LINEAGE**
>
> Abraham
> Isaac
> Jacob
> Judah
> Zarah
> Heremon

the next lecture at the Historical Society."

Smithe now points to the chart with the kings of Scotland and says, "Now over here we have all of the kings of Scotland, including Robert the Bruce, as the throne was then transferred to Scotland, fulfilling the 'second overturn.' These are also the 'sacred families,' as they were called that lay claim to the Zarah bloodline of Jacob, although in reality

> **CHART OF THE KINGS OF SCOTLAND**
>
> **Bruce** McNab Dundasses
> Rosses Wemysses Earls
> **Sinclairs** Abernethys MacKays
> Robertsons MacDuffs Lindsays
> **Stewart** Dunbars Leslies
> Mackenzies Chattan

they may not be. But as long as they think they are, they are suspect."

Genealogy Charts

Smithe then points to the kings of England chart and says, "Now this chart contains the 'third overturn' from Scotland to England, beginning with Edward I or 'Longshanks,' as he was called, who invaded Scotland and removed the Stone of Destiny and took it to England. But then the Stuart dynasty began through King James VI of Scotland, whose title became King of England and Ireland as James I. Am I correct so far, McNair?" asks Smithe.

CHART OF THE KINGS OF ENGLAND

Edward I
Tudors
Stewarts
James I
Queen Elizabeth II

McNair replies, "Right on again, indeed! I will be calling you Professor Smithe pretty soon!"

Smithe now points to the Knights Templar chart and says, "Ok, then, this chart represents all of the families of the Knights Templar, who also have an axe to grind because of being ousted from France and shamed by the Catholic Church and French monarchs for being heretics. Not to mention the amount of money their families lost when they were burnt at the stake during the Inquisition."

CHART OF THE KNIGHTS TEMPLAR

Geoffroi de Saint-Omer; Payen de Montdidier;
Hugues de Payens
Archambaud de St. Agnan; Andre de Montbard;
Geoffrey Bison
Rossal; Gondamer; Sinclair; Douglas Champayne;
St Clair; Anjou
Gisors; Flanders; Jacques de Molay

McNair repeats, "Most impressive, DI Smithe!"

"One thing that I am unsure of, though, is if the stone that was nicked from the abbey is the real stone or a counterfeit," admits Smithe. "I don't believe it could be the real stone, as the weight of it was 335 pounds, and the stone based upon royal seals and copies was around 458 pounds."

McNair concurs by nodding his head thoughtfully, and Smithe tells him of his additional research.

"Several authoritative archaeologists agreed with you that, after due reflection, the stone which was carried by Israel's priests could not have been the same stone nicked from the abbey. Their conclusion was that the real stone would not have cracked in the middle because of the composition; it would have been formed occurring naturally in Israel."

Overwhelmed at Smithe's research, McNair replies, "Good observation, Inspector! I'm glad we agree."

Smithe adds, "One more thing; would the guardian, the Abbot of Scone, and the Archbishop of Canterbury for Scotland, have simply allowed King Edward I to come riding up to Scone and nick the precious relic without at least some attempt to hide it? After all, it was Scotland's most sacred treasure, and the abbot had plenty of warning of King Edward's intention to take it. I think not!"

McNair asks, "So, Inspector, do you think that Bruce made a counterfeit stone?"

"Precisely! It seems incredible that King Robert the Bruce, who was anxious to prove his right to the throne of his ancestors, did not make any attempt to regain his country's most sacred talisman. I also have found out, as you have said, that it has always been the dream of the faithful Knights Templar to keep the stone in Scotland—for succeeding kings to be enthroned—as they believed, as did Robert the Bruce—as it was ordained by God. As you also stated, they were trying to establish a temple in Scotland like the one in Jerusalem for this very purpose," says Smithe.

McNair reiterates, "So, Inspector, you think the Templars hid the stone somewhere?"

Smithe concludes, "Precisely! That's why I think they were gathering the temple artifacts! I don't think the knights were sent to the Holy Land to merely protect would-be travelers. No, I think they were sent there for a mission. In fact, after talking with several experts on this subject, including yourself, I've come to the conclusion that the original stone was probably a much smaller, black stone hidden by Cistercian Abbot Monks of Scone in 1296. So, yes, McNair, I believe they have the original stone, and very possibly, some of the other temple artifacts hidden somewhere."

McNair concludes, "So we agree! Like I have been saying all along, whether these things are so or not, these people believe it."

Smithe provides a motive for revenge and says, "I agree with you, Doctor, and that's why I think a stone will turn up some day with someone claiming it to be the real Stone of Destiny. Now here's another interesting fact for revenge. As you stated in your lecture, and history tells us, when Edward I of England invaded Scotland and gave the order to burn and slay dragons—and finally captured Bruce's spiritual predecessor, Sir William Wallace—they dragged him through the city, then hung him by the neck until he was almost unconscious, cut off and burnt his bowels before him while still alive— then cut off his head, and finally cut the rest of his body into four parts. If that isn't a motive for revenge, I don't know what is!"

McNair acknowledges Smithe's detective work and asks him for his opinion. "Yes, that was a gruesome fate! So, Inspector, give me your opinion as to what happened to the sacred stone, as you seem to have turned into an expert on this subject."

"I wouldn't call me an expert, but that's a fair enough question, Dr. McNair. I will give you my opinion if you will give me yours."

McNair plays along and says, "Fair is fair!"

Smithe begins his hypothesis and says, "Most of the beliefs that surround the mystery of the stone are based on oral history. Some believe the stone was hidden in a cave on Moncrieff Hill, near Scone, or what has been called Macbeth's Castle."

"Yes Inspector, I am familiar with much of this speculation."

Smithe continues with his thoughts. "Then you know there are several more theories, but none of which greatly clears up the fog of mystery. I think as long as there are folks who are proud to call themselves Scots, stories will abound. But it doesn't help me in solving this case."

"I commend you, DI Smithe; you have indeed done your homework!"

"Thanks for the compliment, Doctor, but I think I am still in the dark," confessed Smithe. "I am still getting nowhere. What do you think is going on in all of this conspiracy world domination theory?"

McNair now gives his theory. "Well, since you asked for my opinion, let's start with the tribe of Dan. Samson, a Nazarite of the tribe of Dan, judged Israel during the period of Philistine domination. Recall the Bible story of how his Philistine wife, Delilah, tried to get the secret to his physical strength, which was in his hair."

"Samson, yes, I remember Sara saying something about his connection to what her father believed at the beginning of our investigation. But I didn't see the relevance at that time," ponders Smithe.

"Of course it really wasn't his hair that gave him extraordinary strength, but God gave him power. There are several obscure prophecies in the Bible that point to the fact that the Antichrist will come from the tribe of Dan, as Sara mentioned, and I think this power struggle has been going on ever since the days of Samson. That is, if you believe the Bible," says McNair.

Smithe is beginning to understand and says, "Yes, I just read that story again, of how Samson was blinded by the Philistines after his wife deceived him and they cut his hair, but he still had enough strength in him to push the pillars in the temple of Dagon apart so they came crashing down."

"Sometimes you amaze me, Smithe! Well, I believe the tribe of Dan is still in contention for power with the tribe of Judah over the kingly promise. I also believe that these secret societies formed by many of the European aristocrat families long ago, and who claim to come from the tribe of Judah through Jesus Christ and Mary Magdalene, are still planning to rule the world from a future throne at Jerusalem. However, the weight of evidence indicates that they descended from the tribe of Dan, and not Judah!"

Smithe is anxious and interrupts McNair. "Yeah, I saw *The Da Vinci Code* so I know what you are talking about. But that was just a movie, and I didn't think it really happened. Do you really believe in the Bible and a spirit world? Sorry to interrupt you, Doctor. Please continue your thoughts."

McNair proceeds with his point of view. "Well, to answer your first question, yes, I do believe in a spirit world, and Dr. Flanders did as well. We had many interesting discussions on that subject. Although Scripture says that Samson was of the tribe of Dan, his mother was from the tribe of Judah. The very name 'Dan' means 'judge' in Hebrew, and I believe—as do other scholars—that there is a movement that the Gentiles' world is being prepared to submit to the Noahide laws under a restored Sanhedrin. That's where these ancient families and secret societies enter into the picture."

Smithe is a bit confused and replies, "You lost me, McNair."

McNair obliges. "Recall how the ancient Druids brought their Baal-goddess-worshipping mystic religion to Ireland and influenced the Celts of Scotland, who seem to be connected to the tribe of Dan because of their use of Dan-related place-names, personal names, and peculiar symbols, which are still used by certain secret societies. It seems that the tribe of Dan was involved in a substitute worship system of the Israelites. As we have discussed previously, when the Knights Templar were being persecuted for heresy, many of them fled to Scotland under the protection of King Robert the Bruce who, according to some theories, believed he was a king and priest like his forefather Nimrod!"

"Is there any historical proof of that?" asks Smithe.

"I recently read a book entitled *Symbols of Our Celto-Saxon Heritage* by W. H. Bennett that went into that concept in detail," remarks McNair.

"I'll take your word for it," says Smithe. Still confused, he says again, "You lost me again on this biblical history, McNair."

McNair apologizes and elaborates. "I realize that I have covered a lot of ancient history in my lectures so I will refresh your memory. Recall the time when Emperor Constantine divided his empire into Rome and Constantinople, which is modern-day Turkey. There was a lot of discord within the hierarchy in the Church.

"Remember, it was the French patriarchs that sent the Templars to the Holy Land, and I believe it was to find as many temple artifacts as they could find, including the Ark of the Covenant, to prove their rightful sovereignty and to rebuild the Temple of Solomon. That way, the patriarchs of the East would have more credence than the patriarchs of the West. And that way, the power swing would be enhanced by the East and would reduce the power of Rome.

"Realize, there were two popes at one time. One in Rome, and one in France. I have spoken with several experts on Templar objectives, and some believe that a secondary goal of the Knights Templar was to find as many temple artifacts as they could find."

Smithe's detective mind is working overtime and he says, "So what you're telling me is that the relatives of these ancient families believe they are the rightful heirs of King David, and are entitled to the throne and will rule the world.

That's why they want the Stone of Destiny! To prove their right! I can understand that."

McNair enlightens Smithe further. "Indeed, and here is where these European noble families who had escaped from Jerusalem shortly before, or possibly even just after, the fall of the temple fit into the picture. They believe their families descended from the bloodline of King David, and the proof of these ancient artifacts will prove their rightful inheritance. Supposedly, they have hidden them near the ancient temple in Jerusalem. I think we are already seeing some of these artifacts appear, such as the supposed bones of Jesus' family. I believe when the time is right, other relics will surface, including the real Stone of Destiny and the Ark of the Covenant. Then their leader will emerge as the world's ruler with absolute power. This has been the dream of many a despot, including Adolf Hitler's desperate search for the lost ark during World War II."

Smithe is dumbfounded and replies, "I never knew that!"

McNair provides additional insight. "You can't believe what people believe, Smithe! Have you ever gone to the Hofburg, the treasure house of the Habsburgs in Vienna, Austria, where royal items are on display?"

Smithe has heard of it and responds, "No, but I have heard a lot about it and it is on my bucket list."

"There are people who believe the legendary spear, reputed to have pierced the side of Jesus Christ, is a symbol of power and is now located in the Hofburg Treasure House," McNair says as he gives more illumination to Smithe.

"Really!"

"It's true! Yes, you should go there sometime. Then you will see not only the legendary spear, but also the royal jewels and the cup that Christ supposedly drank from at the Last Supper. It was rumored that when Gaius Cassius, the Roman centurion, took his spear and pierced the side of Jesus, Joseph of Arimathea caught Jesus' blood in the golden cup.

"The cup has now become known as the Holy Grail. These relics are believed to have such power to those who have them in their possession that not only Hitler, but his predecessor, Kaiser Wilhelm, who ruled Germany in 1913, wanted to have the spear in his possession before he launched a war. Did you ever wonder why the Crown of England, also known as St. Edwards Crown, used during the coronation ceremony, has 12 large stones of various colors around it at the base?"

"No, can't say that I was aware of that. What does it signify?" Smithe asks curiously.

"As outlined in Exodus 28:15-21, these are the identical colors of the stones representing the 12 tribes of Israel that the High Priest of Israel wore on his breastplate," McNair explains.

Smithe is still dubious and says, "That's all very intriguing, Doctor, but I still can't believe that people will swallow this conspiracy stuff and nick the stone to prove their legitimate heritage."

"What you don't seem to understand or believe, Smithe, is that we are not talking about real people; we are talking about a spiritual world that has influenced them and is very dangerous," explains McNair.

"Father Benedetti told me the same thing," admits Smithe. "I guess I am skeptical of miracles and a spiritual world, as my job deals in facts!

"Oh, believe it, Detective! Just think about the many supposed miracles that are taking place in the world today, including the ones at Lourdes that you are aware of, where six million people go every year to see the preservation of the body of St. Bernadette. Are these genuine miracles? Is the Stone of Destiny genuine? It doesn't seem to matter to some people. Have you looked on the bookshelves these days to see all of the Masonic books, and books on conspiracy that are glutting the market?"

Genealogy Charts

Smithe responds, "Well, not lately, but I have seen *The DaVinci Code* and *Angels and Demons*. Actually, I kind of liked them."

"People are looking for a priest-king, just like Robert the Bruce and Nimrod of old. And someday he will surface as the False Prophet, according to the prophecies. But first they need substance of genuineness," replies McNair.

"Perhaps you will prove to be right someday, Doctor, and that is a very interesting scenario. But speaking of Robert the Bruce," Smithe points to the Stewart chart and says,

"Let's take a look at the next chart that I would like to show you of the famous Stewart family, as you enlightened us at your last lecture. As you said, it is through marriage with the daughter of Robert the Bruce that we can begin to trace the descent of the Royal House of Stewart. The royal line of male Stewarts continued uninterrupted until the reign of Mary Queen of Scots. As a family, the royal Stewarts held the throne of Scotland, and later that of England, in the direct line until the death of Queen Anne in 1714. In fact, Queen Elizabeth II is thought to have Stewart blood links, as you enunciated in your lecture. Do you think this chart is accurate?"

Dr. McNair is most impressed with DI Smithe's detective work. "Yes indeed, Smithe, very good! Glad to see you paid attention at my lectures. You know, I am very familiar with this Scottish Stewart rivalry, and you've got me thinking about something. This rivalry has also had great religious confrontation over the years as well. Perhaps this is another motive for nicking the stone and killing Dr. Flanders."

Smithe is inquisitive and replies, "How is that?"

McNair explains, "During the sixteenth century, Scotland underwent a Protestant Reformation through the teachings of John Knox. Like the Prophet Jeremiah, Knox wanted to get rid of the idolatry that was taking place in Scotland—as well as the corruption in the Catholic Church. He saw first-hand the rage of the Scottish people with the Church of Rome, who owned half of the land and knew of the promiscuousness that was well known in the Church. Later, Martin Luther and John Calvin had an influence.

> **CHART OF THE STEWART DYNASTY**
>
> Robert the Bruce (King of Scotland)
> King David II (Bruce's son) who died childless
> Walter Stewart, the 6th High Stewart married Marjory, daughter of Robert the Bruce, and therefore started the Stewart dynasty
> Robert Stewart, Bruce's grandson, through Marjory, became King Robert II in 1371, thus
> Mary Stewart (1542-1567) heir of King James V
> James I of England and VI of Scotland (1603-1625) Mary's son.
> James II and VII (1685-1688)
> James III and VIII (1701-1766)
> James Francis Edward Stuart, also known as the Old Pretender
> Charles III (1766-1788) Charles Edward Stuart, also known as Bonnie Prince Charles the Young Pretender
> Henry IX and I (1788-1807)
> Stewart Dynasty, which lasted until the death of Queen Anne in 1714

"In the highlands of Scotland, Roman Catholicism was still very powerful. Mary Stewart, who was the only surviving child of King James V inherited the thrown when she was only six days old and spent most of her life in France. She was raised Catholic but permitted Protestantism. When things were getting tough for her, she fled to England to get help from her cousin Elizabeth, who was Henry VIII's daughter, but supported the Protestantism of her father. Elizabeth, encouraged by her advisors, feared that Mary would try to eventually take over her throne and had her imprisoned.

"Following Mary's imprisonment, her infant son, James VI, who was raised a Protestant in her absence by George Buchanan, eventually took over the throne. When Queen Elizabeth died childless, James I became king of Ireland and took the title James VI of Scotland and England, thus unifying these three countries under his personal rule—thus ending the Tudor rule and beginning the Stewart monarchy."

"I'm with you," says Smithe, "But I'm still a little muddled as to how it helps my case. That's very interesting history; but what does religion have to do with the theft of the stone and the murder of Dr. Flanders?"

"In 1701, a very strange thing occurred in England as to the monarchy, as the Act of Settlement required the monarch to be Protestant, while James Francis Stewart, next in line, was a deeply religious Catholic. Therefore, the crown passed to the Elector of Hanover, who happened to be the great-grandson of James I of England, and Queen Anne's second cousin," explains McNair.

Smithe recalls, "I did read a little of that confusing part of English history."

"You're not the only one, Smithe," says McNair as he continues with his theory. "I believe, as did Sara's father, that this was the last 'overturn' of Jeremiah's prophecy, and why British monarchs are of Scottish royal descent. Despite all of this confusion, the Reformation progressed in both Scotland and England as they both rejected papal authority. However, England continued to have a lot of practicing Catholics, while Calvinism took a foothold in Scotland."

"Is that the reason why there has always been this Catholic/Protestant rift going on in Ireland, Scotland, and England?" wonders Smithe.

"I believe that is partly so, because that is what precipitated the Glorious Revolution, as it was called, in 1688, which impacted Scotland deeply," says McNair.

"How so?" exclaims Smithe.

"After the execution of King Charles I and Oliver Cromwell succeeded the throne, Charles I's sons, Charles and James, fled to France as a safe haven. Upon Cromwell's death there was a political interregnum, although the Fifth Monarchy Men hoped that Robert the Bruce would fill it. However, the new Parliament summoned Charles I's sons from banishment and restored the monarchy by crowning

Charles II. While in exile in France, the two sons of Charles were exposed to the absolute monarchy rule of Louis XIV, which believed in the Divine Right of Kings, and became problematic, to say the least, for the new Parliament," remarks McNair.

Smithe begins to see the connection to a possible religious motive as well and says, "Well then, it seems like we could have a religious motive for confiscating the stone and killing Dr. Flanders. If religion could be a motive," says Smithe.

"Yes, I believe so. Have you ever heard of the Jacobites?" asks McNair.

"You mentioned them before in our discussion on secret societies" recalls Smith.

"Well, there were a lot of different religious beliefs going on during this time period, including the beliefs of the Fifth Monarchy Men, who wanted to make England a theocracy, as we have discussed."

"Yes, I do recall the discussion we had on the Fifth Monarchy Men."

"Jacobites seemed to be believing the same teachings as the Celtic religion, and may have been influenced by the Johoanites. They were a political and religious movement dedicated to the restoration of the Stuart kings to the thrones of England and Scotland, which began from the seventeenth century. This ties in with the reestablishment of the Stuart kings of Charles II and his brother, James.

"When the Catholic James became king, he tried to engage Catholics in public life as well as Protestant dissenters and Quakers, like William Penn. When Jacobitism was introduced in Ireland in 1689, Catholics formed about 75 percent of the population—but in England they were only around 1 percent and in Scotland about 2 percent. The Tories were a more likely source of support, given their commitment to Church and king, but many were reluctant to trust the Church of England to a Catholic king," says McNair.

This idea is starting to gel in Smithe's mind, but he just needs a bit more information to solidify it. He wants to know how this will provide a motive for his case and wants McNair to explain his suspicion that the stone could have been nicked for religious reasons, and asks McNair to explain himself.

"I believe there are families in Scotland that plan to set up an earthly kingdom in Scotland, as far as I can tell. Some of these families still have the same goal. They believe whoever has the stone as a talisman has the power and right to rule. And there will be millions who will follow them. I just finished a book by one of the Stewarts, a Prince Michael Stewart, who has written some very interesting things in his book *The Forgotten Monarchy of Scotland*. It is his belief that early Celtic Christianity was the closest of all religious teachings to the original doctrines of Jesus which also contained many of the old Jewish laws. I can see how someone, someday, somewhere, will try to reinstitute these ways into our society, believing they are doing God's will, and I think this book validates my belief," says McNair.

"Does this Prince Michael have any valid claims to the throne? Are his beliefs very radical?"

"Prince Michael Stewart does seemingly have radical beliefs, but I agree with many of them," admits McNair.

"What do you mean by that, Doctor? Explain yourself!" says Smithe.

"What he says is basically true!" says McNair.

"I'm confused as to why you would say such a thing," says Smithe. "What do you mean? You're not siding with radical ideology, are you?"

McNair explains his viewpoint. "Prince Michael brings out a lot of facts of history that are basically true. The early Church was quite different than what it is today. Paganism was rampant in the early Church, and it was the Celtic Church that tried to get rid of all the statues and idols that were coming into the Church."

Smithe concurs, "Well, being raised Catholic, I never could understand how they justified praying to all of those statues when the first commandment said we shouldn't make any graven images!"

McNair justifies his reasoning and elaborates, "Now you see why I said Stewart was basically right."

Smithe now understands how someone who appears very reasonable and knowledgeable could do some very unreasonable things. But it doesn't help him in solving his case. "So, what can we do to stop these irrational men?"

Bewildered, McNair shakes his head in dismay and provides an unsatisfactory humanistic answer. "We can't, but God can! As long as there is a devil in the world, there will be deception. And as long as there is deception, there will be people in the world believing in true values while doing evil things. But there will also be good people doing good things to stop them. It is my belief that evil is not when evil people do evil things, no, evil is when good people say and do nothing to stop evil people."

They both stare at each other and shake their heads in dismay.

Chapter Fifteen

Five years later detective Smithe is reading the morning paper out on his patio as he is having breakfast on a beautiful morning with the sun shining. He is still thinking about retirement, but is enjoying traveling with his wife Martha when he takes a vacation. He is just relaxing and admiring the rose garden that he and Martha had planted. His murder investigation of Dr. Flanders has gone cold. The headlines read:

> **EXPLOSION ROCKS ISLAM'S THIRD MOST SACRED HOLY SITE,**
> **THE GOLDEN DOME OF THE ROCK AND AL-AQSA MOSQUE**

***

Two years later detective Smithe is reading his morning paper out on his patio as he is having breakfast. The headlines read:

> **ARCHAEOLOGISTS UNCOVER TEMPLE ARTIFACTS NEAR THE DOME OF THE ROCK!** Today, an amazing discovery has been made by Professors Malichi Mazer and Eli Kaufman of Hebrew University. They believe the ancient Ark that was made by the ancient Israelites has been found beneath the rubble of the Dome of the Rock. After thousands of years the Ark which was carried by the ancient priests of Israel containing the 10 commandments, Aaron's Rod that budded, the High Priest's Breastplate has been found.

In Search of the Stone of Destiny

Suddenly and almost simultaneously, DI Smithe gets a call from McGinty of the forensics lab on the phone and tells him that he has something that may be of interest to him on the cold murder case of the Curator at the Abbey! Detective Smithe is all ears and asks McGinty what he has uncovered! McGinty asks him if he has read the morning paper yet? Smithe replies**,** "You mean about the Archeology discovery?"

"No, read page 2 about Israel's insane Coroner," by Barry Chamish."

> **Israel's Insane Occultic Coroner**
> by Barry Chamish
> ...What I said back then was that pathologist Hiss was an occultic madman, lying to save other occultic madmen. Right now there is a head to head clash between the Israeli Supreme Court and the government on who actually rules Israel....In 1998, my Hiss findings were the front page news of a major newspaper, *The Scotsman*. After numerous phone calls concluding that I was right in all my facts, the paper concluded that something "evil and sick" was ruling Israel. On April 14, 1998, 47-year-old Alisdair Sinclair, was stopped by customs officials at Ben Gurion Airport on his way out of the country after a six day stay. They found 9000 Deutsche marks in a false bottom of his handbag and he was arrested without charge... At the airport police station, Sinclair was found strangling on his shoelaces. He was rushed to hospital and pronounced dead. From there his body was transferred to the Abu Kabir Institute for Forensic Medicine and straight into the paws of Dr. Yehuda Hiss, who conducted an autopsy which concluded that Sinclair had killed himself. After that, there was a problem with the body. Sinclair was unmarried, his parents weren't alive and he had been living a rather rootless life in Amsterdam dealing in vintage guitars and strumming them at local pubs. It took three days to track down his family in Scotland and the police offered to bury him in Israel. The family refused and paid about $5000 to fly the corpse home. On May 13, another autopsy was

The Missing Hearts

> conducted, at the University of Glasgow and guess what? The hyoid bone at the base of the tongue was missing and so was the heart. **Both were removed by Dr. Hiss.** But why? ...The Sinclair family started investigating Alisdair's recent life and none of his friends thought him remotely suicidal. "According to Alisdair's brother James, family lore has it that the Sinclairs are descended from the crusading Knights Templars, who journeyed to Jerusalem in the mid-1300s in search of holy artifacts from Herod's Temple to bring back to Scottish hero Robert Bruce. Alisdair himself, says James, was particularly proud of his middle name, Roslyn, the name of a chapel in Scotland whose floor plan is said to be based on Herod's Temple. James mentions these details in attempting to reconstruct his brother's motive for travelling to Israel... This peculiar passage may be of interest to those questioning Britain's early and deep interest in Zionism, their reverence for Chaim Weizmann, the Balfour Declaration, The British-Israel Society, the Round Table policies of Cecil Rhodes and Lord Milner and the like.
>
> How does this Medieval history explain Alisdair Sinclair's missing heart? Whether it does in some way or not, one thing is certain: The doctor who last examined Yitzhak Rabin is one very, weird sicko. *The Skikrret, 2016*

After giving Smithe a few minutes to read the story, McGinty inquires of Smithe, "Well, what do you think Inspector? Does this help with your investigation of Dr. Flanders missing heart?"

DI Smithe recalls the story told to him by Sara about Alisdair Sinclair and the possible connection to Robert the Bruce and her father's missing heart. Now he reads of a Doctor Hiss who appears to be connected as well.

Smithe is unnerved and utters, "It certainly adds to the mystique! Thanks for the info!"

Smithe's phone is ringing off the hook and McNair calls him up on his cell phone, "Smithe here."

"It's happening!" McNair responds in a panicky voice.

Smithe concurs, and says, "I know. I just read about the explosion of the Dome of the Rock and the finding of the artifacts! Call Sara and tell her it's time to open up her father's safety deposit box to see if there are any clues in there that might help us to deter this political plot to take over the human race!"

"Ok, I'll call her and we can all meet at her place."

Smithe declares, "I'll be there!"

**

McNair has arranged a meeting at Sara's house in a few days. Detective Smithe gets in his car and drives frantically over to Sara's house.

As he pulls away, his cell phone is ringing. "Hello, Smithe here! What? Great news, finally. Are they talking? I'll be down to interview them ASAP."

DI Smithe can't wait to talk to the thieves, as he has the uncanny ability to not only see the evil in people, but to bring them to confess. He is glad they have been apprehended, and in his heart of hearts he hopes they will hurt every single day rotting in a cell—but for now he must find out what Dr. Flanders has in his deposit box.

When he arrives at Sara's house, he informs them that the thieves have been apprehended.

Sara says, "Where did they catch them? Why did they do it?"

"They were caught trying to get on a plane to Jerusalem with your father's heart frozen in a metal box. The sensors went off and the guards caught them. They were three young people in their twenties. They are not talking to the police," says Smithe.

"I'm glad they're caught, but it won't bring my father back," exclaims Sara.

After their discussion, they all get into Smithe's car and journey to the Sovergn Bank to open up the Curator's Safety deposit box. They get out of Smithe's car and walk into the bank and Sara walks up to the teller and courteously asks,

"I would like to open my safety deposit box please." Sara hands the Teller her key."

The Teller replies, "Surely, it will be just a moment!" The Teller goes into the closed room and then comes out with the box and hands it to Sara.

"You can go in that room over there for privacy."

"Thank you."

Sara, DI Smithe and McNair enter the private room. Sara gets the box and opens it with the key her father gave her as McNair and Smithe look over her shoulder anxiously. Sara looks into the deposit box and is astonished! She exclaims, "There's just a Bible in here! Wait!" Sara opens the Bible and says, "There's also a sealed letter in here!"

Smithe and McNair respond in unison, "Let's open it and see what the Professor had to say!"

Sara's eyes begin to widen as she opens the letter and reads it out loud.

My dearest Sara. I know that you are reading this letter upon my death, and of course I don't know the circumstances of that death, but I hope it wasn't too painful! I also know that it may have been due to my research of where the Ark of the Covenant may be and what certain sinister and perverted individuals led by the devil himself might do to you and the world if they had this knowledge before them. So I have given you this vital information in a coded form that I know you will be able to decipher along with my good friend and confident Professor McNair. This may be the world's last chance to survive what many call the Great Tribulation perpetrated by these minions of Satan. The first part of this coded message and where the true Ark can be located is in the riddle found in Ezekiel 17:1-24, and the answer to it is found in the coded writing below along with the following scriptures. May God bless you and remember, I'll always love you

Your beloved father.

After reading the letter from her father, startled, Sara articulates, "I can't believe my father knows where the real Ark of the Covenant has been hidden! All of these years he led me to believe it was in Ethiopia!"

McNair introjects, "That's what he wanted you to believe Sara, because it is what a lot of misinformed people believe! And it looks like there is going to be a counterfeit being discovered by this new archaeological find in Jerusalem!"

Sara is bewildered and asks Dr. McNair, "How did you come to that conclusion Robert?"

McNair ponders whether this is the time or place to tell this legend that he came across, when King Solomon married the Queen of Sheba, and they eventually got married and had a son named Menelik. "Well it is a long story, and perhaps I should tell it some other time," says McNair.

"I'm curious Robert," says Sara.

"Me to," says Smithe.

"Ok, why don't we sit down, and I'll give you the gist of it," says McNair. "The story goes that King Solomon wanted his son Menelik to be Ethiopia's first King according to the Ethiopian Chronicles. So, at the age of nineteen, Menelik's mother died, and being educated by the priests in the Temple, he became a strong believer in Jehovah. Being the son of Solomon and a righteous Jew, Prince Menelik saw his father Solomon going back into apostasy, bringing in pagan practices into the house of God from marrying pagan wives.

"Solomon desired that his son return to Ethiopia, 2,000 miles to the south, and be its Emperor. Solomon had a replica Ark made by his craftsman, that consisted of the identical materials and dimensions of the real Ark as a going away present for his son. The only difference in the two Arks was that one contained the glory of God, and the other one did not!"

Smithe is listening intently and puts in his two cents, "A very clever plot! What happened then?"

Realizing they are both very interested, McNair continues with this legend, "I thought you would appreciate this case Smithe being a history buff and all! The following morning Menelik and many of the faithful righteous priests, who despised the abominations of Solomon supposedly switched Arks.

"According to legend, they put the replica Ark in the Holy of Holies, and took the real Ark for safe keeping to Ethiopia, until the nation of Israel would repent, and turn to God once again! Unfortunately, that never materialized, and the nation of Israel consisting of 10 tribes went further and further into idolatry, until they were finally taken captive by the Assyrians in 721 B.C.; but the replica Ark remained in the Temple in Jerusalem."

"Very clever!" Says Smithe as he interjects.

"What happened to the real Ark?" asks Sara.

"The remaining nation of Judah consisting of the tribes of Judah and Benjamin were taken captive by King Nebuchadnezzar's Babylonian conquest in 606 B.C. After the invasion, it is thought that Jeremiah and the priests brought back the true Ark from Ethiopia and took it with them to Egypt. Judah remained captive for seventy years until they were allowed to return to their homeland in 536 B.C. to rebuild their Temple under the Persian King Cyrus.

"It was at this time that the Temple priests supposedly brought back the replica Ark from Ethiopia and put it into the new Temple. Later, when Antiochus threatened to invade, the priests hid the replica Ark in an underground cave. I believe it is this replica Ark that the Archaeologists recently found," Says McNair.

"What an incredible story, and understanding the power contained in the Ark, I now understand why the Ark was so important to find throughout history, and why Mussolini and Hitler wanted to find it? If that story is true then this new archeological discovery is the replica Ark and not the real one. Am I right Dr.?" asks Smithe.

"Yes, the Ark was what made Israel invincible in battle. When the army of Israel escorted the Ark of the Covenant around the city of Jericho seven times, the power of God caused the walls of the city to come crumbling down like a house of cards. That's the reason why Mussolini and Hitler wanted it!"

Smithe nods his head in agreement and then his detective eyes spot something unusual in the letter and says, "I see! What's all this chicken scratch about? And what do these Bible verses imply?" They all look at the unusual markings and read the scriptures that go with it.

Ezekiel 17:1-24

Mathew 7:7 Ask, and it shall be given you; **seek, and ye shall find**; knock, and it shall be opened unto you:

Exodus. 17:9 And Moses said unto Joshua, Choose us out men, and go out, fight with Amalek: tomorrow I will **stand on the top of the hill** with the rod of God in mine hand.

Genesis. 3:3 But of the fruit of **the tree which is in the midst of the garden**, God hath said, Ye shall not eat of it, neither shall ye touch it, lest ye die.

Joshua 24:26 And Joshua wrote these words in the book of the law of God, **and took a great stone, and set it up there under an oak, that was by the sanctuary of the LORD.**

John. 19:34: But one of the soldiers with a spear pierced his **side,** and forthwith came there out blood and water.

After looking at the letter further, McNair declares, "I don't know what those markings mean, but I know someone who might. One thing at a time detective. Let's solve the riddle first, then I think the scriptures will give us additional clues. Sara, let's read the first clue your father spoke of in the book of Ezekiel!"

"You read it Robert, I'm still devastated!" Sara hands McNair the Bible and he thumbs to Ezekiel and reads out loud.

> *And the word of the Lord came unto me, saying, Son of man, put forth a riddle, and speak a parable unto the house of Israel; And say, Thus saith the Lord God; A great eagle with great wings, longwinged, full of feathers, which had different colors, came unto Lebanon, and took the highest branch of the cedar: He cropped off the top of his young twigs, and carried it into a land of traffick; he set it in a city of merchants. He took also of the seed of the land, and planted it in a fruitful field; he placed it by great waters, and set it as a willow tree...*
>
> *There was also another great eagle with great wings and many feathers: and behold, this vine did bend her roots toward him, and shot forth her branches toward him, that he might water it by the furrows of her plantation. It was planted in good soil by great waters, that it might bring forth branches, and that it might bear fruit, that it might be a goodly vine...*
>
> *Thus saith YHWH GOD; I will also take of the highest branch of the high cedar, and will set it; I will crop off from the top of his young twigs a tender one, and will plant it upon an high mountain and eminent:*
>
> *" In the mountain of the height of Israel will I plant it: and it shall bring forth boughs, and bear fruit, and be a goodly cedar: and under it shall dwell all fowl of every wing; in the shadow of the branches thereof shall they dwell.*

"What does all this stuff mean?" inquires Smithe.

"Well, remember that documentary I showed you about the story of Jeremiah in Jerusalem as he explained to King Zedekiah what would happen to him and the nation of Judah?"

Clueless, Smithe replies, "refresh my memory Dr.!"

McNair reciprocates, "Well some commentators on this parable believe **'The great eagle' that went to 'Lebanon' and took the 'highest branch of the cedar'** is explained as to represent king Nebuchadnezzar of Babylon who came to Jerusalem and took captive the king of Judah. That would make reference to king Zedekiah being the highest branch of the cedar.

"The 'cropping' off of the 'young twigs' and carrying them to the land of traffic is explained to picture the captivity of the king's sons. **'He also took the seed of the land'** indicates that the whole house of Judah was taken captive. The **'willow tree' that was 'low in stature'** means, 'Although the Davidic dynasty survived the exile, it was not the noble, tall cedar it had been.'"

"Ok, I'm with you so far but who was the second eagle?" Smithe declares.

"The second eagle in the verse is the Pharaoh of Egypt and the vine is 'Zedekiah who turned his allegiance to Egypt' but God said he shouldn't have done it but rather should have trusted God. Thus, the riddle covers the first half of Jeremiah's commission."

"I'm with you so far, but what happened next?" asks Sara.

McNair adds, "The riddle told us that Nebuchadnezzar took the highest branch of the cedar or the King. The parable now tells us that God, not Nebuchadnezzar will take of the Highest branch. Not *the* branch but *of* the branch. In other words of Zedekiah's children. This is where Jeremiah's commission took place after Nebuchadnezzar killed Zedekiah's sons. God, through Jeremiah was now going to take one of Zedekiah's **young tender twigs and plant it** upon a high mountain."

"What does that mean?" Smithe asks curiously.

"I believe the 'young twigs' in the riddle were the *sons* of Zedekiah. If the young twigs mean the sons, then the **'tender twig'** means obviously **a daughter!**...and I will plant it."

"I think I get it," says Sara. "You mean Queen Teia!"

"Precisely!"

"But where?" Smithe utters.

"I think wherever Jeremiah or Ollam took the tender branch or Teia!"

"You mean Ireland!" as Sara provides the answer.

"I think that is precisely what your father was trying to tell us through this riddle and why he was even helping our drama team."

"But where in Ireland?" Sara responds.

"I think the mysterious writing is the clue we are looking for and I will talk to Professor McDowell, head of our linguistics department in the morning. Meanwhile, Sara please book us three tickets to Ireland as soon as possible."

Sara replies, "Gladly!"

Chapter Sixteen

Sara, McNair and Smithe board a plane to Ireland two days later. It is an early flight and the fog is so thick you could cut it with a knife. They are all seated together in the same row on the plane and Sara looks over to McNair and curiously says: "So Robert, where are we headed in Ireland?"

"I spoke to Professor McDowell and he says the appearance of the so-called chicken scratch as DI Smithe called it, is in fact an ancient dialect called Ogam."

Sara blurts out, "Yes, I have heard about that ancient writing but have never studied it!"

Overhearing the rhetoric, detective Smithe inquires, "Well, what does it tell us?"

Without hesitation, McNair declares, "It suggests that we start our search at Newgrange Ireland!"

Ecstatic, Sara utters, "So that is what my father was trying to tell us in his letter. That we can find the Ark somewhere in Newgrange, also known as the hill of Tara where Queen Teia, my great great grandmother once lived! I'm excited! I can hardly wait!"

"Tell me Doctor, how did McDowell determine the name Newgrange from that chicken scratch?" asks Smithe.

"I'm sure you have heard of the Rosetta Stone Detective?"

"Of course, it was used to decipher the Egyptian language wasn't it?"

"Precisely! The stone was discovered by Napoleon's army in 1799 and until that time we were unable to understand the Egyptian hieroglyphics. But when the stone contained the Greek language side by side of the bilingual Egyptian-Greek edict to celebrate the coronation of the Pharaoh Ptolemy V, we could understand it. It was the same way the name of Christ was put on the cross in Aramaic, Hebrew and Greek."

"I think I get it. Once you have a language you understand next to one you don't, you can interpret the one you didn't understand," Smithe replies.

"Precisely!"

Smithe, still curious asks, "I have another question. What was the Rosetta Stone for Ogam?"

"Good question Smithe! I can see why you are a good detective! Another way decipherers have interpreted different languages is from ancient coins struck with inscriptions in two languages, one of which is known. My search engine found Archeological surveys performed in Vermont and New Hampshire discovered hundreds of inscriptions of Ogam writing among the ruins."

Smithe is a bit baffled and continues his inquisition, "But that would mean that the Celts were in America long before Columbus!"

"Precisely!" says McNair as he once again entertains a new concept from the dubious Smithe.

"Well, how did they get there? They didn't have ships then did they?"

"Ever hear of the Ships of Tarshish Detective?"

Reluctantly, Smithe replies, "Can't say that I have! Open my eyes Doctor!"

"Tarshish was a city built by people in Spain and it is also referred to by that name in the Bible. From the Bible we learn that the ships of Tarshish were the largest seagoing vessels known to the Semitic world, and the name was eventually applied to any large ocean-going vessel.

"On the coasts of Palestine, where the ancient psalmist King David of Israel could watch the vessels of their Phoenician cousins plying their trade with Lebanon and Egypt, the ships of Tarshish became proverbial as an expression of sea power. That's also where the apostle Paul was from and the Bible informs us of his travels on ship. Ironically, the Templars were also known for their ship building and had a fleet that journeyed to the holy land via the Mediterranean."

Sara chimes into the conversation, "I'm familiar with that story as well Robert. My father told me there is documentation that the last time anyone saw the Templars before the majority of them disappeared, they were in 13 ships off the coast of Scotland."

Dumbfounded, Smithe inquires, "Is that true Doctor, where did these Templars go before they wound up in Scotland?"

"Well, no one knows for sure, but it is thought that they may have gone to Switzerland first."

"Why Switzerland? I thought Sara said they went to Scotland as a safe haven under Robert the Bruce?"

"Yes, eventually they could have migrated there. Remember, I said they started one of the first banking systems to hide their wealth. Well, ironically Switzerland started their banking system about the same time the Templars disappeared!"

Astonished, Smithe remarks, "Wow! This gets better all the time. But how do we know that these ships were capable of crossing the Atlantic?"

"Good question Smithe. Most people aren't aware of this, but Julius Caesar wrote a book entitled, *De bello Gallico* in which he described a great battle the Romans had with the Celts. He stated that the Celts had not less than 250 ships and they were so well constructed that they could outride turbulent winds upon the very oceans itself without sustaining injury."

Simultaneously, Sara looks out of the window of the plane and exclaims with excitement, "I think I see it, Oh, what a beautiful site! Truly I think this is God's country! Just think, we are seeing the same beautiful views that the eyes of my great Grandmother Teia observed! Where do we start looking for the Ark Robert?"

The Cliffs of Moher, 10/1/2010, Ronald R. Wlodyga

Doctor McNair replies, "My guess based upon the first two scriptures, **Seek and ye shall find, and stand on the top of the hill,** we should start looking at the top of a hill in Tara!"

***

The next day, before the sun even rises, the trio drive a rented car through the beautiful countryside of Ireland on their way to Teia's Castle in Newgrange. They all hike up to the top of the hill of Tara and Smithe says out of breath, "Wow! I'm pooped! This is a big sucker! Ok, now what Doctor?"

A Hill in Ireland, 10/1/2010, Ronald R. Wlodyga

Once again McNair recalls, "Our next clue, was the scripture that said, **'the tree in the middle of the garden.'** So, we must look for a tree or trees that look like the garden of Eden scene."

The trio continues to look around and suddenly Sara declares, "Look over there, two very beautiful Hawthorn trees! Could that be the trees my father was trying to indicate? I have a feeling!"

The trio walk over to the two beautiful Hawthorn trees standing approximately 10 feet apart and Smithe inquires, "What do we do now? What's our next clue Doctor?"

"Well, the next scripture reference indicated we are to look for a large stone by an Oak near the sanctuary."

Observant, DI Smithe interjects, "Well, I don't see any Oak trees here or a sanctuary! Do you Doctor?"

"No, there are no Oak trees here Detective, but I do see a sanctuary!"

Having a keen eye for clues, Smithe is completely confused and remarks, "Maybe you have Superman eyes McNair, because frankly I don't see anything accept those two trees!"

Hawthorn tree on the hill
cc-by-sa/2.0 - © Nigel Brown - geograph.org.uk/p/1615852

"Precisely Detective! But I think Sara's father has given us enough clues to figure it out! Not one person in a million would be able to understand that what we are now standing on is in fact representative of the sanctuary of God! Dr. Flanders and I took a religious seminar once that described the Garden of Eden scene as the same layout as the Temple, so I think I know what Sara's father was trying to tell us!"

Astonished, Sara replies, "I'm with Smithe on this one Robert. I guess I'm not the one in a million, because I don't get it. Please explain yourself!"

"Yea, I guess I'm not either!" Remarks Smithe.

"Ok, let me show you on paper." McNair gets out a pad and pencil and starts to draw a diagram,

"You see these two Hawthorn trees, they represent the two trees in the garden of Eden where God walked and spoke to Adam and Eve. In a sense, it was a sanctuary because it was where God dwelt! All of the other sanctuaries such as the Tabernacle and the Temple described in the Bible were patterned after it, for that is where God dwelt afterward. In other words, God's sanctuary was wherever He dwelt!"

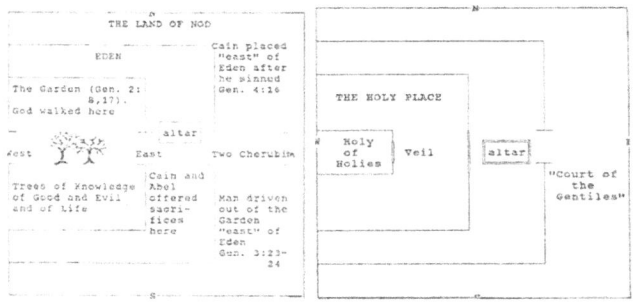

Sara asserts, "I'm beginning to get the picture!"

Smithe is still stymied and replies, "I'm glad you do Sara because you just lost me, Doctor!"

"Ok, let me show you the layout of the tabernacle and later the Temple's floor plan," says McNair as he points to each drawing. "See how similar the layout of the Temple was to the Garden of Eden. The holy place in the Tabernacle and later the Temple was where God dwelt and only the high priest of Israel could enter. Notice how similar the plan is to the garden of Eden and why this is what Sara's father was trying to tell us."

"I think I'm beginning to understand Robert," says Sara.

Smithe mumbles under his breath, "Quite frankly, I'm still lost. I wish I didn't skip so many of those catechism classes when I was going to school."

McNair comforts Smithe as he points to the trees in the drawing, "I don't think you would have learned this in Catechism Detective, but let me continue with my theory. The Garden of Eden was a sanctuary in itself because that is where God walked and therefore it became a holy place. The trees were located similarly to the holy place in the tabernacle and later the Temple where God resided and only the High Priest of Israel could enter once a year on the Day of Atonement. This ceremony is described in Leviticus 16 in the Bible. If I'm right, then the entrance should be on the opposite side."

Sara is now pointing to the drawing and says, "I think I'm getting it! So if this area represents the tabernacle of God, and the Ark was only on the one side, shouldn't it be below the ground right about here!"

"Precisely Sara! It's very possible the Ark is right underneath us, but we don't know how far down to dig!"

"Well, what are we supposed to do now? What's the next clue Doctor?" Smithe inquires.

"Well, our next clue, if I am correct, should be a huge stone under this tree by the sanctuary. Let's start digging over here."

All three start digging until Smithe hits something very hard near the tree and says, "I think I hit something!" He starts to clean off a large stone only to find some very strange circular markings on it and echoes, "What in the world! Professor look at this! It looks like aliens were here!"

McNair and Sara scurry over to see what Smithe has discovered! They are both amazed and Sara remarks,

"Wow! What a weird looking rock! It looks like something from outer space! What do all of those scrolls mean Robert?"

"I'm not sure but I'm going to take a photo of it and send it to my colleague Professor McDowell."

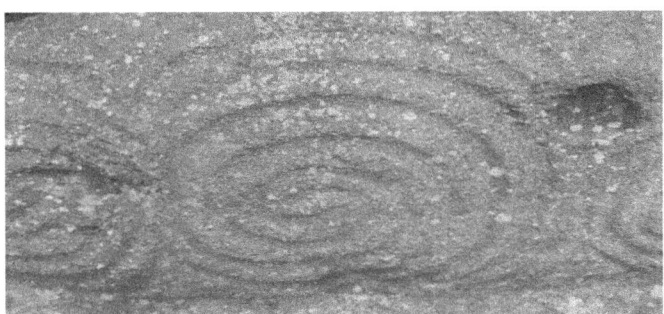

Celtic Stone carving, Free Public Domain Photo, Free Stock
Stone carving at Newgrange in Meath

The next morning Doctor McNair looks at his email message from Professor McDowell of the linguistics department and informs Sara and Smithe, "I just received the answer to my question from Professor McDowell regarding the strange markings on the stone. He said it is old Irish Olgam, the same writing that Sara's father used in his letter."

Inquisitive Smithe asks, "Well, what did McDowell say it meant?"

"He said the scrolls represent many grave chambers underneath us as we are on top of a gravesite. It is very possible that below us is a graveyard where very probably Teia, Heremon and Jeremiah the Prophet were buried and all of their descendants over the years!"

Being a good Catholic, Smithe makes the sign of the cross and inquires, "How then are we supposed to find the chamber in which the Ark is located?"

"We must find the entrance first and then follow the maze around until we come to what appears to be where someone of royalty would be buried! More than likely it will be the one in the middle. Look here!" as he points to a diagram he has drawn of the rock mass.

They all look at the diagram McNair has made of the scrolls on the rock! Sara adds, "I think I can visualize it, but where do we enter the chamber entrance Robert?"

"I believe the answer is found in the next scripture. He takes out his pocket Bible and reads John 19:34, *'But one of the soldiers with a spear pierced his side, and forthwith came there out blood and water.'*

"That's it! That's the clue! The entrance to the tunnel we are looking for is in the side of the hill." Pointing he says, "See those obelisks over there in the side of the hill? That is where an ancient Druid Temple used to be. That's where we will find our answer! You see the Celtic temples were bound to relate to the annual solar cycle whose astronomical axes determine the orientation of the temples and the dates of the year when any given temple celebrates its own special festival. The ancient Druids engaged in these astronomical observations of sun worship."

Left Photo: Hill of Tara, The Holy Well at the Hill of Tara. The Hill of Tara was the ancient capital of Ireland, where the High Kings were crowned and probably the most sacred spot to Irish pagans before the arrival of Christianity, Ireland. Right Photo: The sun entering the passageway Winter Solstice. There is no agreement about what the site was used for, but it has been speculated that it had religious significance – it is aligned with the rising sun and its light floods the chamber on the Winter Solstice. *My Guide to Newgrange Ireland*

Smithe is out of his comfort zone and acquiesces, "I'll take your word for it Doctor!"

McNair has a theory and invites the trio to follow him as he states,

"Come with me. That means that on the three or four days of the winter season when the sun reaches its southernmost limit, a person standing at the altar and looking through the entrance opening will see the sunrise. On all other days of the year the sunrise will not be visible to him. Evidently, the orientation of the temple must be to provide a dramatic event on a selected day of the year appropriate for the temple, in this case the four days of the midwinter festival. If I'm right we should see the light somewhere over here as he points. Yes, there it is! Look over there with your own eyes. Here is the passageway!"

Sara is now very curious as to McNair's theory and asks, "Robert, how did you know we would pick the four possible days out of the year of the winter solstice to be here?"

Smiling facetiously, McNair contributes, "Just lucky I guess! Let's head on in!"

The trio begin their journey into the maze of tunnels. McNair is holding a lantern to see better as it is very dark underground. As they begin their journey after finding the entrance, Sara inquires, "Which way do we go now?"

"Look here!" Doctor McNair replies as He shows them a picture of the rock outside that he took with his cell phone. "See this maze on the entrance rock. My guess is that the King's tomb is located in the center of the maze. That means we must take this tunnel and follow it around."

The pack head further into the tunnel. There are bats flying all over with skulls of deceased bodies everywhere. They walk endlessly until they see a chamber that is fit for a King! There is a huge wooden box there with gold plate on the top that looks like it could be the Ark. There are several smaller boxes around it. McNair opens the box and Sara's eyes dilate as she is aghast! "This place is eerie! Wow, this is incredible. Look at all the gold in this box!"

Smithe is also startled and repeats, "I've never seen anything like it! This is the mother load! There must be billions here! Look at all these diamonds and jewels! This must be King Solomon's gold!"

Chapter Seventeen

As Sara and Smithe are overwhelmed by this incredible discovery of both loot and artefact, McNair is pointing a gun at them and Smithe says as he is both perplexed and in dismay,

"What the heck are you doing McNair?"

Sara echoes, "What's going on Robert?"

"You wouldn't understand, never mind, just stand over there! You to Sara. I'm sorry to have to do this to you Sara but your father gave me strict instructions!"

As McNair puts handcuffs on Smithe, Sara inquires, "My father! What does he have to do with this?"

"Your father was grandmaster of our order!"

"Your order! What order are you talking about?"

"You know all of those meetings your father attended? Well, he was the grandmaster of an order to, to...well I said enough, and I don't think you would understand?"

Smithe chimes in, "So, you and the Curator were partners in crime?"

"Crime Smithe is your job? If you call trying to save the world a crime, then we are guilty! I prefer to call ourselves visionaries! Most people have no idea what is going on in this world, and if it were not for people like us, the world would be run by lunatic despots."

Smithe tries to appease McNair by asking, "So you think what you are doing is not ludicrous?"

McNair ignores Smithe's question and makes a phone call to McDowel and informs him, "I have it! What should I do now?" After hearing McDowel's response, McNair says, "Ok, I'll wait for them!" McNair then says, "good-bye."

Sara asks McNair curiously, "Tell me Robert, did you know all along where the Ark was hidden?" "No, your father was very cautious and didn't reveal that to anyone accept you. That's why we were waiting for the right moment to find out further instructions!"

"Well, I'm grateful for my father's trust. What else can you tell me about this order that you both belonged?"

"Sara, do you respect the sanctity of human life?"

"Yes, I believe in the sacredness of life, but I believe everyone has the right to choose! Why?"

McNair continues his agenda of morality, "Sara, do you believe in the sanctity of marriage?"

"Absolutely! Again, I ask you why are you asking me these moral questions?"

"Do you believe in the Lord Jesus Christ and that He alone is the Savior of the World?"

"Again, I say absolutely, but why are you asking?"

"I believe in those things as well," Says DI Smithe as he chimes into the conversation, "But what does all of this have to do with your order?"

"Being a detective Smithe, do you think that terrorism is getting out of control?"

"Well yea I see it every day on my job!".

"Do you know that in some countries, Christians are being persecuted for singing songs about Jesus in church, and you can be thrown in prison or lose your life if the authorities know you are a Christian?"

"I heard of some of these atrocities, but I thought they were only rumors," says Smithe.

McNair continues to open Smithe's mind as he asks, "Do you want to be ruled someday by some Islamic radical madman that would through gays off of rooftops, or some Jewish Pharisaical Rabbi or some Christian impostor called the Antichrist?"

"Heck no! I believe in democracy, and even though I don't agree with certain lifestyles, I think everyone is entitled to their own opinions. Why are you asking me all of these questions on virtue?"

"Well Sara and DI Smithe, these were the beliefs of Dr. Flanders as well as mine and our organization. As you know, there are many secret societies who are determined to grasp the throne of King David, who are all sincere in their beliefs as we are in ours—but I think they are sincerely wrong! We are in fact in a new crusade!

"A crusade for the sanity of the human race! This is a battle for truth over the forces of deception and evil! Many of these radicals have been influenced by the forces of darkness and many of them would kill in the name of the god they worship. We can't allow that to happen. Your father understood this and that the only way to stop them was to get to these sacred artifacts before them."

Smithe observes, "That's why everyone wants these artifacts and the stone!"

"Yes, because these precious artifacts signify power and credibility! The masses of people will follow whoever has them in their possession, because they are believed to be sacred!"

Smithe adds, "And kill others in the name of their god for them as well!"

"Precisely! And as I have told you before, there are many societies looking for these very artifacts so they can take over the world and run it their way!"

"Isn't that what you propose to do?" asks Smithe.

"Precisely, but I think we are right in the way we would allow freedom without the harsh and extreme laws that most governments are allowing evil and immoral people to control the masses! Would you want to live in a society ruled by a Hitler or madmen that won't allow you religious freedom and would shoot you on the spot if you don't worship god their way?"

"You mean like the religious extremists?" replies Smithe.

"Precisely! You can be killed in some countries under the 'blasphemy law' for preaching Christianity!"

Sara interjects, "I know and that is terrible!"

"Yes Sara, and under the Sharia law, which is an interpretation of what Muhammad preached, a woman can be stoned or hanged for committing adultery. Radical Clerics have gotten this interpretation from the Old Testament, but have not understood the New Testament words of the Prophet and Savior Jesus!"

Sara opinionates, and says, "I know Robert, and although I don't believe in adultery, I wouldn't want a government to kill me for it or make it a crime if I didn't wear a veil over my face."

DI Smithe puts in his two cents, "Yea, even though I am against crime, I wouldn't want to live under a government that would cut off your hand if you nicked something? But I do agree that there is too much sympathy for the criminals these days, and the innocent are being taken advantage of and something has to be done about it!"

McNair pontificates to Sara and Smithe and says, "That's why these extremists want to control the world! It's true that our order wants to control the world as well, but not out of a radical rule but out of kindness, fairness and love!"

"I agree with most of what you said Robert," Sara says as she is beginning to see McNair's viewpoint.

McNair continues his questioning, as he thinks in his mind how he can make a deal with the two potential converts and says, "You both believe in Christian values do you not?"

"Surely!" Says Smithe and Sara as they respond in unison. McNair justifies his organizations views and says, "Well then, you must see how our society has drifted from traditional Judeo, Christian values to a so-called new age philosophy."

"I have heard that term used before. Tell me Doctor, what exactly is the new age movement all about?" Smithe inquires.

"The new Age movement includes elements of older spiritual and religious traditions from both East and West, many of which have been combined with ideas of modern science, particularly psychology and ecology."

"Well, what's so bad about that? Shouldn't we all be concerned about saving our planet?"

"I agree, but these New Age ideas draw inspiration from all the world's major religions with influences from Spiritualism, Occultism and Neo-Paganism. Some of these beliefs are taken from mystical traditions of the world's religions and their practices and beliefs may be characterized as a form of alternative spirituality. Surely you can see why these religions are not and will not lead people to salvation in Jesus Christ as Christians believe." Says McNair as he gives a rebuttal.

Sara concurs as she says, "You are right about that Robert, I have a lot of friends who are into everything from yoga and vegetarianism, to rocks and crystals who believe these things can bring them to higher spiritual consciousness. It seems like our traditional Christian values are being challenged all of the time."

"But I know a lot of good people in some of the religions you mentioned and I would trust them more than many of the so-called Christians I know!" Smithe says as he gives his skeptical opinion.

"Be that as it may, there are a lot of radical groups who want to take over the world and so you both must understand why we need to stop them before the entire world is ruled by the extremist element!"

"Precisely!" Says Smithe as he agrees with McNair and uses one of his cliché expressions.

"Now I will tell you about another element that your father and I feared the most and have been keeping an eye on for many years. Have you ever heard of the term Tzadik?"

"Yes, my father explained to me that they are a mystical Jewish element that believes they have achieved a holiness or piety that very few in this life have attained and are very pleasing to God."

"Your father has taught you well Sara. According to the Jewish Talmud there are 36 of them living among us, but no one knows who they are—and if it were not for their holiness, according to their belief, the world would be annihilated. Some people even believe these pious Tzadik's can perform miracles."

"Robert, you said you and my father feared this group the most. But why?"

"Because we feel these extremists believe that God has placed them on the earth for the express purpose of bringing the world closer to God through their teachings. They are like the ancient pious Pharisees that Jesus continually encountered, and in fact put our Savior to death through their false claims of their council of elders called the Sanhedrin. Their desire is to reinstitute the Torah law on the entire world!"

Smithe interjects, "I have heard of that term before. What exactly is the Sanhedrin?"

"The Sanhedrin is a body of religious leaders in Israel, kind of like the Congress in the U.S. composed of both House of representatives and Senators, always fighting against each other."

Smithe understands and remarks facetiously, "Now I see the parallel except that Congress isn't a religious body in more ways than one!"

"Precisely! Our organization believes the so-called Antichrist will be of Jewish ancestry and be one of the Tzadik's that will come from the newly formed Sanhedrin and deceive the entire world into believing he is actually the Messiah as foretold by the prophecies.

"They will usher him into the Temple as their long-awaited King over Israel and worship him. Because this form of Jewish mysticism is a form of Kabbalah that began during the twelfth century in Europe, we believe they are a part of some of the more extreme secret societies that we have studied. In fact, some of them actually believe that every generation has had a person with the potential to be the long-awaited Jewish Messiah."

"Using his detective instincts, Smithe asks a pertinent question, "Why does your organization believe this Antichrist will be of Jewish descent?"

"Because there are prophecies in the Bible that indicate this! In fact, we think he will most likely come from the tribe of Dan."

"My father told me about this coming Antichrist who will make the whole world worship him and his number is 666 or something. He thought this False Prophet would be a heretical Pope like the one who caused the inquisition or killed the Templars!"

"Yes, that is what a lot of people believed including the Reformers. That is what your father and I believed as well until we changed our minds after further evidence."

"What evidence? Anyway, I'm glad it won't be a Catholic!" says Smithe as he inquires of their substantiation.

"Well, perhaps you will remember some of this from my lectures on church history. Most of the Reformers thought the Catholic church was formed by the Roman Emperor Constantine in 325 A.D. who built the Vatican—but was mostly a pagan and supposedly became a Christian on his death-bed. During his lifetime he supposedly had a vision of a Cross and thought it was a sign from God to conquer in His name.

"He favored Christians in Rome and supported their right for Sunday worship. There were major differences in religious worship by the churches formed by the apostle John in the East. In fact, East and West had many disagreements over issues like Passover being substituted for Easter, etc. Pagan customs and philosophies began coming into the early church."

Curious, Smithe adds, "I always wondered what the heck Easter eggs and bunnies had to do with our Lord's crucifixion. I remember that history in one of your lectures. It sounds like the Machiavelli pattern for success by killing and torturing anyone who disagreed with you."

"Well, look up Quartodeciman sometime in the encyclopedia if you want to know that answer. Emperor Constantine became the Babylonian Pontifex Maximus of the Roman Order. It was both church and state! Remember, Constantine was a pagan sun-worshipper believing as did his forefathers in the secret mysteries of Nimrod and Semiramis. This is how we believe the Papacy brought paganism into the church. In essence, Constantine wanted to enforce certain laws on society that he believed were honoring God."

Smithe inquires further, "You mentioned Easter. I was wondering where that name came from anyway?"

"You're not going to like this Smithe! It came from the old pagan worship of Semiramis or as the Babylonians called her Ishtar."

"Now I remember some of the ancient history you taught me. Let me get this history straight. Not long after Noah's flood, the ancient Babylonian kingdom under Nimrod began these so called "mysteries" as you call them of hidden knowledge similar to what is the Cabbala today."

McNair is impressed by his student's memory, but then again he is a detective, and says, "By golly you've got it Smithe! You have been listening indeed!"

"But how did the Church get hoodwinked into believing they were worshipping the true God, and how did these Tzadik get deceived?"

"All good questions Smithe. When the Jews were taken captive into Babylon after the destruction of the Temple and the killing of their last king Zedekiah, they had to worship King Nebuchadnezzar. Recall how Daniel and a few of his friends refused to worship him and were put into the Lion's den and the fiery furnace?"

"I do recall that biblical story in Sunday school and how they were miraculously saved by God!"

"Well, as you recall most of the captive Jews bowed down to the King and eventually became sun-worshipping idolaters just like the Babylonians. This is where Kabbala developed as well as the Babylonian Talmud. Now realize one thing.

"The Babylonian Talmud is not the same thing as the traditional Talmud of the Jews. This is a perverted version inspired by the fallen Lucifer! However, even that version denies Jesus as Savior. That's why our organization believes all of those obedient to the final Tzadik will be deceived. He will be extremely charismatic and will be learned in the dark sorceries of the Babylonian Mystical Talmud. He will have the power of his father Satan to perform fake miracles to deceive the people because he will be possessed by the devil."

"That's really scary!" Sara exclaims as she becomes nearly hysterical.

"Yea, I'm getting goose bumps myself exclaims Smithe! How could the rest of the Jewish people accept this? Aren't they aware of this coming deception?"

"Actually, there are many Bible prophecies that indicate that the Messiah is to return to Jerusalem and save His people the Jews. That's why the early Jews crucified Christ because they wanted a Messiah that would deliver them from the Romans and restore again their kingdom. But when Christ didn't do it at that time, they thought he was a false Messiah and wanted Him killed." Says McNair as he gives his opinion as to why it is important to know this ancient history.

"Robert, you mentioned that my father eventually changed his mind about who would be the Antichrist. That he would be a Jew coming from the tribe of Dan instead of a famous religious figure like the Pope as so many believe. What changed his mind?"

"Well Sara, after studying the scriptures and history more diligently, your father and I came to this conclusion based upon new evidence."

"What new evidence changed your mind?"

"One day your father was reading the Jewish Encyclopedia and discovered what the respected early church father Irenaeus who lived during the first century had to say regarding the Antichrist. He was a disciple of Polycarp, who was a disciple of the apostle John, the last apostle to die. The early church including the apostle Paul believed the end of the age was near and so they were watching world events very closely. It was Irenaeus' opinion that the Antichrist would come from the tribe of Dan because of its evil doing and certain scriptural references."

"I am quite familiar with the Bible, and I know my father believed the Antichrist would come from the tribe of Dan, because of the Riddle of Samson, but he never explained it to me.

"It's true your father believed part of the mystery is shrouded in the mysterious riddle that Samson gave the Philistines. Do you recall us discussing the relevance of that biblical story previously?"

DI Smithe interjects, "Are you referring to the guy that got his hair cut off by this slag Delilah?"

"One and the same! The story is found in Judges 14. Recall, Samson was a Nazarite of the tribe of Dan who judged Israel during the period of Philistine domination. One day at the feast celebrating his marriage to a Philistine woman, Samson proposed a riddle to the Philistines.

"On the seventh day of the feast, Samson's cunning bride, influenced by the Philistine elite, extracted the interpretation of the riddle and related its meaning to her people. The carcass of a young lion which Samson had killed with his bare hands had attracted a swarm of bees which produced honey therein. Samson paid the wager by slaying thirty Philistines, after which his wife was taken from him. Angered by their treachery, Samson avenged himself by slaughtering many more Philistines and eventually the Philistine lords."

"I recall our conversations in the past regarding Samson, but I still don't see how it relates to the Antichrist being of the tribe of Dan," says Sara.

"Remember, Samson was from the tribe of Dan and your father believed that Samson was representative of a prophecy that God was trying to tell us would happen in the end time. Samson's riddle may be a prophecy that the descendants of the tribe of Dan will one day try to destroy the tribe of Judah in jealous revenge for God's judgment on their idolatry,"

"Yes, he told me that Robert, but what did he think the carcass of the young lion depicted in the riddle?"

"Your father believed as I do that the carcass of the young lion represented Judaism and the tribe of Dan typified by the bees represented the end-time golden age of the Antichrist. Furthermore, your father came to this conclusion after studying the genealogies of the families of the secret societies who plan to rule the world from their future throne at Jerusalem. There is indication that some of them descended from the tribe of Dan.

"That's why your father studied the tribe of Dan and had all of those bloodline charts in his office. Your father being the Bible scholar that he was believed the love story between Judge Samson and the insidious Delilah was God's way of describing what will happen to the church and Satan's counterfeit system during the end time."

Sara is becoming very interested in what her father believed and says, "I'm listening!"

"As you will recollect, Samson's miraculous strength was proportional to his lengthy uncut hair which your father believed symbolized the Holy Spirit. After being betrayed by Delilah, Samson's source of power was revealed to the Philistines, who took him captive, after which his hair was shorn and his eyes were poked out, much like Judah's last King Zedekiah! Samson cried out to God for vengeance upon these wicked Philistines who had taken away his eyesight."

"But didn't Samson's hair grow back eventually?"

"That's right! Samson's hair eventually grew back, and one day a 'lad' led the spiritually restored Samson between two supporting pillars of the pagan temple Dagon where he brought the entire temple down with him! Your father believed that this was God's way of explaining what was going to happen to the many people in the last days before Jesus returns to restore the Kingdom of God. He believed many people would go through a refining process to reawaken their conscience out of spiritual slumber and blindness through what is called the Great Tribulation."

"My father told me that this would be a terrible time and that there would be none like it! But aren't Christians supposed to be raptured off the earth during this time?"

"There is indication that Irenaeus may have believed that, but your father didn't buy into that theory and neither did the early church fathers. Instead he believed many saints will cry out to God like Samson to take vengeance upon their wicked Philistine oppressors of the 'Beast' power!

"Many will be martyred at this time, only to be delivered by our Savior just as the 'lad' helped Samson. Essentially, the kingdom of the 'powers of darkness' will come crashing down like a house of cards and the prince of the powers of evil will be smitten like the idol of Dagon!"

"Forgive my ignorance McNair," Says Smithe, "But I still don't understand how all of this confusion got stated anyway. I mean how did this paganism and mysteries of Nimrod and Semiramis and Kabballa get into the Jewish community when God spoke directly to them and performed all of those miracles. Why didn't they remain faithful?"

"You indeed have on your thinking cap once again! As you stated, the Israelites became unfaithful to God when they were in captivity. The worship of the goddess Ashtoreth as the Hebrews called her, and Ishtar by the Assyrians was extremely strong in the known world.

"But during the days of King Solomon, the nation of Israel began to go astray and follow the customs of the heathen nations around them. Semiramis became the

Goddess of Fertility and Reproduction. She was worshipped in the royal household of Solomon and was part of temple worship during the time of Jezebel, who was spitefully critical of her by the Levite prophets of the Bible. She was denounced as the Mother Goddess and all kinds of terrible practices were attributed to her."

"Wasn't Solomon the one who had all of those wives?" says Smithe sarcastically as he gives his recollection of King Solomon.

"That's correct! He had 300 wives!"

"Unbelievable! I can barely take care of one let alone a 300!" Smithe replies with humorous amazement.

Because of his criminal background, Smithe is still curious and inquires of McNair, "Tell me more about this Babylonian Kabbalah that is supposed to deceive the world."

"The Kabbalah has been traced to the ancient mysteries of Babylon and Egypt and never originated with the Hebrew nation under God. Instead, these Jews got their ideas from the Babylonians and the Egyptians when in their captivity.

"Kabbalah is one of the most grossly misunderstood parts of Judaism. It was legend that God taught the Kabbalah to some angels, who in turn after the Fall, taught it to Adam. Originally, based upon tradition, it was to help humanity return to God. It then supposedly passed to Noah, to Abraham and Moses. It is believed by the adherents of this belief, the oral tradition ended and the knowledge was written down."

"My father told me that extreme Kaballah was tied to black magic and very dangerous!"

"Some of my Jewish friends have described extreme Kabbalah as 'the dark side of Judaism,' describing it as evil or black magic. There are certainly many traditional Jewish stories that involve the use of hidden knowledge to affect the world in ways that could be described as magic. The Talmud and other sources credit supernatural activities to many great rabbis. In fact, the Bible does as well."

"I do recall the account of a sorcerer named Simon Magus in the Bible, who bewitched the people," says Sara.

"Yes, that's in Acts 8 and that is a perfect example of what we believe is a forerunner of what the Antichrist will do as he will have supernatural powers. Justin Martyr, considered a Saint in most Christian churches, wrote that he had formed a formidable following in the days of Claudius Caesar because of his magical powers, and was honored as a god with a statue being erected to him on the Tiber, between the two bridges, bearing the inscription, 'holy god Simon.' We believe he had demonic influence," says McNair.

"Father Benedetti warned me about such possibilities," says Smithe.

Sara is once again dismayed and remarks, "This all seems so eerie and probably why my father didn't explain all this to me! That sounds like something the devil would do to imitate God!"

"I agree, but it's important to note that all of these magical effects were achieved through supernatural power, generally by calling upon the name of God. Those practicing this kind of Kabballah, believe these practices are no more 'evil' than the miracles of the prophets, or the miracles that Christians ascribe to Jesus," says McNair.

"What did my father think these people will do in the future, Robert?"

"Your father believed that someday an individual whose bloodline is from one of these old families practicing mysticism—will rise to power just like Simon Magus and implement the Noahide Laws!"

"You mentioned these Noahide Laws before says Smithe. I checked it out and didn't the U.S. Congress sign a bill under President Bush to impose them on the people of the United States?"

"Precisely, but it must be understood that we are not dealing with the Noah of the Bible when the religion of Judaism refers to 'Noahide law.' There is even a debate among Jewish scholars as to the interpretation of 'The

Noahide law' as binding upon non-Jews," says McNair as he explains the difference between these laws.

Smithe doesn't completely understand the Talmud and asks, "The Talmud, isn't that the Jewish version of the scriptures?"

"Actually, it is a record of rabbinic oral discussions of Jewish law, ethics and history. The Talmud also states the penalties for disobedience, but some radicals who interpret the Noahide laws believe that violation of any one of the seven laws are subject to capital punishment."

Smithe is now getting the picture and exclaims, "Bloody hell, that sounds a lot like some of these radical Middle Eastern beliefs who want to enforce their laws on everyone!"

"Our organization believes the Antichrist will claim to be the Jewish Messiah for whom the Jews have been waiting since Abraham. He will have to fulfill all the Old Testament prophecies concerning the appearance of Messiah if he has any hope of deceiving Orthodox Jews.

"The main point to be grasped is that this false messiah will most likely be an orthodox Jew. He will probably be living according to the ancient Judaic Law and the Talmud, but have his own spin regarding idol worship. Smithe, you asked about some of the Noahide laws. Basically, they are the 10 commandments with oral interpretation."

"Bloody hell, in other words, if one or two people step forward to accuse someone of violating any one of these seven laws, that testimony alone would be enough to kill the accused."

"You've got it!" says McNair.

The detective in Smithe foresees the real problem, and says, "And a person could be put to death for the flimsy accusation of being cruel to animals based on the lying testimony of one person!"

"Precisely! And notice, there is no assumption of innocence until proven guilty, nor of the prosecution having to prove their case. No, on the accusation of one person, the accused may be legally put to death. Recall the Pharisees also succeeded in killing Jesus Christ on the basis that He blasphemed God, which is Noahide Law number 2. Remember Jesus' prediction to His followers in Matthew 10:24-25, that the disciples of the Master will be treated in just the same way as the Master has been treated."

Smithe is startled and states, "Unbelievable! As bad as our system is, I think I'll take it over this tyrannical system!"

Sara is flabbergasted and comments, "O my Lor... O, guess I can't say that anymore, O my my, this is really frightening!"

McNair is in agreement and responds to Sara's concerns, "Yes, this is frightening stuff, and that is why our organization has been so adamant about exposing these secret societies of today which are powering the drive into the New World Order. Without realizing it, they are playing into the hands of this mystic Jewish group, which has its active roots in the ancient Kabbal, a group which is a soul-mate to today's secret societies."

"I wonder if the Devil is setting the stage where Christians could be legally charged with violation of Noahide Law Number 2, of blaspheming God? They may think our belief that Jesus is God in the flesh, as well as the Father is God and The Holy Spirit is God is three Gods and a violation?" Says Sara.

"Maybe, and they probably will think the punishment of decapitation is a much more humane way to die than crucifixion, but I wouldn't want either one!" Says Smithe.

Sara concurs and says, "Me neither!"

Smithe is still playing detective and inquires of McNair, "Hold on now McNair, I want to see if I understand this end-time scenario correctly and how it ties into the death of Dr. Flanders. I heard that there are two individuals described in this end-time plot to take over the world. The Antichrist and the false Prophet. Am I correct in that assumption?"

"Precisely, and I can see the detective instinct in you to find out more about them!"

"Heck yea! Give me some more clues!"

"The Antichrist and the False Prophet are the two super world rulers described in the biblical end time, and are Satan's counterfeit two witnesses. Satan will be using these two counterfeits to bring forth his counterfeit kingdom, while God will be using His Two Witnesses to bring forth His Kingdom.

"Because of their delusion, many people the world over will believe these counterfeits are the 'good guys' and that the true servants of God are the 'bad guys.' Just exactly opposite of the truth naturally. It will be a similar experience as to what happened in Egypt when Moses and his brother Aaron were God's two witnesses and the Pharaoh had his two fake witnesses Jannes and Jambres duplicating miracles!"

"I know what you're talking about because I saw the 10 Commandment movie where Charlton Heston played Moses!" says Smithe as he recalls the biblical account.

"Tell me more about these two charlatans that will deceive the world Robert, because I certainly don't want to be deceived!" says Sara as she is very inquisitive.

"We are told in the book of Revelation these two individuals will be possessed by demons and will perform sorceries. Their false system, using a metaphor, is called Babylon!"

Smithe is flippant and exclaims, "You're not going to tell me that you believe in ghosts, now are you?"

"No Smithe, I believe in something more sinister and more powerful than ghosts! The Bible calls them demons or fallen angels!"

"I read a little in the book of Revelation, but had to stop because it was filled with so much gruesome stuff and symbolism, I couldn't understand it. What is Babylon all about?" asks Sara.

Seeing the two are very interested to know more, McNair continues with his biblical knowledge, "The book of Revelation describes Babylon as something that is the epitome of sin and compares it to a harlot full of lust. This lust is compared to material abundance and goods, earthly treasure.

"She has gained the whole world, but has lost her soul! She is rich and luxurious, and all the merchandisers of the world are dependent upon her. In other words, she looks beautiful on the outside, but on the inside, she is full of corruption." Revelation 17-18.

"Sounds a little like someone in Hollywood!" says DI Smithe as he gives his uncanny observation.

"Remember this is not a person but the Bible is using physical metaphors to describe a spiritual condition. She is made up of peoples and tongues, gathered out from all the nations of the world. She sits gloriously in her pride, thinking she is so great and powerful, that she is safe, and will see no sorrow.

"By her looks, her sorceries, and her wealth, she has deceived all the nations into lusting after her, and becoming like her. Through her wealth and economic control, she rules over all the kings of the earth. She will force the entire world to receive the 'Mark of the Beast' through a buying and selling system."

"That sounds like the U.S.A.!" says DI Smithe.

"That's true! So how do we know?"

"Our organization believes whoever this world leader will be, he will be a Jewish leader familiar with the customs and traditions of the Jews in order to go into a rebuilt Temple and declare himself as God as the prophecies suggest! Certainly, no orthodox Jew would accept him otherwise! No Orthodox Jew would accept a gentile to be their leader!"

"I see why my father no longer believed he will be a radical Pope as most of the Reformers thought!"

"That's correct Sara! Most of us thought that would be the end-time scenario after reading books like Alexander Hislop's *Two Babylons*, portraying the Catholic Church as the so-called whore or false church of Revelation 17.

"But upon further investigation, we found this book to be fallacious and we changed our mind and realized that the pattern that the Catholic Church's clergy and structure was not after the paganism and mysteries of Nimrod and Semiramis, but after the Israelite system of High Priest that God ordained! The Catholic church certainly fit the mold during the Middle Ages and that's why all the Reformers believed this scenario."

"Wew! I'm glad to hear that the Catholics won't be involved!" says Smithe as he is relieved.

"Well, there still might be some concern that the Catholic Church will be used by this radical Kabbala, and in fact may be what the Bible calls the 'Image of the Beast' if they have copied their ecclesiastical and political structure. We will just have to watch future events! But we must realize also that things will be different during the end-time. The Bible informs us that demons or spirit beings with supernatural powers will be inhabiting the bodies of these two individuals!"

Once again, Sara is startled and says, "That sounds really frightening!"

In a surprise and unexpected move, McNair concurs Sara's feelings and then provides a solution to their dilemma, "I'll tell you what I'm going to do. In the morning, McDowell is sending several men to take these artifacts to a safe place and then I will let you go free. If you would like to know more about our organization, I'll be glad to answer any of your questions or concerns and we can discuss it in an intelligent fashion."

Smithe gives his Ok, and says, "That sounds fair enough!"

Sara is also in agreement but then inquires, "What is the name of your organization Robert?"

"We call ourselves the CCC, an acronym for Christian Crusaders for Christ."

Sara gasps, "My father requested me to donate his organs to that organization."

"That's quite right Sara, and we have his organs in our possession per his request."

"So, my father was instrumental in creating the CCC!"

"He was our apostle!"

"One more thing Robert. Did my father have anything to do with the Stone of Destiny being nicked?"

"Absolutely not! Your father believed it was genuine, and he was guarding it. He told me about the safety deposit box and that you were the only one who could access it."

Smithe looks at Sara for a moment and contemplates whether he should ask his next question in front of her. "What . . . about . . . Dr. Flanders's heart? The perpetrators are still not talking as to why they cut out his heart. Do you know why they did this?"

Sara flinches and turns away. The thought of what those monsters did to her father haunts her every night when she tries to go to sleep.

Robert sighs and shakes his head. "Dr. Flanders believed he had the spirit of Robert the Bruce, and it was well known from his lectures that he desired that his heart, like Robert the Bruce's heart, be returned to Jerusalem to rest with Jesus. I believe the thieves are descendants of some secret society who believe they are satisfying an ancient religious ritual that when a person of royal blood was killed, their powers would be transferred to them. Thank God they were apprehended before they got on that plane to Jerusalem. Now that they have been caught, our organization will carry out Dr. Flanders's wishes, as we have his heart that was embalmed in a metal casket."

"I think there is some validity to that as I did some research on Bruce's heart as it was buried in Melrose Abbey after it was found in an archaeological find in 1921 and dug up again in 1996."

"Very good Smithe, I'm impressed with your research. Our organization is aware of that and tried to get some DNA samples, but his heart is under lock and key."

It's all starting to make sense to Smithe, but there are still so many unanswered questions. "I have another puzzling question," he says. "Do you know who nicked his ashes and why?"

"Our organization took Dr. Flanders's ashes for DNA evidence to trace his ancestry, also at his request. Any more questions?"

Smithe in disbelief replies, "I still can't believe that humanity would be so radical as to lead the human race into utter destruction!"

"So, Smithe, you are still skeptical and you don't think intelligent people would act in a beast-like fashion to take over the world?"

"Well, yes I have seen a lot of intelligent people lose it when they put themselves in bad situations, but I guess I have more faith in humanity!"

McNair challenges the two skeptics and says, "Then I would like to show you something that is going on in England even as we speak! Something that I am sure you are aware of, but perhaps have never witnessed with your own eyes."

"Well, I guess we can't see what you're talking about as long as we're held here!" says Smithe as he replies reluctantly.

"All right then, do I have your word that if I release you that you will come with me to England to see this strange event that is going on right now?"

"You have our word!"

McNair says apologetically to Sara, "I am so sorry that I had to do this to you Sara, but I hope you will understand the wishes of your father. Would you please book us on the next available flight to England?"

"I'll admit it was hard to understand your motives Robert, but now I understand completely. Surely I will arrange for our transportation to England!"

The next morning, before dawn, the trio board a plane home for the long journey to England!

Chapter Eighteen

It is a beautiful morning as the sun begins to rise and the sky is filled with beautiful yellow and purple hues as the trio arrive at Stonehenge England, and McNair drives Smithe and Sara to see people dancing and singing in the streets as 20,000 Druids bring in the summer solstice.

Drummers, dressed up in pagan costumes looking like ancient Druids and people partying like tailgaters at a football game—welcome the sun as it rises above the primeval monument of Stonehenge on the longest day of the year. People appear to be having fun as though it was a New Year's Eve celebration and they are dressed in strange costumes consisting of black cloaks with deer antlers and oak leaves. Several are doing a weird dance at the Heel stone, a twisted, pockmarked pillar at the edge of Stonehenge.

DI Smithe and Sara observe this festival with McNair in disbelief as Smithe remarks, "I have heard of this festival, but never observed it myself. I can't believe that civilized people would act in this horrid fashion. It's just like they worshipped the sun in the days of old as pagans."

"This is really strange," admits Sara.

"Can you now see how so called rational intelligent people can act and why they will be ripe to follow the Antichrist. These are the intelligentsia of the world. Doctors, computer programmers, Scientists, Psychologists, Teachers, etc." Remarks McNair as he expresses his concern as well, and the reason for his organizations mission.

"After all these centuries, I guess things haven't changed all that much!" says DI Smithe as he agrees with McNair's assessment.

Stonehenge Summer Solstice, Media & Culture, by Philip Ross 06/21/15

"Precisely! Remember all of the Celtic history that I lectured on regarding the ancient Druids? I took this picture when we were in Ireland looking for the Ark," *handing his cell phone to Smithe*. "Do you see any similarities to Stonehenge and it's connection to Ireland?"

Ireland, 2010, Ronald R. Wlodyga

They all look at each other mystified and return home!
***

Two years have gone by as DI Smithe seems to have solved the murder of Dr. Flanders, his missing heart and ashes. He no longer has frightening dreams of the bloody death of Dr. Flanders. But everything he had discussed with Dr. McNair has still resonated in his mind. His wife Martha has since died and he reminisces about the joyous things they have done during their lifetime. He thinks about how Martha wanted him to retire so they could do more traveling, but he couldn't because he loved his job so much. He is still contemplating retirement as he looks at the beautiful roses he and Martha planted. He is on his patio reading the morning paper and having breakfast. Suddenly his eyes focus on the headlines which read:

> **ISRAEL TO BUILD 3RD TEMPLE**
> **Noahide Laws will be administered by a restored Sanhedrin.**
> **Simonides receives Noble Peace Prize**
> **Jerusalem Post**: Jewish Cleric Simonides has accomplished the most colossal human achievement of the ages. This miracle worker has persuaded the Jews, Arabs and Christian world to allow the Temple's construction and has been hailed as the all-time peace maker and given the Nobel peace prize!

DI Smithe rushes into his house to watch the breaking news. The entire world is glued to the TV watching the evening news broadcast from New York.

Katie Koranski the News-anchor woman on channel 13 is reporting what is going on and says to her audience, "Ever since religious Cleric Simonides has unified the Middle East by negotiating a peace settlement between Arabs and Jews and Christians, the holy city has undergone some major changes. Here to explain is our correspondent in the Middle East Betsy Starktan.

Betsy is the Middle East Journalist speaking on live TV from Jerusalem and says, "Thanks Katie, behind me is the newly built Temple where a newly formed Sanhedrin of 70 Rabbis have made some dramatic changes to this holy city, pilgrimage to Jews, Arabs and Christians. Any moment now we are going to hear from Nobel Peace Laurette Simonides who has been so instrumental in bringing all of this about through his charismatic nature. Everyone seems to just love this man of peace! Oh, here he comes to make a major announcement."

Simonides addresses the excited crowd and speaks in a calm mellow voice, "Friends and righteous people of all nations. People have come from all over the world to share in the blessings of this holy city. And now we of the Sanhedrin have just made a major decision and pray that all nations will follow our example to bring peace and stability to the world. We are reinstituting the Noahide laws immediately and encourage all nations to follow suite in accordance with the United States President.

"These timeless laws apply to all human's through humanity's descendant from one paternal ancestor who Hebrew tradition is called Noah. Any non-Jew who lives according to these laws is regarded as one of the righteous among the Gentiles. We are also encouraging gentiles to keep our seventh day Sabbath according to the commandments given our forefather Moses. The death penalty will be enforced in Jerusalem to anyone who violates the Sabbath including non-Jews according to Maimonides teaching."

The TV camera shifts back to correspondent Betsy Starktan as she replies to Katie, "There you have it Katie, the ancient Noahide laws will be enforced in Jerusalem by the newly formed Sanhedrin and all violators including non-Jews will be subject to the death penalty!"

Katie askes inquisitively, "What exactly are the Noahide laws?"

"Basically, they are laws that the Jews have felt come from divine origin and considered compelling for good living such as no idolatry, no blasphemy, no sorcerers, no witchcraft, no murder, no adultery, and no sodomy."

Katie inquires further, "Did I understand Simonides to say they are also enforcing the Jewish Sabbath as part of them?"

"Yes Katie, and that may be a tough one to swallow, but I heard that many Christians are now willing to keep it as well out of respect and honor as it is the fourth commandment! The major Christian bodies of Catholic and Eastern Orthodox churches and the Protestants held a meeting with Simonides and believe the Ten Commandments to be binding on them as well and have accepted this practice for unity sake!"

Katie abruptly ends the conversation to continue other world news, "Thanks for your report Betsy and now on to other world news!"

The camera shifts back to Betsy as she is nodding her head in unbelief as she says, "Back to you Katie!"

Meanwhile, DI Smithe gets on the phone with Sara and then calls Dr. McNair to see if he has been watching the news.

"I've been watching the news and bloody hell, it's happening just as you said it would! I think it's time to do something. What is your organization going to do?"

"As I've told you previously, my organization has been waiting for the Antichrist to appear on the scene and we believe this Simonides fits the bill! He is very charismatic, a peace maker and is changing the laws of his father's just as the prophecies concur. We are watching to see if he will start to perform miracles."

DI Smithe is intrusive and with his detective mind desires to know more. He has caught a lot of criminals during his lifetime, but now his interest has focused on catching the biggest of them all. "How will we know if he is the Antichrist?"

"Remember my lecture about the types in the Bible being patterns of future events?" says McNair.

"Yea, like the death of Samson being representative of the end time."

"Good memory Smithe! We believe that God has revealed the future by several significant events that occurred in the past and that is God's way of showing us what will happen next!"

Smithe adds, "You mean by the types!"

"Precisely!" says McNair in his Professor-like response.

"Go on, I'm listening!" says Smithe as he desires McNair to provide more information.

"That will take a lot of time and I would prefer if we didn't do it over the phone. I'll tell you what Smithe, I'm planning on having dinner with Sara this week-end and perhaps we can get together to discuss this."

"That's fine with me. Let me know where and when."

***

It's a cloudy day, as McNair comes to visit Sara and go to their favorite Irish restaurant. The two have been dating on a regular basis, although not as often as they would like because of their busy schedules. After a delightful dinner, McNair drives to Sara's house where they have arranged to meet DI Smithe. Smithe has been waiting in his care for 15 minutes and spots them driving up. Smithe gets out of his car and greets both of them with a big bear hug!

"Good to see you Smithe," says Sara as she gives him a peck on the cheek. They have gone through so much together over the years that they feel almost like family.

"Good to see both of you as well," echoes Smithe. They all walk into Sara's home and the two men sit down. Sara rushes into the kitchen for some snacks and puts on a pot of tea. McNair and Smithe start to engage in a serious Bible discussion.

McNair begins by getting out his Bible that he has brought along. He thumbs to a book in the Old Testament, and says, "There is a prophecy in the Old Testament that has to do with the character of the individual who will be the Antichrist as we were discussing on the phone."

Sara has now come back with the snacks and overhears the conversation. "Where is that Robert?"

"It's in the second chapter of the book of Daniel."

"Oh, that's the book that showed the dream that the King of Babylon had and wanted someone to interpret it for him. After none of his smart people could, he called upon the prophet Daniel who explained it."

McNair is impressed and replies, "Sometimes you amaze me Smithe!"

"Well you are a good teacher, and I took very good notes on your lecture comparing some of the Roman Emperors to Daniel's fourth Beast or the Roman Empire. In order to be a good detective you have to know your enemies. Besides, you got my interest in this prophecy stuff and I'm not sure if I'm even a good Catholic anymore. Anyway, I have been doing a lot of reading on my own and took a lot of notes at your lectures."

"Good for you Smithe, then you know that the dream Daniel interpreted for King Nebuchadnezzar of a great image represented the four world ruling empires that would come on the scene down to the very end of the world as we know it. It started with the head of gold symbolic of King Nebuchadnezzar's kingdom as Daniel explained the dream!"

"I remembered that! Then the Babylonian kingdom was defeated by the Kingdom of the Medes and Persians under King Cyrus. Then the Persians were conquered by the Greeks under Alexander the Great. Then finally the Romans defeated them!"

"Precisely! You catch on quickly Smithe and know your history!"

"As I said, before I became a detective my major was history. But one thing I'm not clear on is who is represented by the stone made without hands that smashes the toes of this image?"

"I think I know the answer to that, it will be our returning Savior," says Sara as she is getting involved and interjects.

McNair agrees, and says, "Precisely!"

"Oh, I see, yes that makes sense!"

"Anyway, when we get to the 8th through the 11th chapter of Daniel, we learn more about end-time events characterized by the longest prophecy in the Bible known as the King of the North and South. But we must first start with chapter 8 where it talks about a little horn who stands up to the prince of hosts or the returning Christ!"

Sara turns to the chapter in her Bible and says she will read the prophecy aloud. She begins to read the eighth chapter of Daniel.

After Sara finishes, Smithe is confused and asks McNair, "What does it mean his power shall be mighty but not his own power?"

"Many have attempted to interpret the Bible out of their own human reasoning," says McNair, "But we must let the Bible interpret itself! The explanation of the little horns power in verse 24: *'But not by his own power'* literally means he is not using his own power, but is getting his power from somewhere else.

"In other words, this king will not accomplish his great deeds by his own strength. Now realize that the book of Daniel is a parallel account of the end time events. Revelation 17:17 reveals why. Ten lesser kings give their military power and strength unto 'the Beast.' Furthermore, this little horn of Daniel 8:24 *'shall destroy wonderfully.'*

Sara is now confused and asks, "What does that mean Robert?"

"The Bible tells us the Antichrist will have marvelous, frightening supernatural military powers 'and shall destroy the mighty and the holy people' as it says in verse 24."

"Who are the holy people? Is it referring to Christians? Aren't they the holy people?" asks Smithe.

"Based upon additional scriptures, our organization believes this 'Beast power' will be a persecuting power of the end-time—a union of church and state similar to that of the Holy Roman Empire that will destroy the hosts or armies of the 'mighty people' or the Jewish people.

"Remember, when Daniel wrote his book, there were no Christians as of yet. We came to that conclusion based upon past events or the 'types' as I keep referring to them."

"What event occurred in the past that will be similar to the end-time?" Smithe asks.

"Our organization believes the Bible interprets this 'little horn' as a great ruler who shall exist at the second coming of our Savior when world sin has reached its climax as it says in Daniel 8:23. We believe *this 'little horn'* is described again in Revelation 17:14 where we read that he makes war with the Lamb or Jesus Christ, but the Lamb will overcome him and his allies.

"Our organization believes this war will be a supernatural war between fallen angels fighting against the returning Savior!"

"Fallen angels! This sounds like 'Star Wars'! So, you really believe in a spirit world?" DI Smithe askes as he is astonished.

"Absolutely, and the Bible reveals such, that is if you believe the Bible is the word of God. That's what Dr. Flanders believed and why he quoted the scripture, *'For we wrestle not against flesh and blood, but against the rulers of the darkness of this world, against spiritual wickedness in high places,* as it says in the book of Ephesians."

Smithe replies facetiously, "Maybe Father Benedetti was right, and Ok, let's say I do, where is the Bible proof of what you believe?"

"Remember the story I told you about Nimrod's Babylon?"

"Refresh my memory!"

"Nimrod, who was an evil man and built the tower of Babel and started sun-worship?"

"Yes, now I remember and his connection to the Druids and one of their most common symbols was a sun-god with a serpent around it. Even the ancient Israelites got caught up in this false worship system and were sacrificing their children."

"I can't believe any mother would do that," says Sara.

"It is hard to believe," says McNair, "But then something else happened as described in Genesis 6 that was so horrid.

The Bible says that fallen angels or demons called 'sons of God' actually had sexual relations with human woman—and produced a race of giants called Nephilim!"

Smithe is flabbergasted and asks, "You mean there really are demons or what most people call ghosts?"

"Yes, Father Benedetti was spot on because there really is a spiritual world that most people know nothing about. These demons are fallen angels that rebelled against God and Satan is there leader. Their human offspring were destroyed in the flood, but the Bible informs us that another group of fallen angels will do similar things in the last days as happened previously."

Sara is especially concerned and asks Robert more questions, "I guess that's why it is so important to understand the types. How did you come to the conclusion that the 'little horn' of Daniel is the same being as the 'Antichrist' in the New Testament?"

"Sara, I believe the Bible answers that question, so would you please read Revelation 17 to us because this 'little horn' causes the same events as the final world power of Revelation 17.

Sara begins reading Revelation 17 out loud. After reading she asks, "Robert, who do you think will be the little horn that will be a persecuting power and what 10 nations will be affiliated with him?"

"It's really anyone's guess who it is and what it will do, but we can learn from what was done previously in history as I keep stating."

"You mean from the types!"

"Precisely!"

"I'm glad you and Sara understand these types. I never heard that term used in all my Sunday school classes! I wish I knew more about them!"

Sara explains what she understands about types to Smithe, "A type in the Bible is a person, place or thing in the Old Testament that represents a future person place or thing in the New Testament as a fulfillment. Isn't that right Robert?"

"Yes, Sara has given a good definition. A type is simply God's kindergarten method of teaching us His plan of future events by events that have already occurred. It's been said what was concealed in the Old Testament has been revealed in the New!"

"Give me another example Sara."

"Well, the Passover lamb in Israel represented the Christian's Savior and therefore the lamb was a type of Jesus being led to the slaughter as John the Baptist called him the Lamb of God!"

Smithe finally understands and provides his own example, "Ah! I get it! It's like coke, there are substitutes and then there is the real thing!"

"I guess you could put it that way," says McNair. "Other words that could be used instead of type, are shadow, picture or an object lesson by which God taught His people. So when we read of this prophecy in the Old Covenant, we can learn what happened in the past and apply it to what will happen in the future."

"Go ahead Doctor explain how this prophecy was fulfilled in the Old Covenant and how you think it will happen in the final fulfillment," says Smithe.

Realizing they are both engaged, McNair continues his hypothesis, "Ok. Sara, please read the eleventh chapter of the book of Daniel aloud and I'll make comments! This is one of the longest prophecies of the Bible, but it is crucial to understanding the end times."

Sara begins reading the eleventh chapter of Daniel. Afterwards, McNair gives his comments, "The background that we spoke of earlier about Nebuchadnezzar's dream in chapter two, is necessary to understand this chapter. Most students of history understand that after Alexander the Great died at an unexpected early age of 33, his kingdom was divided up between his four generals.

"That was the Grecian Kingdom," says Smithe.

"Yes, the Grecian kingdom was envisioned by the bronze belly and thighs of Daniels interpreted image. From here the prophecy foretells the activities of only two of these four divisions: Many prophecy writers believe Egypt is the 'king of the south,' because it is south of Jerusalem; and the Syrian kingdom, the king of the north, just north of Judea. While this scenario is plausible, I am keeping my eyes on Saudi Arabia.

"History further informs us that Seleueus conquered Lysimachus in 281 B.C. and controlled the North while the Ptolemies became the controlling power in the South. Thus, eventually only two powers existed; that of the Seleucidae in the North and the Ptolemies in the South. The general who eventually inherited Egypt was Antiochus. A long and bitter struggle between these two families is recorded by historians. The Holy land changed hands many times over the years between these two kingdoms, but then in 167 B.C. something dramatic happened."

"What was that?" asks Sara.

"In 167 B.C., Antiochus sent troops to the Holy Land and desecrated the Temple and sanctuary, abolished the daily sacrifice and placed an abominable image on the altar in the Temple. The prophecy then comes to Christ and the apostles in verse 32. Antiochus took away the daily sacrifice, forbade the ministration at the Temple, and perverted by flatteries the Jews who were willing to forsake their religion. But right here, the prophecy cuts off from the continuation of events in the history of those ancient north and south kingdoms."

"So, we should be looking for some madman who will do similar things," says Smithe as he gives his professional opinion.

"Precisely, those three years under Antiochus were to be among the most trying in Jewish history. The Jewish historian Josephus says that Alexander requested that his statue be placed in the Temple at Jerusalem upon his death. Antiochus tried to end the religion of the Jews. Jews were forced to eat pork and worship pagan gods. Those who refused were mercilessly killed. Many of them therefore acquiesced to adopting Hellenistic customs."

Once again Smithe observes, "Then what you are saying based upon the types, is that this coming Antichrist will do similar things as this despot Antiochus?"

"That's anyone's guess, but we believe he will do similar things!"

"Didn't that time period have something to do with the Jewish custom of Lights?" says Sara as she chimes into the conversation.

"That's absolutely correct. When the Maccabees liberated Jerusalem, they tore down the pagan gods from the Temple Mount and relit the lights of the Menorah. To this day the Jewish eight-day winter festival of Hanukkah, or Festival of Lights, recalls the cleansing of the Temple in the days of the Maccabees. Our organization believes the coming Antichrist will do similar things as did Antiochus. This will begin a time the Bible calls The Great Tribulation."

"There are many people who believe that all of these events have all been fulfilled by Antiochus in 167 B.C. How do we know that they were not?"

"Excellent question Sara! Because Jesus indicated in Matthew 24 that the Great Tribulation spoken of by Daniel the prophet had not yet occurred! Jesus said these things in around 31 A.D."

"Many scholars on prophecy believe this coming dictator will unite 10 countries in Europe reviving the ancient Holy Roman Empire. The book of Daniel indicates the time setting is at the resurrection of the just at the Second Coming of our Savior." Rev. 17:12; Daniel 12:1.

"My father also told me of a special mark that the Antichrist would place upon people that would cause them to be martyred if they did not have it. What is that Robert?"

"Yes, this mark of the Antichrist is described in Revelation 17 to a Great Harlot seated on a seven-headed ten horned Beast and has been interpreted by many including the Reformers as the Papal church at Rome as I have already mentioned."

"Now hold on there, McNair! You're not going to imply the Catholic church is involved in this end-time plot to take over the world, are you?"

"Don't get your feathers ruffled Smithe, I didn't say that I necessarily believed it, only that many of the prophetic writers of today do, as did the Reformers. I already said that Dr. Flanders and I used to believe that but later came to a different conclusion."

"I see, well then how did the Reformers arrive at that conclusion?"

"Because nothing else in World History seemed to fit. The desire for Worldly Power began to manifest itself in the Catholic church on a broad scale in the fourth century when the Roman Empire ceased its persecutions of Christians, and made Christianity it's State Religion under Constantine. The spirit of Imperial Rome passed into the church.

"The church gradually developed itself into the pattern of the Empire it had conquered. Rome fell. But Rome came to life again, as a World-Power, in the name of the Church. The Popes of Rome were the heirs and successors of the Caesars of Rome.

"The Vatican is where the Palace of the Caesars were and Emperor Constantine gave Pope Militades the land in 313 AD. In 326, the Constantinian Basilica was built on what is thought by many to be the tomb of St. Peter."

Smithe is appreciative of this ancient history and remarks, "I didn't know that!"

"Not many do but It's true! As time went on the church at Rome took its nose-dive into the millennium of Papal abominations. The Popes claimed all the authority the Caesars claimed, and more. The Papal Palace, throughout the centuries, has been among the most luxurious in all the world!"

Smithe agrees and replies, "I'm not naïve of the abdominal things that have gone on in the early church that wasn't reflective of the kind of church Jesus desired. I always wondered why they spent our hard-earned money on those lavish statues and things. It didn't seem right considering how meager our Lord lived!"

"How true, perhaps now you can see why the Reformers thought the apostle John described the church of Rome as the fallen church in Revelation 17.

"It appeared to be full of names of blasphemy and its no secret that Popes have claimed to hold on earth the place of God and to have supreme authority to even forgive sin.

"The age of Indulgences was also an atrocity that led Martin Luther to rebel and helped start the Reformation. How could anything be more blasphemous?" Declares McNair as he elaborates on the prophecy's connection, and why the Reformers came to their conclusion.

Smithe asks another pertinent question, "True, the church did those things in the past and I guess the people and clergy all looked the other way. But are you telling me that martyrs are going to occur again?"

McNair says he will let the Bible answer that question as he asks Sara to continue reading some scriptures. "Sara, would you please read a few more verses for us that may clarify some things?"

Sara agreeably replies, "Surely, Robert."

"Please read Revelation 6:11 concerning end-time martyrs." Sara begins to read,

> **And white robes were given unto every one of them; and it was said unto them, that they should rest yet for a little season, until their fellow servants also and their brethren, that should be killed as they were, should be fulfilled.**

McNair now asks Sara to read Revelation 20:4. Sara reads,

> *And I saw thrones, and they sat upon them, and judgment was given unto them: and I saw the souls of them that were beheaded for the witness of Jesus, and for the word of God, and which had not worshipped the beast, neither his image; neither had received his mark upon their foreheads, or in their hands; and they lived and reigned with Christ a thousand years.*

"For over 500 years the horrors of the Inquisition ordered by the Popes, in which millions of innocent people were tortured, imprisoned and burned—account for one of the darkest periods in all of human history. These things are not pleasant to talk about, but truth is truth," says McNair.

"And people think water-boarding is bad!" remarks Smithe facetiously.

McNair concurs, "Yes! I know!"

Being defensive of his faith, Smithe echoes, "Well it's true the Church has had a dark history, but they have changed a lot over the years."

"I totally agree," says McNair. "But history is history, and most amazing of all, it seems exactly pre-figured into what John the reveler described. Can you now understand why Dr. Flanders and I along with the Reformers believed the Bible labeled the church at Rome as the 'Image of the Beast'?"

"Well, since you put it that way! You've got me thinking now! But how does all this fit into your theory that all deception came from Babylon where this Nimrod and Semiramis deceived the world? Doesn't this scripture in Revelation mention something about Babylon?"

"That's a valid point Smithe, and I'm glad you're thinking. But the big question we must ask is, was Kabala the image of this system or was the Catholic church its image? Or were both influenced by them? You see, religion determined the sexual morals of the people.

"Normally, when a country was overthrown, and a new government came to power, a new religion was introduced. But when Nebuchadnezzar's Babylonian Empire was overthrown, their Assyrian Babylonian Mystery religion did not die! By the time of Jesus, the prevailing religion throughout the Roman Empire was Roman Paganism, a religion of Emperor worship."

"Robert, you said Constantine was one of the first Roman Pontifex's, and isn't it questionable whether he was really a Christian?"

"That's true Sara, and there are many opinions on that as he killed members of his own family—but supposedly he repented and was baptized on his death bed!"

"Nimrod was the King and founder of Babylon, and was not only its political leader, but he stood as the priest king, or its religious leader as well just like the Pontifex's of Rome. From Nimrod descended a line of priest-kings, each standing at the head of the occult Babylonian Mystery Religion. That is why the Reformers saw this connection to the church at Rome," declares McNair.

Sara is more than curious and begins to question McNair's reasoning and says, "Let's say the church at Rome is the Image of the 'Beast of Revelation' who many have identified as the Roman Empire. What is this mysterious mark they will impose on everyone that will cause these future martyrdoms?"

"Let me put this in perspective! Thus far we have established several remarkable points. There are many prophetic thinkers who believe the church at Rome is the *image* of the Roman Empire and someday a False Prophet will emerge who will perform fake miracles. You ask what possible mark or identifying sign could the church brand on people to cause the eventual martyrdom of those that don't have it by a future Roman Empire? I have thought long and hard on this one and there are many theories."

Smithe is more than defensive, and he is curious and speculates, "I am curious about your conclusion! I heard this mysterious Mark had something to do with the number 666 and it was some kind of computer code in Brussels or something."

"I heard that one as well," McNair replies, "and believe me I have heard them all, but a few additional scriptures will give us more insight as to why such a mark could cause martyrdom. The apostle John describes the 'Image of the Beast' as a great harlot that rides or is affiliated with the Roman Empire. Sara would you please read Revelation 17:6 for us?"

Sara eagerly reads Revelation 17:6,

> ***And upon her forehead was a name written, MYSTERY BABYLON, THE GREAT, THE MOTHEER OF HARLOTS AND AMOMINATIONS OF THE EARTH.***

Inquisitive, Smithe asks a valid question, "I have a question about what Sara just read."

"Go ahead Smithe, what is it?"

"You have been saying all along that these verses may imply the Roman Catholic church is the 'Image of the Beast', and yet this verse is speaking about a woman."

"Remember the types as I keep referring? Here, God uses a physical woman to describe a spiritual church as He does in several other places."

"Oh, you mean like the church is to become the Bride of Christ?"

"By golly you've got it! So, let's continue our study as to what this mysterious mark could be assuming it applies to the church at Rome. Sara please read Revelation 6:9-10."

Sara begins reading,

> ***And when he had opened the fifth seal, I saw under the altar the souls of them that were slain for the word of God, and for the testimony which they held: And they cried***

> *with a loud voice, saying, How long, O Lord, holy and true, dost thou not judge and avenge our blood on them that dwell on the earth?*

"The book of Revelation describes The Great Tribulation and a time of martyrdom during the last days prior to the Saviors return. Jesus said there would never be a time like it, including past martyrdoms.

"I believe the martyrs here are those of the past, symbolically crying out for vengeance of martyrs yet to occur. I believe these martyrs occurred during the Inquisition of the Middle Ages when millions were put to death by the Holy Roman Empire as I have already discussed in my lectures on church history.

"Many of our relatives also left England for freedom of religion from this persecution to America. Sara, would you please continue reading Revelation 13:15-16."

Sara continues reading the scripture,

> *And he had power to give life unto the image of the beast, that the image of the beast should both speak, and cause that as many as would not worship the image of the beast should be killed. And he causeth all both small and great; rich and poor, free and bond, to receive a mark in their right hand, or in their foreheads: and that no man might buy or sell, except he that had the mark, or the name of the beast, or the number of his name. Here is wisdom. Let him that hath understanding count the number of the beast: for it is the number of a man; and his number is Six hundred threescore and six.*

"Thank you, Sara. Now we get down to brass tax and the most important and fundamental question as to what could be this mysterious mark that the Beast power will kill people who do not have this mark on their forehead or hand. In order to answer that question, once again we must resort to past history and to the Bible for answers. Let's notice several significant things here. The Bible says it is a mark in the forehead or right hand and if you don't have it you can't buy or sell anything. And also, the number of the individual known as the beast is Six hundred threescore and six, or 666."

"What does all that mean, I don't understand!" Says Sara as she is startled and inquires.

"It's gobbly gook to me!" Says Smithe. "Can you think of any types in the Bible that have reference to a mark in the forehead or hand?"

McNair appeals to Smithe's detective prowess and provides additional clues.

"By golly Smithe you are a good detective! To know if you have the Mark of the Beast you must first know what a mark is symbolic of in the Bible. If you look up the word 'mark' in the dictionary, you'll find it means token, or *sign* to designate ownership. So, let's look up some scriptures that have reference to a sign or mark."

McNair brings out a concordance out of his briefcase that he has brought along, and says he will look up the word 'mark.'

Smithe shows his biblical ignorance and asks, "What's a concordance?"

"It's like a dictionary with all the words listed in the Bible," Says Sara as she obliges cordially.

"McNair thumbs to the word 'sign' in his concordance and asks Sara to read Exodus 31:12-17. Sara begins to read:

> **And the LORD spake unto Moses, saying, Speak thou also unto the children of Israel, saying, Verily my sabbaths ye shall**

> *keep: for it is a sign between me and you throughout your generations; that ye may know that I am the LORD that doth sanctify you. You shall keep the Sabbath therefore; for it is holy unto you; every one that defileth it shall be put to death; for whosoever doeth any work therein that soul shall be cut off from among his people. [16] Wherefore the children of Israel shall keep the sabbath, to observe the sabbath throughout their generations, for a perpetual covenant.[17] It is a sign between me and the children of Israel forever: for in six days the LORD made heaven and earth, and on the seventh day he rested, and was refreshed.*

"Did you get it? Did you get the sign?"

Smithe shows his detective competence, "Yes, the sign was God's Sabbath that he gave the nation of Israel! And if any one defiles it shall be put to death! It doesn't sound like something that Jesus would say. He only spoke of loving your neighbor."

"Well, believe it or not Smithe, Jesus is the same God of the Old Covenant as the New. Most Christians don't realize that!" McNair drops another bombshell on Smithe.

Smithe is dumbfounded and questions, "Really, I never was taught that! Where does the Bible say that?"

Sara would you please 1 Corinthians 10:1-4. Sara complies and reads:

> *Moreover, brethren, I would not that ye should be ignorant, how that all our fathers were under the cloud, and all passed through the sea; and were all baptized unto Moses in the cloud and in the sea; and all did eat the same spiritual meat; and did all*

> ***drink the same spiritual drink: for they drank of that spiritual Rock that followed them: and that Rock was Christ.***

Smithe is still dubious and inquires, "Is that in the Catholic Bible?"

"You can read it in any Bible!"

"Being put to death for not resting on the Sabbath day! That sounds serious! Now I can understand how someone could implement these Noahide laws and think they are doing God's service!" says Smithe.

"Precisely, but remember, the Noahide law that a future False Prophet may want to implement is a perversion of the Noahide laws that are stated in the Jewish Talmud!"

"Ok, so let's say we know what the sign is, but how does it apply to the mark in one's right hand and forehead? I have already acquiesced to fact that the Catholic church had a dark history of martyrdom, but how does the Jewish Sabbath sign have anything to do with the Catholic church?

"What is this mysterious mark these people have been branded with in their foreheads and right hand? Is this coming Beast power going to write something on people's hand and head like a bar code or something?" asks DI Smithe as he inquires further.

"Now you are thinking and getting to the root of the matter! As Sara just read, the seventh day Sabbath to the nation of Israel was a special sign between God and them. In essence it was an invisible sign marked on their forehead or mind and the hand was symbolic of working.

"Israel's mindset was not to work on the weekly Sabbath or the annual Sabbaths! That was their invisible relationship between them and God only known to them! Sara, would you now please read what God said to the nation of Israel in Exodus 13:9."

Sara begins reading,

> **And it shall be for a sign unto thee upon thine hand, and for a memorial between thine eyes, that the Lord's law may be in thy mouth: for with a strong hand hath the Lord brought thee out of Egypt.**

"You can read similar words describing the keeping of God's laws in Deuteronomy 6:1, 6-8; 11:18."

Sara provides an interesting question, "I get it! But how does the church fit into this picture? They don't keep the seventh day Sabbath! I did read somewhere where Emperor Constantine changed the day of rest in the Roman Empire from the seventh day to the first day of the week. Is that true Robert?"

***

"After Rome conquered the world, the paganism that had spread from Babylon and developed into various forms, was merged into the religious system of Rome, including the idea of a Supreme Pontiff or Pontifex Maximus. Thus. Babylonian paganism which had originally been carried out under the rulership of Nimrod, was united under Julius Caesar of Rome, who was recognized as the 'Pontifex Maximus' in 63 B.C.

"The Romans regarded Neptune, Saturn, Mars and Liber as 'gods' and Rome was regarded as 'the city of the gods' in the first century. During the reign of Nero in 64 A.D. Christians were falsely charged with burning the city. Perhaps some three years after this burning, the apostle Paul was seized near Troas. 11 Tim. 4:13. As the Roman world began to be Christianized, the people heard that their traditional religions of sacrifice to their Roman gods was no longer required as the God of the Christians did not require sacrifice—because Jesus Christ provided the only required sacrifice for their sins!

"The neophyte Christians began to be noticed from their pagan counterparts as they refused to eat meat that was sacrificed to the Roman gods and refused to worship in the

Roman temples. As Christianity began to flourish, the Roman leaders became alarmed and began blaming the new Christians for any accident or natural catastrophe that caused great damage or loss of life. They claimed the gods were punishing them for forsaking their sacrifices.

"That's why Emperor Nero blamed the Christians for the burning of the city in A.D. 64 and many were tortured by being torn by dogs, nailed to crosses, doomed to the flames and burnt. Emperor Domitian continued the persecution of Christians from A.D. 81 to 96. Over the next century, waves of persecution swept through the Empire, particularly during the reigns of Diocletian who had a mission to 'to tear down the churches to the foundations and to destroy the Sacred Scriptures by fire.' He issued several edicts including a law requiring church officials to be imprisoned and tortured if they refused to make a sacrifice to the Emperor. Ironically, the more the Christians were persecuted, the more they seemed to flourish."

***

"I heard it was a very trying time for the early Church and many of the leaders of the Church were martyred," says Sara.

"Yes, that's true Sara, but then an apparent miracle happened in 306 A.D. as the Roman Emperor Constantine reigned and sympathized with Christians and allowed them to practice their religion. It is uncertain as to why he preferred the Christians and there is much debate if he was ever a Christian among historians. He most likely was influenced by his mother Helena, who was a Christian and made a remarkable pilgrimage to Judea when she was eighty. The Roman Bishop Eusebius, who favored Constantine, wrote much about his life and one of the most controversial changes he authorized being the change of Saturday and Sunday rest.

"The opening of the fourth century was tumultuous for the Roman Empire. It witnessed the final struggle between the pagan Roman Empire and Christianity. The Christian religion suddenly emerged to freedom under the Edict of Toleration because of Emperor Constantine and his promotion of Christianity as the future state religion.

"His edict, often designated as the earliest Sunday law gave jurisdiction over civil observance of the day of rest from Saturday to Sunday, but not over the religious observance of the day of worship. This benefited Christians as it stopped the persecution of them by making Sunday a legal day of rest, so they would not be discriminated against by the pagan populous, who were required to work on Sunday. Previously, Saturday was the only day of rest in the empire.

***

"During what has been termed The Great Persecution, which lasted about two centuries, many Christians died under the Roman Emperor Diocletian, who had the reputation of being the most loathsome of all the Roman Emperors. Some Catholic biographies of the popes allege that 17,000 martyrs occurred within a single thirty-day period, although this number is much disputed by other historians. Although there is much controversy over the life of Constantine and his influence over paganism and Christianity, one thing is for certain. Eastern Orthodox Christians, Anglicans, and Byzantine Catholics venerate him and his mother as a saint.

"Historians tell us he was not baptized until on his deathbed, and he was still officially the high priest of Roman paganism. Christianity was his favorite religion and he participated in heretical disputes including the Trinity at the council of Nicaea. Unlike many previous emperors, it appears he did not want conflict between the Christian and pagan religions to divide his empire."

***

Smithe has been listening to every word Dr. McNair has just said and gives his opinion.

"Didn't you say Doctor that the Roman Empire put many Christians to death during the first few centuries if they didn't observe their old pagan worship?"

"That is the dark history of the early Christians!" says McNair.

Smithe makes an interesting detective observation, "If what you say is true history, well, maybe a similar thing will occur down the road! I mean this religious cleric Simonides could be the Antichrist as you said, and do a similar thing that the Roman empire did during the first century! After all he has everyone keeping the Jewish Sabbath in Israel with the threat of death to all those who violate it!"

"You are indeed observant and propose an interesting concept. That is entirely possible and that is why we are watching him!"

"He does fit the scenario that a Jew will one day go into the Temple and declare himself to be God?" Sara agrees.

"That's what our organization believes! That's why we are watching him very closely!"

Smithe has on his detective hat and says, "Yea, that certainly would take the Catholic church off the hook! After all he has gotten the Sanhedrin in Israel to impose the Jewish Noahide Law so that anyone who doesn't keep the Jewish Sabbath would be put to death? How can we stop him McNair before all of these people are killed once again?"

"I think the answer will be found in the power that the newly discovered artifacts will give. The offspring of the person God considers to be heir to the Stone of Destiny and the High Priest's breastplate will tell us who it is?"

Smithe is inquisitive and asks, "But where do we start looking for this person?"

"We have ruled out getting results from Westminster where most of the English Kings have been buried because they won't give us permission to exhume any bones, but our organization is getting DNA samples from the bones we found in the King's chamber at Tara."

As Smithe leaves Sara's house, he gives Sara a hug and shakes McNair's hand and says, "Keep me posted!"

***

A year goes by and Dr. McNair is on his patio and reads the headlines in his morning newspaper,

> **RELIGIOUS CLERIC SIMONIDES PERFOMS MIRACLES IN JERUSALEM: THE SICK ARE MADE WELL! SIMONIDES HAILED AS NEW MESSIAH!**

DI Smithe is watching Satellite TV in his home along with the entire world as religious cleric Simonides is performing unbelievable miracles including bringing fire down from heaven. He walks around the grounds looking for people to heal of their infirmities near the newly built Temple in Jerusalem.

Anxious, DI Smithe calls up McNair and inquires of him, "World events appear to be moving very fast as this Simonides is performing miracles, just as you said the Antichrist would. Has your organization made any progress in finding the person you think can stop him?"

"The Bible predicted the Antichrist would perform fake miracles," says McNair. I will be coming to England next week to give a lecture at the Heritage Center that I think you will find very informative. We can talk then."

"Yes," says Smithe. "I'll see you then."

Chapter Nineteen

Dr. McNair is shaking hands at the Historical Heritage Center, and looking around at the packed house of 230 people including DI Smithe, DC Humphrey, Father Benedetti and Sara that have come to hear his lecture on the age of Giants. He walks up to the podium gingerly with his notes in hand. He greets his audience and says,

"Good evening everyone. This is going to be an eye opener for most of you regarding end time events or what is called eschatology. If you have been watching the news these days you have noticed some very unusual things going on in the world, especially in Jerusalem. Many have wondered if this new religious cleric Simonides could be the False Prophet as he is doing some very unusual things.

"But how can we know for sure? For this lecture I will be using past historical events as well as the biblical scriptures to enlighten you. For those of you who have Bibles I will be quoting extensively. To begin our story, which is really God's story we must go back to the beginning of time.

"To understand and comprehend the whole picture of the universe and all supernatural things in it, in order of time and sequence, we must go all the way back into pre-history. Most people would probably tell you that the beginning of pre-history of the Bible is found in Genesis I, but the event recorded in John 1:1 reveals an existence perhaps long prior to the time God created the earth and the material universe. Let's read it together. "McNair opens his Bible and reads:

In the beginning was the Word, and the Word was with God and the Word was

> *God. The same was in the beginning with God. All things were made by him; and without him was not anything made that was made.*

"The term 'all things' can be translated in the book of Hebrews as 'the universe.' In other words, the entire universe was made by the Word of God! Clearly, the 'Word' is also God who created the World! The fourteenth verse of John 1 says,

> ***And the Word was made flesh, and dwelt among us, 'and we beheld his glory, the glory as of the only begotten of the Father,' full of grace and truth.***

"The Personage called the Word was the one who ultimately was born Jesus Christ. The name 'the Word,' is translated from the original Greek word 'Logos' which means 'Spokesman.'

"It was the personage that later became Jesus Christ that did the creating as we read in Ephesians 3:9:

> ***God created all things by Jesus Christ. Whom he hath appointed heir of all by whom he also made the worlds. Heb. 1:2,10. For by him 'Christ' were all things created, that are in heaven, and that are in earth, visible, and invisible, whether they be thrones or dominions, or principalities or powers; all things, were created by him, and for him. Col. 1:16-17.***

"Truly, all things were made by 'the Word' or the one who became the Savior of the world He created—Jesus Christ! John 1-3, 10. There was no sin at this time and it was a perfect creation! Now we come to the creation of Angels as I will read Psalm 148:2,5,

> *Praise ye Him, all His angels: praise ye Him, all His hosts. Let them praise the name of the Lord: for He commanded, and they were created.*

"Yes, angels are created beings—perhaps there are millions of them that God created. Angels are spirit beings, composed of spirit, immortal, with life inherent. Jesus, their Creator, said so in Luke 20:34,

> *The children of this world marry, and are given in marriage; but they which shall be accounted worthy to obtain that world 'age', and the resurrection from the dead, neither marry, nor are given in marriage: neither can they die any more, for they are equal unto the angels.*

"Three levels of angels were created; ordinary angels which do not have wings; Seraphs, which do have wings. Isa. 6:2, 6, and Cherubs who also-have wings and are the supreme creation in angel life. There are three cherubs mentioned in the Bible—Michael, Gabriel, and Lucifer—all of which are also Archangels! "The prophet Ezekiel saw the strange creatures covering God's throne and knew they were cherubs. Ezek. 1.

"These cherubs appeared to men in ancient times and were known from the time of Adam until Noah as the guardians of the garden of Eden. When God placed two cherubim with 'flaming swords' there to guard the way to the tree of life, they remained there from that day until the destruction of Eden in the Flood. Gen. 3:4. That was a considerable amount of time since that was about one-sixth of all recorded history.

"There was a time when Michael the Archangel contested with Satan over the body of Moses. Jude 9.

Michael came to help Daniel. Dan. 10:13. Concerning future prophecy, the Bible tells us Michael will help God's people in the last days. Dan. 12:1. Michael and his angels will cast the Devil and his angels out of heaven in the last days. Rev. 12:7. It was Gabriel who appeared to Daniel and gave him understanding of prophecy. Dan. 8:16, 9:21. Gabriel appeared to Zacharias. Luke 1:11-20 and Mary. Luke 1:26 to tell them of their new offspring.

"Cherubim were able to manifest themselves as lions, oxen, men, and eagles—or as an aggregate of all four. These huge spirit creatures were preserved in stone as the *winged bulls of Baashan* on ancient Assyrian kings' palaces.

"One can search the great museums of Britain, France, Germany, and Egypt, and you will see hundreds of examples of worship of 'the host of heaven' as gods in the form of men with 'eagles heads'—which incidentally were common in the inscriptions of ancient Egypt. In Egyptian tombs, archaeologists have found winged bulls featuring the heads of men and lions' claws, and other assorted mixtures of these four.

"Remember what I said about the *'winged bulls of Baashan'* as this will become very significant as I continue this lecture!

"The tales of the children of Noah, all of whom had seen those cherubim, repeated down through time gave rise to the mythologies about winged dragons, flying serpents whose mouths breathed fire, which guarded mysterious castles filled with fabulously valuable treasures at the top of craggy mountains. These all undoubtedly are mythological tales endlessly repeated and embellished, stemming from human encounters with cherubim.

"The Bible tells us that the earth was originally populated by Angels. In Job 38:4, 7 we read *'All the angels shouted for joy at the creation of the earth.'* This reveals that the angels were created before the creation of the earth and the material universe!

"When God told Moses to decorate the interior of the tabernacle in the wilderness with cherubim' Ex. 25: 18, Moses didn't ask God, 'What do they look like?' He knew, especially since he had come from a background of the royal courts of Egypt. In Hebrews 8:2, 9:1, 2, 13:11 the apostle Paul enlightens us to the meaning of the earthly tabernacle. The earthly tabernacle was a type of the true heavenly throne of God of which Christ is our high Priest. Heb. 10:1-18.

"But notice that God told Moses to make only *two* cherubim. Why only two if there were originally *three* cherubim that covered God's heavenly throne? The answer is astounding! God placed the great cherub Lucifer on the newly created, perfect earth, in charge of apparently a third of the angels. This Lucifer was a super being of awesome, majestic beauty, dazzling brightness, supreme knowledge, wisdom and power—perfect as God created him. God created Lucifer with the ability to have 'free choice' as He does with all of His created beings so they can make their own decisions. God's ultimate goal is for them to make the right choices, else they would not have individuality and character.

"In Isaiah 14:12-14 we read of what happened to Lucifer, the archangel that once covered God's throne. Starting in verse four, we read of the physical king of Babylon who is pictured as a grasping, conquering tyrant, who is the lesser or type, the great anti-type who controlled him—Satan the devil. You will notice that things are said of the great former cherub, Lucifer, who now becomes Satan the devil!

> ***How are you fallen from heaven, O Lucifer, son of the morning . . . who did weaken the nations?***

"The name Lucifer means 'shining one' or 'shining of the dawn.' He was the light bringer—the one who had tremendous truth, knowledge and understanding. He had been given authority over many angels and it was his responsibility to teach and to educate them. He was the Illuminator of his day.

"But what was his attitude towards the responsibilities and power he had been given by his Creator? *he wanted more power*! He became filled with jealousy, vanity, lust and greed. He wanted to take over the whole universe. He said in verse 13:

> *I will ascend into heaven. I will exalt my throne 'position of rulership' above the stars 'angels' of God. I will also sit upon the mount of the congregation in the sides of the north.*
>
> *Verse 14. I will ascend above the heights of the clouds, I will be like the most High.*

"In the original Hebrew the words should read: 'I will be the most high.' Lucifer wanted to be God! The total boss of the universe! This is how Lucifer became Satan the Devil. It was God who changed his name when Lucifer changed his character. More insight into this amazing truth is found in Ezekiel 28.

"Here again we see a human despot, this time it is the prince of Tyre, who is a human instrument in the hands of Satan, the real ruler of this world. Verses 2-6 plainly reveal that the prince was a 'sharp operator' who had accumulated a tremendous amount of wealth and power. In verses 12-16 we see the real power behind the throne—Satan.

"Please note, once again, just as in Isaiah 14, that these words can in no way apply to a mere mortal human being. Notice verse 13:

> *Thou hast been in Eden the garden of God ... thy tabrets and of thy pipes was prepared in thee in the day that thou wast created. Verse 14: Thou art the anointed*

> *cherub that covereth; and I have set thee so: thou wast upon the holy mountain of God; thou hast walked up and down in the midst of the stones of fire. Verse 15.*
>
> *Thou wast perfect in thy ways from the day that thou wast created, till iniquity 'sin' was found in thee. Verse 16.*

"This could not be speaking of the human king of Tyre, for he was never created. The only individuals that could possibly fulfill being created were Adam, Eve or Lucifer! All were created and in the Garden and all sinned! But the only one of these that was ever a cherub was Lucifer!

"The first sin, even before man's, was made by the angels. Lucifer sinned, Ezek. 28:16 and convinced one third of the angels to rebel with him against the throne of God. Rev. 12:4. Stars are symbolic for angels in the Bible as noted in Revelation. 1:20. In II Peter 2:4 we read:

> *For if God spared not the angels that sinned, but cast them down to hell 'Gr. Tartaros—a condition of restraint', and delivered them into chains 'restraint' of darkness, to be reserved unto judgment.*
>
> *Jude 6 sheds more light on this...**And the angels which kept not their first estate 'earth,' but left their own habitation, he hath reserved in everlasting chains under darkness unto the judgment of the great day.***

"What caused the angels on earth to sin, to turn to lawlessness? Certainly, the ordinary angels did not persuade Lucifer, this great super being, to turn on God. No, it was Lucifer that rebelled first and convinced one third of the angels to rebel with him. How long did this take after the angels were created is not known. God does not reveal this. It could have been one or less to millions of years! "How then did this Lucifer, this shining Star that God created become Satan the Devil is revealed in Isaiah 14: 12. Notice,

> *How art thou fallen from heaven, O Lucifer, son of the morning? How art thou cut down to the ground, which didst weaken the nations?*

"Jesus answers this question in Luke 10:18. *'And he said unto them, I beheld Satan as lightning fall from heaven.'* Jesus, remember, was there in His glorified form as God!

> *And there was war in heaven: Michael and his angels fought against the dragon; 'another name for Satan—Rev. 12:9' and the dragon fought and his angels. And prevailed not; neither was their place found any more in heaven. And the great dragon was cast out, that old serpent, called the Devil, and Satan, which deceiveth the whole world: he was cast into the earth, and his angels were cast out with him. Rev. 12:8-9.*

"The power of the Creator was loosed upon Lucifer and his angels with such terrible destructive force that he and his followers were blasted out of heaven and back to earth. Jude 6, II Pet. 2:4, Isa. 14:15. Lucifer's name was changed to Satan, which means enemy or adversary." Rev. 12:9.

Chapter Twenty

Doctor McNair continues the background of God's story as it unfolds with Jacob's end-time prophecy. "Let's continue this story in the Old Testament with the prophecies of Jacob and Moses concerning the twelve tribes and their descendants in the 'last days' that provide us with a clue to the revealing of the Antichrist as recorded in Genesis 49.

> *And Jacob called unto his sons, and said, Gather yourselves together, that I may tell you that which shall befall you in the last days. Gen. 49:1.*

"Now notice what Jacob prophesied of the tribe of Dan and why many prophetic writers believe the Antichrist will be a blood descendant from the tribe of Dan:

> *Dan shall judge his people, as one of the tribes of Israel. Dan shall be a serpent by the way, an adder in the path, that biteth the horse heels, so that his rider shall fall backward. I have waited for thy salvation, O LORD. Genesis 49:1, 16-18.*

"Notice, Jacob identified the tribe of Dan as a serpent!

"Moses also prophesied of the tribe of Dan, that Dan would emigrate from its territory in the northern part of Israel, which is today the Golan Heights, notice:

> **And this is the blessing, wherewith Moses the man of God blessed the children of Israel before his death... And of Dan he said, Dan is a lion's whelp: he shall leap from Bashan. Deuteronomy 33:1, 22.**

"These and other Scriptures further indicate that the Antichrist will most likely be from the tribe of Dan as we shall see, who is also possessed by demonic beings." *Smithe and Humphrey look at Father Benedetti and grin and he reciprocates!*

"This is where the story gets very interesting," says McNair.

"When the nation of Israel occupied the Promised Land, the tribe of Dan moved from their God-appointed territory on the coast to the Canaanite territory of northern Israel. There they occupied Leshem/Laish near *Mount Hermon*, which is also called Mount Sion. Joshua 19:40-48. Pay particularly attention to *Mount Hermon* as we will study this very important location.

"Well, before we continue our study in more depth, let us take a fifteen-minute break."

DI Smithe is beginning to be a believer in the spirit world. He recalls the scripture on Dr. Flanders's wall. 'For we wrestle not against flesh and blood, but against the rulers of the darkness of this world...'

***

As soon as the break begins, Smithe, Humphrey, Father Benedetti and Sara congregate in a discussion. Dr. McNair walks over to them and DI Smithe introduces Father Benedetti to him.

"This is Father Benedetti," says Smithe as he introduces him to Dr. McNair.

"Please to meet your Father," says McNair.

"I'm pleased to meet you as well," says Father Benedetti as he reaches out to shake McNair's hand. "I'm thoroughly enjoying your lecture as I have been warning people for years about the dangers of the spirit world," says Father Benedetti.

Smithe chimes in and says, "Yes Father Benedetti warned Humphrey and me after we visited him when we first realized this was no ordinary case, and wanted to know more about the occult. Because of his warning and your lectures, I have found out more about the spirit world myself as I have done my own research."

"What research was that," says McNair.

"In studying the history of Freemasonry, which uses a lot of symbolic or esoteric language as you know, many people have made an erroneous connection to the occult. It is true that they have many rituals that are based upon allegory, but too many have taken them literally and that is very dangerous.

"How is that?" inquires Father Benedetti."

"I have concluded that Freemasony is not a religion but more like a fraternity that encourages personal character development, much like Christianity. As one develops individual virtue through community service, he attains what is called a degree. Like many fraternities there are many, the most popular is the York Rite and the Scottish Rite. The Scottish Rite attains the last degree one can earn as the 33rd. One can earn all 32 degrees in a single eight-hour class, but only about 20% of members attain the 33rd degree which is an honorary degree given for exceptional service."

"I still don't see the occult connection," says Benedetti.

"I found out that when King Louis XIV of France had an observatory built in 1666 to measure longitude, called the Paris Zero Meridian, the ancient territory of Dan and Mount Hermon were located 33 degrees east of the Paris Meridian, and get this, 33 degrees north of the Equator."

"That is truly amazing," says Sara.

"So, the number 33 is the connection." says Father Benedetti.

"Yes, the pieces are starting to fall into place. Well, I guess I better start the rest of my lecture," says McNair as he walks up to the microphone and welcomes everyone back.

"Let's continue with our story of the renegade tribe of Dan. In Judges 1:34, we find the tribe of Dan was defeated by the Amorites:

> **And the Amorites forced the children of Dan into the mountain: for they would not suffer 'permit' them to come down to the valley: But the Amorites would dwell in mount Heres in Aijalon, and in Shaalbim: yet the hand of the house of Joseph prevailed, so that they became tributaries. Judges 1:34-35.**

"Who were these Amorites that forced the children of Dan into the mountain? This is very important to our study. Many Bible scholars believe the Amorites were *Nephilim* or the seed of fallen angels, whose great height was described by the prophet Amos:

> **I destroyed the Amorites, though they were as tall as cedars and as strong as oaks. I destroyed the fruit on their branches and dug out their roots. Amos 2:9.**

"God had commanded the Israelites to destroy the Amorites who were described as 'tall as cedars,' and also the inhabitants of Bashan, which was called the land of giants where the giant Og lived as recorded in Deuteronomy. 3:13.

"Believe it or not, Bashan is mentioned 60 times in the Old Testament. It was the name of the region east of the Jordan River, which is, in part, today called the Golan Heights. It was known as good cattle grazing land and was the very land into which the tribes of Reuben, Dan and Manasseh chose to settle. Numbers 32:1-5.

"Bashan was a kingdom and its king was named Og. We hear of him 22 times in the Old Testament but learn little about him, except that he and his people were the Rephaim, a remnant of the giants, also known in Hebrew as the 'walking dead.' These can be traced to Genesis 6:4 where Moses tells us:

> ***That the sons of God saw the daughters of men that they were fair, and they took them wives of all which these chose... There were giants in the earth in those days, and also after that when the sons of God came unto the daughters of men, and they bear children to them, the same became mighty men which were of old, men of renown.***

Chapter Twenty-One

Dr. McNair has just explained that there is a scripture in the Bible indicating that angels can procreate and is very strange and difficult to accept.

"But that is precisely what Scripture says. The Hebrew word '*Bene Ha Eloheim*' always means angels in the Old Testament. Some point to Matthew 22:3 as evidence that angels cannot have sex, because Jesus said, 'they neither marry nor are given in marriage, but are like the angels of God in heaven.' However, this says nothing about the capabilities of angels.

"We can now also see why God ordered them and other tribes of similar lineage such as the Anakins, Numbers 13:33, to be utterly destroyed as He Himself destroyed those who polluted the earth before the flood. Scripture records that Jesus dealt a great deal with demons.

"The area in which Jesus preached as part of His ministry was heavily populated with them, there being as many as 2000 in the one man called Legion. All of the demons knew Jesus and knew His mission. Mark 5:7. They also knew their ultimate destiny, as they complained to Him that their time had not yet come. Matthew 8:31.

"Scripture tells us demons exist and that they seek to occupy human bodies, unlike angels who are capable of appearing in human form without invading human bodies. Satan and his legions of demons have deluded the world and oppose God's plan by influencing world art, literature, music, education, politics, as well as religion. They also accomplish their purpose through direct possession of the minds and bodies of individuals."

***

Once again DI Smithe and DC Humphrey look over to Father Benedetti and nod. Father Benedetti smiles back with a big grin. Dr. McNair sees them grinning at each other and tells the audience that they have the privilege of having Father Benedetti in the audience who is experienced in this sort of thing and invites him to say a few words on this subject. Father Benedetti comes up to the lectern and says.

"Thank you, Dr. McNair. It is important to distinguish between 'demon possession' or control and 'demon influence.' To demon possession mostly unbelievers are exposed; to demon influence, both believers and non-believers are exposed. In order to conquer Satan and overcome his influence, we must understand how he operates.

"In 'demon possession' the personality is literally invaded, the body inhabited by a fallen angel, and dominating control is gained. No one choosing God's way can be invaded by the forces of darkness. It is only as the enlightened deliberately choose darkness or sin, that he exposes himself to demonic influence."

***

Father Benedetti thanks Dr. McNair and steps down. Dr. McNair thanks Father Benedetti for his insight and continues with his lecture.

"It was Saul's repeated deliberate rebellion and disobedience to God's divine will, 1 Sam. 3:13, 15:22,23 that rendered his weakened will susceptible to demonic influence 1 Sam. 16:14. Josephus, the Jewish historian attributes Saul's persecution mania to actual demon possession in his book, *Antiquities of the Jews*, 6:8:2, 6:11:2.

"Job was turned over to Satan because he needed to learn a spiritual lesson. Job 1:8. The apostle Paul turned one over to Satan in the early church to save his eternal life 11 Cor. 5:5. Satan does not, however, have power to touch Christians as Father Benedetti said, who do not practice sin. 1 John. 5:18. But the non-believing are his to utilize at his will 11 Tim. 2:26.

"Demons, which are fallen angels that were originally created by Jesus Christ, possess along with all God's created beings, personality, intelligence and are voluntary agents. It would appear that they would also have individual names like Legion, as did the angels such as Gabriel, Michael and Lucifer.

"Demons knew Jesus very well, since He created them and stood in deep respect of His name and called Him 'Son of the High God' Mark 5:7, Luke 4:34, Mark 1:24. They even bow before Him. Mark 5:6, 3:11. They believe that there is one God. James 2:19. They asked His permission to go into the swine. Mark 5:10. They obey Jesus completely. Matt. 8:16, 3:11. They know and are aware of their own doom. Matt. 8:29.

"Jesus spoke of Satan as a 'murderer' in John 8:44, notice:

> ***You are of your father the devil and the lusts of your father ye will do. He was a murderer from the beginning and abode not in the truth, because there is no truth in him: when he speaketh a lie, he speaketh of his own: for he is a liar and the father of it.***

"Realize, the Bible says Satan was a murderer from the beginning—but where? When?

> ***For this is the message that ye heard from the beginning, that we should love one another. Not as Cain, who was of that wicked one, and slew his brother. 1 John. 3:11-12.***

"It was Satan's influence that made Cain kill his brother! Jesus, very plainly tells us Satan is a murderer! Murder is not something that is natural to man—It is satanically inspired by demon possession or demon influence!

"Not in all cases, but Demons can make one try to kill himself, like the boy who tried to tear himself or fall into the fire and water, Matt. 17:14-18, or by cutting oneself with stones, Mark. 5:1-5 or any kind of suicide.

"Remember it was Satan that entered into Judas personally, Luke 22:3 and he tried to kill Jesus Christ! He wanted to destroy Peter, but Christ wouldn't let him.

"It was Satan who tried to kill Moses through Pharaoh when he was a baby. It was Satan that tried to kill Jesus when He was a baby through Herod and by trying to taunt Him into jumping off a pinnacle of the temple. Matt. 4:5. The apostle Paul knew that Satan would try to destroy a man's flesh if he were put out of God's Church. 1 Cor. 5:5. It will be Satan's armies that will kill the Two Witnesses of God prior to Christ's return. Rev. 11.

"We must recognize that these demon spirits exist, and that some of them populated Bashan. There is a photo of a winged bull found in the Persian palace of Cyrus and now found in the Louvre. One must wonder if this was what a fallen angel looked like as we read what the cherubs looked like in Ezekiel as they transported God's throne!

"Mount Hermon/Sion, also known as Mount Baal-Hermon, is located at the 33rd degree latitude and longitude of the Paris Zero Meridian. According to the Book of Enoch, the fallen angels descended on the summit of Mount Hermon and mated with human women. Here is what is written about them in the book of Enoch:

> *And the angels, the children of heaven, saw them 'handsome and beautiful daughters' and desired them... And they were altogether two hundred; and they descended into Ardos, which is the summit of Hermon. And they called the mount Armon, for they swore and bound one another by a curse. I Enoch VI.6, vs.1-5.*

Chapter Twenty-Two

Dr. McNair has just provided scripture reference that **the offspring of the unholy union** between demons and human woman were destroyed in the flood. "However, according to Genesis 6:4, there was a second invasion of fallen angels who mated with the Canaanite women:

> *And GOD saw that the wickedness of man was great in the earth, and that every imagination of the thoughts of his heart was only evil continually. Gen. 6:4-5.*

'After that' seems to refer to Numbers 13:31-33, where in the report of the spies to Moses they speak of the men of Canaan as of *'great stature,'* adding: *'And there we saw the nephilim, the sons of Anak which come of the nephilim.'*

"According to *Gray's Concise Bible Commentary,* this suggests that the culminating sin of the Canaanites was not different from that of the antediluvians. Observe further that the offspring of these sinful unions became *the 'mighty men which were of old, the men of renown.'* Most likely, this is where the ancient classics got their ideas of the gods and demi-gods.

"Here is what the *Pulpit Commentary, Part 9: Appendix 23 & 25* says of them: *'giants. Heb. Nephilim'* Those mentioned in Gen, 6:4 were all destroyed in the Flood; these came from a second irruption of fallen angels, 'after that': or after 'those days' = the days of Noah.

"Prophetic author J.R. Church writes on page 76 of his book, *Daniel Reveals the Blood Line of the Antichrist:*

> *Moreover, the tribe of Dan led the other nine tribes into the idolatrous worship of the Canaanites: In the region of northern Israel, the tribe of Dan readily adopted the pre-flood Baal worship of the Canaanites, who were the descendants of Ham and his cursed son, Canaan. As stated above, 'It is certainly observable that the first introduction of idolatry in Israel is ascribed to the tribe of Dan. Judges 18.' There in the Canaanite area of Mount Hermon, the tribe of Dan intermarried with the Canaanites, who were offspring of the Nephilim. Jacob's prophecy implied that Dan would therefore become the offspring or seed of the Serpent, Satan.*

"In the Bible, Bashan is linked to the Nephilim. Og was king of Bashan and he was described as being 9 cubits '14 feet' tall. For only Og king of Bashan remained of the remnant of giants; behold, his bedstead was a bedstead of iron; is it not in Rabbath of the children of Ammon? nine cubits was the length thereof, and four cubits the breadth of it, after the cubit of a man. Deut. 3:11.

"The Bible tells us that there is going to come a head-on collision between the Satanic powers of pagan darkness of centuries, with strong demonic activity focusing on the supernatural as the end of this dark age draws near. To this end 'the man of sin,' or 'the son of perdition' who opposes and exalts himself against every so-called object of worship so that he takes his seat in the temple of God will proclaim himself to be God. 11 Thes. 2:3-4.

"Power will be given to him over all kindreds, and tongues and nations Rev. 13:8. He will inaugurate a world-wide reign of terror, blasphemy, and murder.

> *He shall speak words against the Most High, and shall wear out the saints of the Most High, and think to change times and laws.* **Dan. 7:25.**

"It will be Satan's supreme and most desperate attempt to be 'like the Most High.' Isa. 14:14.

> *And then shall that wicked one be revealed, whom the Lord shall consume with the spirit of his mouth and shall destroy with the brightness of his coming. Even him, whose coming is after the working of Satan with all power and signs and lying wonders. And for this cause God shall send them strong delusion, that they should believe a lie.* **II Thes. 2:8-9, 11.**

> *And I saw three unclean spirits like frogs come out of the mouth of the beast, and out of the mouth of the false prophet. For they are the spirits of devils 'demons' working miracles, which go forth unto the kings of the earth and of the whole world, to gather them to the battle of that great day of God Almighty.* **Rev. 16:13-14.**

"When Christ returns, the Devil and his demons will not be able to deceive the world any longer. Rev. 20:2-3. In Matthew 12:26, Jesus confirms the fact that Satan has a Kingdom*: 'And if Satan cast out Satan, he is divided himself: How shall then his kingdom stand?'* Jesus calls him 'the prince of this world' *age* in John 12:31, 14:30, 16:11. also 1 John 5:19, John 7:7, 14:27, 1 Cor. 1:21, 11:32, 1 5:9, 1 John 3:1, 13.

"Further, the apostle Paul tells of Satan's world in Ephesians 6:1;

> *For we wrestle 'contend' not against flesh and blood 'humans', but against principalities, against powers, against rulers of the darkness of this world 'age', against wickedness 'wicked spirits' in high places.*

Chapter Twenty-Three

DI Smithe and DC Humphrey look at each other and nod as they recall the scripture on the wall in Dr. Flanders office, as Dr. McNair continues his lecture.

"The apostle John connects the 'spirit of antichrist' with 'the world' or the Satanic system 1 John 4:3. John declares that 'whatsoever is born of God, overcomes the world' or Satan's system. 1 John 5:4.

"I have just mentioned that certain 'sons of God' descended to the summit of Mount Hermon and lived for a while among men, taking human wives and producing 'giants.'

"In addition to the biblical account, several ancient sources mention these Nephilim, including Rabbinic literature, the Zohar, and the Book of Enoch. God incarcerated those fallen angels in *Hell*, where the Greek word *Tartarus*, is used which means, a subterranean abyss or 'bottomless pit.' Rev. 9:1,2. As previously mentioned, their human offspring were destroyed in the flood. However, Genesis indicates that another group of these fallen angels descended after the flood and continued their abominable practices. They also established a form of idolatrous worship, known as the Canaanite religion of Baal and Ashtaroth.

"The Jewish Talmud informs us that Nimrod was a mighty man or tyrant on earth, after the flood. In Genesis 6 we find the curious story of the invasion of the 'sons of God' into the human race, that resulted in a race of giants called Nephilim. Apparently, Nimrod was one of these 'mighty men,' that introduced a false system of religious worship into the world. From Babylon, it spread to Nineveh, and then to the rest of the world.

"The Prophet Daniel offered a very strange statement concerning the iron and clay in his famous explanation of King Nebuchadnezzar's dream. It may be a reference to the perverted sexual relationship between physical humans and these renegade angels, notice:

> **And whereas thou sawest iron mixed with miry clay, they shall mingle themselves with the seed of men: but they shall not cleave one to another, even as iron is not mixed with clay. Dan. 2:43.**

"He said that *they* would mingle with *'the seed of men'*. It is possible that he was referring to a situation similar to the one that occurred in the days before the Flood, when the 'sons of God' or fallen angels, took human wives. Ancient sources tell us that fallen angels descended to the summit of Mount Hermon and lived in the area that eventually became the territory of Dan.

"According to the *Encyclopedia Britannica*, Hermon means 'forbidden place.' Jerome, the 4th-century translator of the *Latin Vulgate Bible*, interpreted Hermon as 'anathema.' Evidently, mount Hermon was the port of entry for a group of wicked angels, who corrupted the human race in the days of Noah.

"The apocryphal *Books of Enoch* and *Barnabus* enlarge upon the story of the Nephilim. Although these have been called apocryphal Books among the Apostolic leaders, the *Epistle of Barnabas* has been referred to by the early theologians Justin Martyr, Clement of Alexandria, Origen, Irenaeus, Tertullian, Eusebius, Jerome, Hilary, Epiphanius, Augustine, and others.

"The books of II Peter and Jude add further insight about the fate of these fallen angels. The apostle Peter wrote of them:

> *God spared not the angels that sinned, but cast them down to hell 'Greek, Tartarus, meaning a place of restraint', and delivered them into chains of darkness, to be reserved unto judgment; and spared not the old world, but saved Noah the eighth person, a preacher of righteousness, bringing in the flood upon the world of the ungodly. II Peter 2:4,5.*

"Jude put it this way:

> *And the angels which kept not their first estate 'Heaven', but left their habitation, he hath reserved in everlasting chains under 'darkness' unto the judgment of the great day. Jude 6.*

"Both passages tell of severe punishment upon the fallen angels or what the Bible calls demons. Yet, Moses said that 'sons of God' reappeared after the Flood Gen. 6:4. How can this be? We find the answer in Genesis 6:4:…" *and also after that"*, meaning after the flood more fallen angels returned to the earth and established what Joshua called the 'land of giants.' Moses and Joshua conquered those giants, of whom, Og was king in Mount Hermon. Joshua wrote:

> *And the coast of Og king of Bashan, which was of the remnant of the giants, that dwelt at Ashtaroth and at Edrei, and reigned in mount Hermon, and in Salcah, and in all Bashan, unto the border of the Geshurites and the Maachathites, and half Gilead, the border of Sihon king of Heshbon. Them did Moses the servant of the LORD and the children of Israel smite. Joshua 12:4-6.*

"The tribe of Dan moved to this area during the days of the Judges, and adopted the Canaanite worship of these angels. It was an ancient idolatry that opposed the worship of God. In fact, Baal and Ashtaroth were Canaanite deities, whose origin began in the vacinity of *Mount Hermon!* The book of Judges even calls Mount Hermon 'Baalhermon,' saying:

Namely, five lords of the Philistines, and all the Canaanites, the Sidonians, and the Hivites that dwelt in mount Lebanon, from mount Baalhermon unto the entering in of Hamath. Judges 3:3.

"It is evident from this nefarious history, the devil was determined to replace the *seed* of the woman with the *seed* of the serpent.

"When the Israelite spies explored the land in Numbers 13:33 they reported seeing giants or Anakim. Here is how they described them, notice:

And there we saw the giants, the sons of Anak, which come of the giants: and we were in our own sight as grasshoppers, and so we were in their sight.

"The human race has never seen a battle between angels and demons before. It is a subject most theologians would rather not talk about. However, there appears to be scriptures that support a past and future battle. Scriptures tell us that the Antichrist will be possessed and not completely human."

Chapter Twenty-Four

The bell rings as John walks eagerly to his classroom in a Catholic school for boys.. At thirteen, John is rather large for his age, and he is destined to be pope someday. John rushes into the classroom and sits at a desk in the far-left corner. Sweat drips down his brow and he pushes up his thick wire-rimmed glasses. He pulls out his books and the teacher begins the lesson on doctrines.

Concurrently, Simonides is reciting the Hebrew scriptures and preparing for his bar mitzvah in a synagogue. At thirteen, Simonides is also large for his age. He wears thick wire-rimmed glasses, has black hair, and is dressed in a black suit with black tie. A Jewish boy is considered to be an adult when he turns thirteen. The occasion is marked by him becoming a bar mitzvah, which means he is a son of the commandments. He is destined to be the future Prime Minister and high priest of Israel.

Rabbi Feineberg stands at the altar and finishes his reading. He looks over at the young boy. "Simonides, please come forward to read the Torah scroll."

Simonides recites the commandments that make up the Jewish law. His father recites to his son, "My God-given son Simonides, I give my blessing to you and thank God that he has now freed you from sin, and I rejoice along with all of my family and friends that on this day you have become a man."

Simonides's parents arrange a *Seudah* meal for him and family and friends join them after the ceremony at which the boy delivers a sermon of thanks. Simonides is showered with gifts. He feels elated that he is finally considered a man in the eyes of God.

Years pass, and the two boys have grown into adults and their careers are flourishing in their respective faiths. John, now twenty-seven, stands at seven-two and is being ordained as a priest in the Catholic faith.

Similarly, Simonides, age twenty-seven, stands at a whopping seven-two and is being ordained as a Rabbi.

The years fly by, and Father John, now forty-five, is being ordained a Cardinal in the Catholic Church in Vatican City. He is dressed in traditional red garments along with sixty-nine other priests.

Simonides, now forty-five, is being ordained as High Priest in Israel. He is dressed in white garments and addresses the crowd assembled at the newly rebuilt Jerusalem temple.

Five more years pass, and Simonides is fifty years old. He has gray hair and a peppered beard. He is dressed in white vesture clothing that is worn by the High Priest of Israel. It is Yom Kippur, and he is standing near the Temple and says a prayer before the gathered crowd who have come to worship on this most sacred holy day.

Meanwhile, Father John stands at the altar in a Catholic church. Sunlight shines through the stained-glass windows. The church is packed with people on Easter Sunday. He is fifty years old, clean shaven, with gray hair and a circular bald spot on the back of his head. He looks up to the heavens and holds a piece of wafer in his hand as he recites a prayer in Latin and prepares to give communion to the faithful during Mass.

Father John is dressed in traditional white clergy robes with miter for this is a special Easter-Sunday service. He has on gold vestures.

For over five decades, two men have lived their lives by their faith, praying to a god they believe in, and helping others discover and find their spirituality. But under the surface lurks a dark force, churning to break free . . . and one of these men will eventually succumb to it, becoming the Antichrist.

Chapter Twenty-Five

It is a beautiful fall day as the sun peeks through the leaves, casting shadows on the ground. The air is crisp and fresh. Smithe is sitting on his patio sipping on a cup of black bitter coffee and reading the morning paper when he is startled by what he reads.

"Bloody hell," he says. He quickly calls McNair. After three rings, he picks up.

"Have you seen the morning paper yet?" Smithe asks.

"No, I haven't. What's going on?" McNair responds with a yawn. It's barely eight and the two cups of coffee he's had are burning his insides.

Smithe holds the paper in front of him and recites the story to McNair.

With rates near zero, the Feds mulls its options as High Priest Simonides provides solution

Policymakers digging in the Feds' toolbox for ways to jolt economy.
The Washington Press
Updated 8:22 a.m. ET, Wed., March 18, 2019
WASHINGTON, DC — With a key interest rate already near zero, Federal Reserve policymakers are weighing what other tools they can use to jolt the country out of recession.

Fed Chairman Benjamin Yokoloff and his colleagues resume their two-day meeting Wednesday with Simonides, a High Priest in Israel, and at its conclusion they are all but certain to leave a key bank lending rate at a record low to try to bolster the economy, which has been stuck in a recession since December.

After Smithe finishes, he sighs. Since the day one, this case has been nothing but a headache. "It's happening, isn't it?"

"Yes, it appears so," McNair huffs. "We need to act fast! It seems Simonides is making his move. Our organization, the Christian Crusaders for Christ, has been very busy these last few years collecting DNA samples from all of the bones we found in the king's chamber at Tara. I believe we have found the remains of King Heremon and Teia, and if we can match their DNA to a modern descendant, I believe God will give the descendant the power to counter the wiles of the devil as he works through Simonides."

"But who could be of their bloodline? Where can they be?" Smithe asks. Then it dawns on him. "Could Sara be of the royal bloodline?"

"Yes, I believe Sara is the key," McNair states.

Smithe furiously rubs his forehead in an attempt to make sense of it all. "How do you mean?"

McNair collapses into a large blue chair and takes a few deep breaths to slow his breathing. There's a lot of information to spew out, and he's been told that he has a habit of talking too fast. There's also a lot at stake, and with each day, they seem closer to the truth. In a slow manner, McNair says,

"Our molecular geneticist lab has confirmed that all of the bones found in the king's chamber at Tara are a match. Therefore, all of them represent the kingly lineage to King David."

"Are you absolutely positively sure? Sometimes DNA can be contaminated and can be bullocks," Smithe says.

"Done correctly, Forensic evidence doesn't lie!" McNair snaps. "Our evidence is based upon Mitochondrial DNA, which is only passed down from mothers to their children. It's not just two hundred to four hundred building blocks of DNA molecules, but sixteen thousand or more base pairs."

Smithe grunts in frustration. "Professor, please talk in laymen's terms."

"Well, think of it this way. Its like comparing random sentences to having all the chapters of a book. We were especially fortunate that the DNA samples were not destroyed by sunlight as they were well preserved below the ground."

Smithe clicks his tongue. It made sense. Sentences on their own can have more meaning when they are part of a chapter. "I get it," he says.

"Another key connection came through the male Y chromosomes. The lab compared the bones of the males, and all of the Y-chromosome markers from the males matched!"

"Okay, let me get this straight," Smithe says. He takes a sip of his lukewarm coffee. "So, you have what most likely represents the kingly line of King David, but how is that going to determine who and where that lineage is today?"

McNair smiles. "Basically, we have determined that the DNA of the King Heremon, Queen Teia, and the Tudor–Stuart lineages going all the way back to Queen Elizabeth I are a perfect match."

Frustration flares up once more and Smithe clenches his right hand into a fist. Sometimes he lacks the patience, especially when it seems that the professor could easily—and quickly—get to the point. "Okay, so you have a lot of matching DNA samples of past generations, but how is that going to help us with this case?"

"By comparing existing DNA databases of the descendants of King James from various populations we can find a match in the Stuart line of today," McNair responds.

Smithe is confused. "Why pursue the King James lineage of the Stuart dynasty and not Queen Elizabeth of the Tudor dynasty?" he says.

"Because Queen Elizabeth I never married and was known to be a virgin."

Smithe chuckles. *Of course, the Virgin Queen.* "Okay, where do we start looking for this modern-day kingly descendant?" he asks.

"We started with the children of King James I. Of the seven children, only two survived that lived longer than age eighteen. Elizabeth of Bohemia died at age sixty-five. The other was Charles I of England, who was executed at age forty-eight. We have traced their bloodlines and have gotten nowhere. Although Elizabeth and Charles had children, we were unable to locate their remains. It seems the trail ended with them, but we are still searching for possible descendants."

"Where does that leave us?" Smithe inquires.

"It leaves us searching for another clue. As I said earlier, I think Sara is the key."

"What do you mean by that? How does she figure in?" Smithe asks.

McNair sits up in his chair and puts his cellphone on speaker. His heart races. "Remember when I said that our organization took the ashes of Sara's father Alexander when he died? Well, our lab found that Alexander, as well as Sara's DNA, match the DNA of the Heremon and Teia lineage going back to King Zedekiah and King David. They also match the Stuart lineage DNA of all the kings and queens of England, Scotland, and Ireland."

Smithe gasps. "Incredible! So, you think Sara has these . . . hidden powers . . . to stop this madman antichrist who wants to kill anyone who disagrees with his way of life?"

"No, I don't because it seems that the powers of past lineages of kings were of the male gender to be a future king. But we have another lineage to pursue because of a recent archeological find."

"What is that?"

"The discovery of King Richard III's skeleton!"

Smithe nods. "I read about that a few years ago."

"Then you know that the DNA analysis supports the claim that a skeleton dug up from beneath a parking lot in the English city of Leicester represents the mortal remains of King Richard III, according to British experts. It's the academic conclusion of the University of Leicester that beyond reasonable doubt the individual exhumed at Greyfriars in September 2012 is indeed Richard III, the last Plantagenet king of England."

"That does sound like a good lead, but getting back to Sara's possible connection, where does that leave us since Sara is not married and doesn't have any children?" Smithe asks.

"Yes, I realize that, but she may hold the key to her father's past as she has informed me of some very intimate things. Let's go have a talk with her. I'll call her and arrange for a meeting,"

"Sounds good, let me know when." Smithe agrees as they both say good-bye and hang up.

Smithe takes another sip of his coffee and leans back in his chair. *It's going to be another long day*, he thinks, but at least they are one step closer to the truth.

Chapter Twenty-Six

It's a blustery morning and the sun is shining as Smithe pulls up to Sara's house. He walks up the manicured walkway that's brimming with orange and yellow flowers and knocks on the door. McNair comes to the door and welcomes him inside.

From a distance, Sara says in an excited voice, "Come in, Detective, I can hardly wait to hear the new evidence Robert has, and I have something to show you as well!"

McNair smiles eagerly. "You go first, Sara, what did you want to tell us?"

Sara enters the room and says hello to Smithe and gives him a big bear hug. Then she motions for the men to sit down in the living room. A pot of tea and three teacups and saucers with flower designs sits on the coffee table. The tea is hot and bitter, but Smithe gulps it down regardless.

"You said you may have some new evidence linking me to the kingly bloodline of King Heremon and Queen Teia," Sara says.

"Yes, Sara . . . we think you are the key to stopping the antichrist, and that key is in your bloodline through DNA evidence that our lab has verified." Says McNair as he obliges.

Sara is dumbfounded. She looks at Smithe and then to McNair, and she looks away. A picture of her father sits on the fireplace mantle. He's standing next to Sara smiling and holding up a large gray fish, a trophy he pulled out of the river on a weekend getaway with Sara. Sara will never forget the look on his face when he pulled the fish out of the water. His blue eyes sparkled and he laughed that deep belly laugh that she always loved.

McNair places his teacup down on the saucer with a shaky hand. "Your DNA is identical to all the kings and queens of England, Scotland, and Ireland, which also matches the DNA of the Heremon and Teia lineage all the way back to King David."

Bewildered, Sara is silent for a moment. She can hear her father's voice in her head. "Wow! I guess my father was right about our ancestry." She stands up quickly and rushes down the hallway. She comes back a moment later carrying a few things in her arms.

"Now I will show you something," Sara says. "I have been looking through Father's things and I found some very interesting paintings. Look at this one first."

Sara gently places the painting on the coffee table and unwraps it. The painting is of Queen Teia holding a cat. The paint on the canvas is thick and cracked, and it smells dusty and old. At the bottom is an inscription that reads, *'Fromm'*.

"Wow, that is old," Smithe says as he examines the painting. "That's a very nice painting of Queen Teia and she is very beautiful. But how does that link you to the kingly bloodline?"

Sara then reveals another painting of Queen Elizabeth I. She looks stern and upright in her royal garb. The inscription at the bottom reads, *'From.'*

"Now I'm going to play detective, gentleman," Sara says. "Do you see anything that is common to both paintings and yet very unusual?"

McNair and Smithe look intensely at the paintings.

Smithe replies, "Can't say that I can. I don't see anything unusual about the queens. They both seem to like cats."

"I agree with Smithe," McNair says.

Smithe widens his eyes as he notices a detail he didn't see before. "It's the same big, bushy cat!" he exclaims.

"Yes!" McNair chimes in.

"That's correct, gentleman, but that is no ordinary cat. Do you see the unusual spelling of the word *'from'* on the bottom of the painting of Queen Teia?" Sara says.

Observant, Smithe utters, "Yeah, but I just thought whoever painted it made a mistake."

McNair articulates, "That lettering is Old Irish! It was thought that certain words, numbers, grammatical marks, and individual letters on inscriptions were not found among English writing until the fourteenth-century. So, this painting gives credence to the time period going back to King Heremon and Teia."

"That's right Robert, but there is more to substantiate our premise. This cat, with its unusually large dark brown and white bushy tail and hind legs that resemble a raccoon, is no ordinary cat."

Surprised, McNair interjects, "I didn't look at it closely before, but it looks like a rare Norwegian Coon cat. Is it, Sara?"

"Yes, it is, Robert."

Smithe is confused and asks sheepishly, "What's a Coon cat?"

"It's a very rare breed of cat that has been considered extinct. The Coon cat was believed to be a cross between a raccoon and a cat," McNair explains.

Sara quickly stands up and says, "Hold that thought, Detective," as she leaves the room and returns with a cat.

"What on earth!" Smithe says.

"This is our cat Bessy, and she has been in our family for as long as I can remember. Father said the cat is like a family logo. Over the years, we have been breeding her with a family that only my father knows."

"I'll bet if we find out who they are we'll find another relative of yours," McNair says. "Perhaps a relative who has some psychic powers to stop this antichrist Simonides. Sara, maybe it's you who has these powers. Did you ever read tarot cards or have telepathic powers to move objects?"

Sara provides a clue

"No, I have never felt any unusual power in my life," Sara says, furrowing her brow in confusion.

McNair chimes in, "I don't think it is you who possesses this supernatural power, but perhaps a relative of yours or a bloodline from your father. Is there anything or anyone in his past that you know that might carry his genes?"

"Well, as far as I know he didn't have any brothers or sisters, but..."

Sara scrunches her nose to keep the tears from falling. Whenever she thinks of her father, she feels a deep sense of sadness. It wasn't fair what had happened to him. She never got the chance to say goodbye.

"Well, right after my mother passed away, my father told me that when he started his first job, long before he met my mother, he had an affair with a woman whom he wanted to marry, but when she got pregnant, she disappeared."

"What do you mean she disappeared?" Smithe asks.

Sara sighs. "My father told me she was pregnant with his child and that she might have had an abortion or she might have had the baby. I don't know. I may have a brother or sister somewhere. I don't even know if my father knew anything, and if he did, he never told me about it."

"Did he tell you the woman's name?" Smithe asks. "Did he ever try to find her?"

"No, he didn't want to talk about it so I dropped it," Sara says, frustrated.

Smithe continues his interrogation as respectful as he can be, knowing this is a sensitive issue. "Did he say where she worked?"

"No, but I know his first job was at the British Museum as curator of the Middle Eastern Arts."

"That's a start," Smithe says. "Thanks for the lead. I'll get down there right away."

"I'm going too," McNair declares.

"Don't think you're going without me," Sara echoes. She is not about to be left out.

Chapter Twenty-Seven

The next morning, before the sun rises, the troop arrive at the **British Museum**, an ornate building with tall columns. They scurry the 72 concrete steps leading to the museums grand entrance. Smithe is gasping for air and nearly out of breath as he is the oldest and a little out of shape,

"I thought climbing the hill of Tara was tough, but that was a piece of cake," he exclaims. When they approach the front desk, they ask the secretary to see the administrator.

"Do you have an appointment?" she asks.

Smithe shows her his badge. "Ms. Kelly is expecting us. I called earlier."

The secretary picks up her phone and dials a few numbers. After a brief moment, she hangs up and says, "Administrator Kelly is on her way."

After a brief wait, an attractive woman walks up to the trio. Katherine Kelly is sixty-five and her gray hair is tied up into a bun at the base of her neck. Her face and eyes are kind. "I understand you want to see me. What is this regarding?"

Smithe nods and holds up his badge. Politely, he says, "Yes, Ms. Kelly, I'm Detective Smithe and this is Dr. McNair and Sara Flanders. I would like to ask you a few questions regarding a case I am investigating."

Kelly squints her eyes and looks confused. "Okay . . . how can I help?"

Impatient, Sara chimes in, "Do you know of a man named Alexander Flanders? He worked here some fifty years ago. He is my father."

Kelly is startled as she looks at Sara, and then she raises her eyebrows. "Why yes, I remember Alex. Wow, that takes me back." She looks over Sara's face. "So, you are Alex's daughter? Well, I can certainly see the resemblance. You have his eyes. Yes, I knew your father very well. I hope he is quite well." Suddenly, her face drops. "Nothing has happened to him, has it?"

Somber, Sara informs Kelly that her father died, but she doesn't go into the detail about what happened because it's just too painful.

Kelly stares at Sara in shock and tries to compose herself. "Oh, oh . . . I'm so sorry to hear that. I really loved . . . I mean, I was very fond of your father."

Smithe notices that Kelly's cheeks have turned red. *'She's stumbling over her words,'* he thinks. *She knows more than she is implying.* He clears his throat and says, "I must ask you some more questions, Ms. Kelly. Is there somewhere more private?"

"Oh, why yes, of course," Kelly says. "Follow me."

They venture down a long hallway that is lined with various paintings and approach an empty conference room. Kelly turns on the light and shuts the door behind them. They all have a seat at the table.

Smithe bluntly asks, "Do you know if Alexander Flanders had a girlfriend while he worked here?"

"Well, well . . . yes! In fact, we dated for over a year," Kelly says. Her cheeks are burning.

'I knew it,' Smithe thinks. After years of being on the force and countless cases, he is able to read people before they even spoke a word. Smithe leans forward and says, "Sara told us that her father said the woman he was once in love with worked here and that she was pregnant at the time. Do you know anything about that?"

Kelly remains silent, and then she starts crying. Sara and McNair look confused, but Smithe knows he has pushed the right buttons.

Kelly turns to Sara and says, "Your father told you that he was in love with me?"

Sara gasps. "Wait . . . are you . . . ?"

"If you have the time, I would like to show you something that I think you will find very interesting," Kelly says.

At that, everyone stands up in unison and follows Kelly down a long hallway. Smithe is feeling anxious. Sara looks as if she's seen a ghost.

Kelly leads them to the parking lot and invites them all to her car.

"Where are we going?" Smithe asks. He doesn't like surprises.

"Please trust me."

Reluctantly, Smithe agrees. Kelly winds down tree-lined streets, and after a few moments, they arrive at a Catholic church. Once inside, they follow Kelly past the podium to the sanctuary where a priest is sitting behind a desk. When he sees them, he smiles and gives Kelly a big hug and a kiss.

"Hello, Mother, what are you doing here? And who are these wonderful people?"

"This is my son, John," Kelly says.

Smithe, McNair, and Sara stare at Father John in astonishment. Sara can't believe her eyes. He looks so familiar . . . his eyes, his brow, his nose. *Can it be?* she thinks.

"Will you please tell us what's going on here, Kelly?" Smithe says impatiently.

"I think it is quite obvious, don't you? Sara and John are stepbrother and sister." Kelly turns to Sara. "I loved your father," she says.

"I think we all need to sit down and have a cup of coffee," Smithe says.

"Yes, that would be perfect. Come with me," Father John says.

Father John leads them down the hall to a quiet room set up for visitors with snacks and coffee. They all take a seat. Sara is shaking. She can't believe this is happening. She and

Sara meets her father's old flame

her father were close—they told each other everything—but never in her wildest dreams has she imagined that one day she would be reunited with a long-lost sibling.

Chapter Twenty-Eight

Kelly looks around the room and tries not to linger on Sara's face. *'She thinks she looks so much like Alex.'* She thinks of their past relationship and what could have been and bites back tears. After mustering up the courage, she clears her throat and says,

"The cat's out the bag. Alex and I were once in love, but we were so young at the time. I got pregnant and I was scared and didn't know what to do."

Kelly pauses for a moment, then continues. "There is something else I must tell you . . . something I haven't told anyone. I left to get an abortion, but a wonderful woman talked me out of it, and it was the best decision I had ever made." She looks at John.

"But it wasn't until my third trimester when the doctor heard two heartbeats. I had . . . twins."

"Mother, did I hear you say twins?" Father John asks. He is in disbelief.

"Yes, John, you are a twin! You have a twin brother."

"A twin? Mother, why didn't you tell me this before?"

"You mean I have *another* brother somewhere in this world?" Sara interjects.

"Yes, it's true. But you must all understand. I was a young woman of twenty. I had no money. I had no place to go. I was an only child and my parents were killed in a car accident when I was ten. This woman and her husband took me in and said they would raise one of you. I wasn't making much money at the museum at the time, being only an intern, so I had to quit my job to raise John. I was embarrassed and I didn't think Alex was in love with me as he was just starting his career and was ambitious. We were so young and naive. I didn't think I had much of a choice."

Sara is hysterical and repeats in astonishment, "You mean I have another brother somewhere in this world?"

Father John shakes his head in disbelief. "I can't believe what I'm hearing! I have a twin brother!"

"Do you have any idea where your other son might be?" Smithe asks.

"Yes, I have kept in contact with the Helzburgs for a few years when he was young, but then they sent him to school in Israel and I lost touch. I spoke with them occasionally to see how he is doing, but they passed away when he was twenty. They told me he was much involved in his career and didn't correspond much. I have seen his name in the paper several times."

McNair plays the detective and asks Kelly a pertinent question, "Do you know his name and where he is now?"

Proudly, Kelly declares, "Oh yes, he was raised as a Jew and went to school in Israel to be a rabbi. I'm sure you've heard of him. His name is Simonides."

Startled, Sara shouts, "Oh my God! Oh my God!"

"Please don't mind Sara, as she has gone through so much recently," McNair says, and he gently places his arm around her shoulder.

Feeling proud of her son's accomplishments, Kelly pulls out several newspaper articles from her purse with headlines of Simonides's escapades. "Look, here is a recent story of my son Simonides being hailed the world over as a great peacemaker and politician. He is helping to solve all of the world's problems. People all over the world respect and love him. I'm so proud of him."

Smithe just shakes his head. Never in a million years did he think this investigation would somehow lead to Simonides.

Sara whispers into McNair's ear, "It's as though we have a modern-day scarlet thread."

"Precisely, we have a set of twins from the same bloodline. One good and one evil," McNair responds.

Sara looks at Father John and says, "I think I would like to meet our other brother."

"Yes, indeed!" Father John responds after he has ingested what he believes to be wonderful news.

"Now that I have told you everything, can you please tell me why you have come to find me and want to know about my past?" Kelly says. It feels like a weight has been lifted. After all these years, her secret is out.

"I am investigating the murder of Dr. Alexander Flanders, and I believe his relatives may be in danger," Smithe says.

Kelly gasps. Sara said that her father had died, but she hadn't gone into any detail.

"I really can't give you any more information than that, as this is a murder investigation," says Smithe. "But I would like to contact your son Simonides to ask him some questions."

"I have a brilliant idea," says McNair. "Let's all go to Jerusalem to meet Simonides."

Smithe scoffs at the idea; he is investigating a murder and he usually doesn't work with other people in the field, but in this case, it will be beneficial to have McNair by his side. He hasn't quite figured out how Simonides, a high-profile religious cleric, fits into all of this and is still not convinced he is the antichrist, but if he is, and the entire world hangs in the balance, he wants to do his part in saving humanity.

Sara feels as if she's just ridden a loopy rollercoaster with no end in sight. "Let's go to Jerusalem," she says.

Chapter Twenty-Nine

> **Simonides reaches out to Iran. World Council Religious Cleric Simonides wants to end decades-old strained relationship**
> *The Corresponding Press*
> By Bernard Peres
> Updated 7:03 a.m. ET, Fri., March 20, 2025
>
> Jerusalem: World Council Religious Cleric Simonides told Iran's people and leaders that the free world wants to engage with their country and end decades of strained relationship, but not unless their officials stop making threats.
>
> On Friday Simonides spoke with Farsi subtitles that urged Iraq and the international community to resolve their long-standing differences. His speech was timed to the festival of Nowruz, which means "new day." It marks the arrival of spring and is a major holiday in Iran.
>
> "So, in this season of new beginnings I would like to speak clearly to Iran's leaders," Simonides said. "We have serious differences that have grown over time, but now is the time to commit to diplomacy that addresses the full range of issues before us, and to pursuing constructive ties among the international community and Iran."

> **Incoming Israeli prime minister Simonides tries to temper image as opponent of talks "partner for peace"**
> *The Corresponding Press*
> By Bernard Peres
> Updated 7:55 a.m. ET, Wed., March 25, 2025
> JERUSALEM—Israel's incoming Prime Minister, Simonides, on Wednesday promised to resume peace talks with the Palestinians after he takes office, saying his government will be a "partner for peace."
>
> The comments were the latest sign that Simonides is trying to temper his image as an opponent of the peace process. But facing the prospect of a clash with the United States administration and the rest of the international community, Simonides has been softening his line in recent days. Speaking at an economic conference in Jerusalem, Simonides said his development plan is not a substitute for political negotiations. "It's a complement to them," he said, calling a strong economy a "strong foundation for peace."

> **After deal in north, Simonides aims to install religious law nationwide**
> By Bernard Peres
> *The Corresponding Press*
> Updated 12:49 a.m. ET, Mon., April 20, 2025
> ISRAEL—Speaking to thousands of followers in an address aired live from Jerusalem on national news channels, Israel Prime Minister and cleric Simonides bluntly defied the constitution and federal judiciary, saying he would not allow any appeals to state courts under the system of Noahide law that will prevail there as a result of the peace accord signed by the president Tuesday.

Chapter Thirty

It was a turbulent flight to Jerusalem, and the group sat behind a child who screamed the entire time. Needless to say, they are more than anxious to get off the plane.

After they get off the plane and retrieve their luggage, Father John is walking and talking with Sara. "Can I carry some of your luggage?"

"That would be very helpful, Father John."

"You can call me John, if you wish. We are related, after all," he says with a smile.

They briefly discuss their upbringings and what they are going to say to their newly found brother Simonides. Father John has been briefed as to the potential identity of Simonides.

"So, what do think about our brother potentially being the antichrist?" inquires Sara.

"I agree he looks suspicious, but people have said some pretty disturbing things about our church over the past centuries as well, and I only take it with a grain of salt. But how can we stop him if it is true?"

"I don't know, but Dr. McNair has some ideas."

"So, McNair is the one who holds the key to stopping the antichrist?" Says Father John in a curious tone.

"Well, it does sound silly when you put it that way," Sara responds. "He is a biblical scholar and has studied this subject more than anyone else."

"Does he know about exorcisms?" Father John asks.

"I'm not sure. He's not a priest, only a historian."

Father John furrows his brow and has a faraway look in his eye. "There is only one person who can stop . . ."

Sara pauses for a moment and wonders why John looks so disturbed and didn't finish his sentence. It's as if a cloud has passed over him. "Are you okay, John?" she asks. She touches his arm and he flinches.

"Yes, yes," Father John stammers. "It's all so crazy when you think about it."

"What are you going to say to Simonides when you see him?"

"I'm not sure, but I am going to pray for wisdom," Father John says.

***

The next day, after a good night of rest, the group rent a car and McNair drives to the Temple Mount in Jerusalem. Sara is in awe of the building that sits at the center of the plaza. There's a large golden dome that glistens in the sunlight that is being repaired from an attempted explosion. They emerge from their car and begin walking up to the Temple.

McNair provides a history lesson for the troupe as he is astonished at what they are seeing before them, "We are witnessing ancient history here in this holy place of three major religions. This is the place that Abraham sacrificed his son Isaac, where Jesus was crucified, and where the Islamic prophet Muhammad visited.

"The golden Dome of the Rock is an Islamic shrine built near the Temple Mount where it is believed Muhammad ascended into heaven. This has been a bone of contention between these religious factions as the Jews have always wanted to build their Temple where the original one was built by King Solomon. As you can see it is being repaired due to an attempted explosion by extremists."

"I want to see the Church of the Holy Sepulcher where Jesus was crucified on Calvary according to tradition, and also where He was buried in the Garden Tomb," says Sara.

Just then, a man emerges from the Temple dressed in a white robe with facial hair. He is surrounded by an immense

Simonides heals the sick

crowd. He places his hands on a man's head and says, "Do you believe that I have the power in my hands to heal you?"

The man, covered in sores, looks up and shouts, "Yes, Rabbi, I believe!"

In a blink of an eye, the man's sores slowly disappear. The man shouts to the dismayed crowd, "Look! My sores are gone! Praise be to Simonides! I am healed!"

Smithe almost chokes on his own tongue. He is not religious, though he does believe in a higher power . . . but this is something else altogether. *How can it be?* he questions.

Simonides moves through the crowd to an arthritic woman who is crying out and cannot walk. He lays hands on her head and says, "Do you believe that I have the power in my hands to heal you?"

"Yes, Rabbi, I believe!"

Then the woman gets up and starts walking on shaky legs. "I can walk! It's a miracle! It has been twenty years since I have walked. Praise be to Simonides, I can walk!"

Simonides then moves toward a blind man. He lays hands on his head and says to him, "Do you believe that I have the power in my hands to heal you?"

"Yes, Simonides! I believe!"

The man opens his eyes and exclaims to the startled crowd, "Simonides has healed me, I can see! I can see! It's a miracle!"

The man runs toward Smithe's group and shouts, "I can see! I can see! Simonides has healed me!"

Smithe is baffled. What he's just witnessed goes against anything he's ever known. He works with facts—cold, hard facts. He starts to doubt, thinking these are paid actors and Simonides is trying to pull the wool over everyone's eyes, *he thinks to himself,* 'can he really be the antichrist?'

He puts the thought out of his mind for the moment and says, "Come on, let's go," hurriedly, and the group follows.

As they approach Simonides, he turns around and stops and stares. He can't help noticing the uncanny resemblance to Father John who is his size and build. His eyes graze over Sara and Kelly who has tears in her eyes.

"Who are you? Do I know you?" Simonides says to Father John.

"You do not know me, but I know who you are and I have some very important information for you. Can we speak in private?"

Simonides seems hesitant. "What is this regarding?" he asks.

"Simonides, please," Kelly says. She holds his gaze for a moment and there is a flicker of recognition in his eyes.

Simonides takes a step closer and says, "Come with me and we will talk."

The group enters a building adjacent to the Temple. Simonides tells everyone to wait outside while he talks with Father John in a private room.

Smithe doesn't like this one bit, but he must play this right, otherwise he will scare off Simonides and that's the last thing he wants. He stands there in silence.

Frustrated and somewhat angry, Father John looks at Sara and provides reassurance. "It's okay, Sara, wait here."

Father John follows Simonides down a hallway and into an empty room that's lined with bookcases. Simonides quickly closes the door, looks at Father John, and says impatiently, "Tell me who are you and what do you want from me."

Father John clears his throat. He has seen this look before—a look of skepticism—but there is something else under the surface. It's almost as if Simonides wants to do him harm.

"My name is John, and I'm a Catholic priest in the UK. My mother, Katherine, is an amazing woman, but we are all human and we all have our faults. She revealed to me recently a deep, dark secret she has been holding onto for all this time . . . that I have a brother. You see, you and I are related . . . twins, in fact."

Simonides heals the sick

There's a moment of silence while Simonides processes what Father John has said. Then, out of the depths of his belly, Simonides laughs hysterically. His laughter fills the room.

"I have no brother! I am he who has come to prepare the world for peace. My father is not of this world and has sent me to save the world and bring peace. Can't you see the healings I am performing?"

"You are a fake and a liar," Father John replies.

With uncontrolled anger, Simonides snaps, "Get out of here now!"

"If only you could see the truth," Father John says, and he storms out of the room and down the hall.

A few moments later, Simonides emerges from the building alone. His jaw is tight, and it's clear he's annoyed.

"Where is Father John?" Sara asks with deep concern and curiosity.

"He is wandering about the Temple grounds. Am I my brother's keeper?" Simonides says with a sneer.

Sara is getting perturbed. "So, I see that Father John told you that he is your brother, and I can also see that you don't believe him. I don't suppose he told you that we are also siblings?"

Simonides grits his teeth in anger. "Siblings, you say? Who told you this lie?"

Sara looks to Kelly, who is softly crying. "It is not a lie," Kelly says, stepping forward. "I am your mother. You and Father John are twins separated at birth, and you and Sara are stepbrother and sister of the same father."

Full of venom, Simonides replies, "I have no human father! My father is in heaven!"

"What are you talking about?" Sara asks. "Where is Father John?"

But before anyone can say another word, Simonides charges through the crowd and disappears.

Chapter Thirty-One

After searching for Father John for almost an hour, the group decides it best to go to the hotel and hope that he will show up.

'It doesn't make any sense,' Smithe thinks. But he feels confident that all will end well and Father John will show up sooner or later . . . or so he hopes.

The hotel sits on the outskirts of a bustling neighborhood. The rooms are decent—Smithe, McNair, and Father John in one room, and Sara and Kelly sharing the other. After unloading their luggage, they convene in the men's room.

"Something very sinister has happened to Father John," Sara says as she sits on one of the beds. "I can feel it. Father John seemed so angry. He went into a room with Simonides and never came out."

"Let's not jump to conclusions," Smithe says. He knows how these sorts of things can get out of hand.

"If only you could have seen the look he gave me when he told us to stay outside and wait for him. I don't know . . . it was weird. Don't you all agree?"

McNair pipes in, "While I do think it's quite strange that Father John disappeared after the meeting, it may be something quite innocent, such as him wanting to visit some holy sites. He is a holy man, after all."

"Sara's right," Kelly says, and everyone turns around to see her standing in the doorway. Her nose is red from crying.

"So, Father John is missing and both of them went into a room and only Simonides came out!" Sara says, boarding on hysterics.

"We don't know that," Smithe says. He paces around the room. "All we know is that they went into the building, they most likely went into a private room, but that is all we know."

"So where is Father John?" McNair says. "I see what you're saying, Detective, and you are the detective, but it does seem a little odd that Father John is missing."

"I agree. There may be something fishy going on. If he doesn't turn up tonight, I will contact the local police in the morning."

***

The next morning, there is still no sign of Father John. Kelly told them last night that she always found it frustrating that her son didn't have a cell phone. "I have no need for one," he would say.

After a quick breakfast, Smithe heads to the police department while McNair and Sara return to the Temple grounds. Kelly stays behind in case Father John shows up at the hotel.

McNair and Sara find a quiet place to sit, away from the crowd, while they wait for Smithe to return.

"I never got a chance to ask you how you're doing with all of this," McNair says. He gently takes her hand.

Sara sighs. "It's all so overwhelming. There are moments where I think I'm going to wake up from a dream, but when I pinch myself I'm still stuck in this same nightmare. I miss my father so much, and I can't even begin to process what all of this means about having *two* stepbrothers."

"You know, I find it helpful to take a deep breath when I'm feeling overwhelmed. Our minds are racing and our bodies are trying to catch up. Sometimes you just need to step back and give yourself a breather . . . so to speak," McNair says.

Sara chuckles. "You love the puns," she jokes, and kisses him on the cheek.

Just then, Smithe appears from around the corner. "I've filed a report with the local PD. They are now aware of Father John's disappearance, but it's more likely that he got stopped somewhere and didn't have his proper paperwork. Let's stay positive."

"Thank you," Sara says.

The crowd erupts into cheers. The trio watch as Simonides stands on the steps and speaks to the crowd. Behind him there is a white curtain on a metal frame. He is performing what appears to be miracle after miracle.

"And now, my friends, I am going to perform one of the most spectacular, one of the most unbelievable miracles that you have ever witnessed."

The crowd cheers.

"This should be good," Smithe says sarcastically.

"Throughout history there have been many great magicians who have performed many amazing tricks, but they have been mere charlatans. Now I will show you the power of heaven. I will show you what only God can do and no one else has ever done before. I am going to resurrect the dead!" The crowd oohs and ahhs at this and they can't take their eyes of Simonides.

"What the . . . ?" McNair trails off.

Simonides claps his hands and shouts, "Yes, that is what I said! I am going to bring back people from the dead, many of whom you know very well. In fact, many of these people are adversaries of mine, in a way. I want to bring them back because I want to expose them before all the world for what they are! I want the whole world to know that the Christ of the Christian world is false and only I, Simonides, is the true son of God!"

The crowd gasps.

Simonides walks over to a curtain and pulls it back to reveal two small boxes on a wooden table. "My friends, this box contains the ashes of a very famous president that you all know. I will bring back someone the whole world has admired and he will also tell you who I am."

Simonides is worshipped

Sara feels fear rising in her body and her heart races. Immediately she is drawn back to images of her poor father who was sacrificed in the name of these bizarre rituals. Her hands shake with anger, and McNair clasps it, trying to calm her.

"Let's see what happens," Smithe whispers. "I don't know what to expect, but let's stay here for a moment."

The crowd is silent as Simonides prays over the box. Suddenly, gray smoke emerges from the box and curls into the air, then a foul odor permeates the scene. It smells like death. Everyone is mystified! Then a loud thunderous noise occurs and out of the smoke and fog comes a figure of a man.

"Is that . . . ? No, it can't be . . ." Smithe says in shock. He can't believe his eyes. "It's someone who looks like him, that's all. It's not the real JFK, right?" He turns to McNair and Sara, but they remain silent, their eyes as large as saucers.

John F. Kennedy flashes the crowd a dazzling smile. He stands at six feet, his brown hair combed to the side with precision, and his blue suit is tailored.

"President Kennedy, tell the people who I am," Simonides says with a wicked smile.

President Kennedy expounds some unbelievable comments to the stymied crowd. "My fellow servants of Simonides. You know my famous saying: 'Ask not what your country can do for you—ask what you can do for your country.' But I am here now to tell you that even though I was a practicing Catholic in my former life, I now serve Simonides."

The bewildered crowd chants in unison, "hail Simonides, God of all Catholics and the universe!"

"I don't believe this," Smithe scoffs. It all seems so ridiculous to him, but deep down there is a nagging feeling that just won't go away: *What if it's real?*

Simonides prays over the next box and just like before smoke and a foul odor emerge from the box. Everyone is silent. Some are afraid. Then a loud thunderous noise occurs and figure of a man emerges from the fog. It is Pope Innocent

III whose orders killed thousands during the Inquisition of the Middle Ages.

The pope is dressed in traditional garments of red and gold that barely cover his protruding belly, and his tall hat is shaped liked an egg.

McNair can barely contain himself. "Pope Innocent III will go down in history as the inquisition Pope.

Pope Innocent III raises his hands upward to heaven and says, "Peace be to all of you who now know as I do that Simonides is in fact the almighty and powerful god who can resurrect the dead and give life to all.

"It is I who owe him and the entire Christian world an apology for the things I unknowingly did, as my orders were responsible for the deaths of millions of Jews, Templars, and Christians who I branded as Judaizers and heretics during my inquisition."

Pope Innocent III pauses for a moment and looks upon the crowd. There is sadness in his eyes.

"I believed it was my duty from God to persecute those who were influencing wrongly the church. These Jewish people kept the seventh day Sabbath as did their ancestor Moses, and were influenced by the Jewish way of life. I made decisions based upon the principles of the law of Moses, but it didn't turn out the way I had intended. I now ask for your forgiveness and submit my life to serving Simonides and honor the keeping of the Noahide Laws."

Simonides chuckles and paces around the humbled pope. "I understand, my friend and servant. The mobs were out of control and the local bishops did not uphold your ideas. They were filled with prejudicial passion, as are most local mobs and heresy hunters."

Simonides turns to the crowd. "Yes, it is true that in the law of Moses, if there was found a man or woman who had gone and served other gods and worshiped them, then you shall inquire diligently, and if it is true and certain, that such an abominable thing has been done, then you shall bring forth that man or woman who has done this evil thing, and you shall stone that man or woman to death with stones."

"But the people you persecuted were not heretics!" Simonides shouts at the pope, and the crowd takes a step back. "They were heretics according to *your* law, but they were keeping my father's laws. You should have been dispelling pagans, not our Jewish brothers who had to hide their true faith!"

Pope Innocent III kneels down before Simonides and says in a repentant voice, "Yes, Simonides, my master, I ask for your forgiveness!"

"Is this real? What am I witnessing?" Sara says.

Smithe grunts in agreement. He still can't believe what he is witnessing—the madness of it all.

Simonides takes a few deep breaths to calm himself. "Now, my friends, let me tell you about this Jesus who the Christians worship falsely as a god and who supposedly turned water into wine, walked on water, and healed the sick. This Jesus who the Christians worship and who supposedly brought people back to life. But this is not the truth and you have seen it with your own eyes what I have done! Jesus was a bastard, born illegitimately and nothing more than a mere man. Let the truth be known!"

Simonides eyes narrow and his chest is pounding. He looks like a man possessed.

The frenzied crowd prostrates before Simonides. One man shouts, "Our redeemer has come back! Our messiah is here! Our god has come back to deliver and help us!" The crowd echoes this sentiment, and it isn't long before the arena is filled with the mantra.

Suddenly, a loud voice from the crowd shouts, "You are the bastard, Simonides, the son of the devil himself!"

The crowd quickly quiets down. Smithe feels on edge. *'This could get ugly,'* he thinks.

Simonides's eyes focus wildly on the crowd to see who spoke the pointed remarks. "Who said this? Who are you to rebuke me?" he yells.

Another voice rings out, "It must be Moses himself!"

The First Witness of Jesus Christ confronts Simonides and says in a commanding voice, "You know who I am, Simonides!"

The Second Witness takes a step forward and repeats what the First Witness said: "And you know who I am, Simonides!"

The crowd murmurs. Someone shouts, "It's Moses and Elijah. They have come back!"

The Second Witness turns to Simonides and says, "We are here to warn you and confront you. We are the witnesses of the true Almighty God!"

The crowd, shocked and confused, talks among themselves. Simonides looks as if he's seen a ghost. But he straightens his posture. He will not go down without a fight.

"Who are they to rebuke Simonides?" a woman shouts. "It must be Moses and Elijah who have come back!"

The crowd bursts into cheers and jeers, and Simonides grows nervous. Quickly he responds to the Witnesses, "I know who you are and I know you cannot touch me for my time is not yet!"

The crowd pushes forward, still shouting and some cheering.

"I don't know what is going on, but we need to leave before this really gets out of hand," Smithe says.

The trio quickly disappears into the shadows. They can hear the crowd chanting in the distance for the longest while.

Chapter Thirty-Two

Smithe lies in the hotel bed staring at the ceiling as McNair snores in the bed next to him. He can't stop replaying what happened earlier at the Temple. Growing up, his parents made him go to Catholic school and he hated it. The nuns were always yelling at him, he disliked the uniforms, and he never really understood the meaning of the Scriptures when he and his classmates were forced to sit through Mass.

It wasn't until he was older and met his wife that he found some meaning in the spiritual aspect of religion, as she was a week-end and holiday-only Catholic. Yes, he believes in a higher power—he knows there has to be something else out there and the afterlife—but never has he had a spiritual 'epiphany,' so to speak, something that has altered his way of life and beliefs. But today was something different altogether.

'What did I see?' he thinks. Simonides is a strange man, someone who seeks too much power, Smithe reasoned, but he can't quite put his finger on what he saw today. Was it all smoke and mirrors? Or is there some truth to it?

'No, that's impossible. Pope Innocent III and John F. Kennedy didn't just rise from the dead to have a conversation with a crazed man. But what if it is true?'

Regardless, Smithe knows that Simonides is the key to finding out more in his case, and maybe he is one step closer to bringing Alexander Flanders some justice. But more than that, if he really is the antichrist as foretold by the scriptures, he will take away religious freedom and kill anyone who opposes him.

'What game are you playing at, Simonides?' Smithe whispers.

***

The next morning the troupe prepares to depart and head home. Smithe is eager to see the newspapers and he is not disappointed. With his suitcase in hand, Smithe picks up a newspaper in the hotel lobby and reads the headlines in the *Jerusalem Gazette*:

**RELIGIOUS ZEALOT PROCLAIMS
THE GOD OF CHRISTIANS TO BE A FAKE!
RESURRECTS THE DEAD!**

**RELIGIOUS CLERIC SIMONIDES BLASPHEMES THE GOD
OF CHRISTIANS AND PROCLAIMS HIMSELF TO BE GOD!**

Smithe shakes his head. He grabs a cup of coffee and a scone and finds a chair to sit in while he waits for the rest of his group to join him. The room is abuzz with murmur about what happened yesterday on the Temple grounds, but Smithe tunes them out.

Twenty minutes later, McNair, Sara, and Kelly arrive with their luggage and Smithe can't help but feel defeated. There still isn't any sign of Father John and it's tying his stomach in knots.

Kelly's eyes are puffy and it's clear that she has done nothing but cry since they arrived. "I can't leave without my John," she says.

"I can assure you that the police are doing everything they can to locate Father John. Captain Fieneberg gave me his word that he will contact me as soon as they know anything . . . and I mean *anything*," Smithe says.

"None of this is right," Kelly cries.

"You have to trust Detective Smithe," Sara says, and places her arm around Kelly's shoulder. "I know that I have the most talented detective on the case who is trying to bring justice to my father, and I know he will do whatever he can to find your son."

Kelly nods in agreement.

It's a long flight back home, and the travelers are tired and weary. Everywhere they turn there are breaking-news stories reporting of the miracles of Simonides. They all agree to go home, get some rest, and resume at Sara's house in the morning to discuss what to do about Simonides.

***

As usual, Sara invites everyone to sit in the living room and offers tea and biscuits. Everyone is tired but eager to push forward with the case.

Smithe takes a sip of his tea—a little bitter for his tastes—and dives right in. "Now that we have seen what Simonides has done, performing miracles, killing Christians, even claiming to be God, I'm becoming a believer. But what can anyone do about it?"

"You have to admit those miracles really looked real," Sara says.

"I saw a very clever trick on a TV show in which a famous singer appeared to be singing with Elvis!" Smithe declares. "I'm still not convinced it was anything more than a magic trick."

Sara huffs. "You *really* think it was a trick?"

Smithe is a man of facts, not tricks and illusions. His job is to spot illusions—intentional or otherwise—to reveal the cold, hard facts. "Really, Sara, I do. On the TV show, it was like Elvis was raised from the dead. The audience went wild. Turns out it was a hologram. Totally amazing what they can do these days with technology."

McNair chimes in, "True, Detective. I recently saw a video that made it appear as if Michael Jackson is still alive shopping for groceries in small store. The maker of the video said he came up with the idea to show how easily people can be fooled."

Sara is beginning to see behind the mask. "I've been to Disney World and have seen holograms as well. But it looked so real. Part of me is terrified to learn that it is real, because the concept of resurrecting the dead is not something I can wrap my head around. But there's another part of me that wishes it is real, because in some way I think it will explain what happened to my father."

She grows angry for a moment and shouts, "This is not to say that it in any way justifies what happened to my father! He didn't deserve to be taken from this world in such a brutal, horrific manner. But I'm grieving and I'm in shock, and I'm trying to make sense of all of this."

Sara breaks down in tears and Kelly slides closer and comforts her.

"I agree with the detective," McNair says. "Remember, the Bible says that in the last days, the antichrist would perform false miracles."

Just then, Smithe's cell phone vibrates in his pocket. He pulls it out and sees that it's Captain Fieneberg from Jerusalem.

"I gotta take this," Smithe says, and answers the phone, "Hello, this is Detective Smithe."

"Detective, this is Captain Fieneberg. I have information regarding the disappearance of John Kelly."

"Yes, please continue," Smithe says as he gets up and hurries into the kitchen away from prying eyes and listening ears.

"I'm sorry to inform you, but we found three bodies in a room on the Temple grounds. One has been identified as John Kelly. It looks like they were killed by mysterious means as there were no marks on their bodies, but this is now an open investigation. More will come to light in the coming days. I wanted to do you the courtesy to call you first before I call his next of kin."

Smithe's stomach drops. *No, this can't be,* he thinks.

"Thank you, Captain," Smithe says, gaining his composure. "I'm actually with John's mother Katherine Kelly, if it's okay with you and your department's protocol, I can tell her the news and that she should expect to receive a call from your department soon."

"That is fine," Captain Fieneberg says. "I really wish I had good news."

"It comes with the job," Smithe says sadly, and hangs up. He sighs heavily. This is his least favorite part of the job, but even he is a little unprepared for this. He knows Kelly and Sara are not going to take the news well.

Slowly, Smithe walks back into the living room and is met with expecting faces.

"Any news?" McNair says.

Smithe sits down on the couch across from Kelly. Her eyes are tearing, and her lips are quivering, and he knows that she knows. He's been at this long enough to know that mothers have that instinct, and it makes his heart heavy.

"I'm sorry, Katherine, but I have some bad news. Your son John was found murdered on the Temple grounds. I don't have any words right now to express how sorry I am for the loss of your son."

"Not my boy John!" Kelly wails, and she cries uncontrollably, collapsing into Sara's arms. "Not my boy!" They hug each other and Sara with tears in her eyes mumbles, "I wish I had the right words, just know that I care."

McNair also comforts her as he gives her a hug and whispers in her ear, "We all need help at a time like this, and I just want you to know that I am here for you."

Smithe shakes his head. "What are we going to do?" he whispers to himself.

Chapter Thirty-Three

The next day, Sara storms into Smithe's office. She is **frustrated, heartbroken**, and angry, and she will stop at nothing to bring the murderers of her father and her stepbrother to justice.

Smithe is sitting behind his desk while McNair is hovering over a table reading over various pieces of paper.

"Robert, is there anything in the Bible that can tell us what we can do as individuals to stop this madman Simonides? Now that Father John is dead, he was our last hope to find someone with the genes that God would recognize as the legitimate kingly lineage."

McNair clicks his tongue and speaks in a rapid tone, "As I have said previously, our organization, The Christian Crusaders for Christ, has been very busy these past few years getting DNA samples from all the bones we found in the King's chamber at Tara. I believe we have the DNA of King Heremon, Teia, their children, and all of the kings of Ireland, Scotland, and England."

"What have you concluded?" Smithe asks.

"It was my hope that we would find an individual who matched their DNA to a modern descendant. I even thought Father John would be a match, but he was not. But we must keep looking, for I believe God will give them power to counter the wiles of the devil."

Smithe, again, is confused, and at this point, he's just as frustrated as Sara. "Can you please, for once, just spit it all out?"

McNair, not fazed by the insult, says, "The only DNA sample that was an exact match to the royal bloodline of King David was Dr. Alexander Flanders. None of their modern descendants living today are a match and therefore not capable to possess supernatural powers to stop the antichrist. None of them except Sara's father! I'm sorry to say."

Smithe wants to scream. He is still skeptical concerning the exploits of Simonides and that he is the antichrist. He also doesn't understand why Sara can't be a match, something that McNair has explained to him a few times.

"Can you explain why Sara's DNA isn't the same?" Smithe asks. McNair gives caution, "Absolutely, Sara doesn't seem to have any supernatural powers and usually the powers went to the male offspring in the family just as inheritance rights. That's why we thought Sara's stepbrother, John, was a possibility, as his DNA was close but not a perfect match. The Bible clearly shows this through the family of Abraham, Isaac and Jacob. Furthermore, God also shows an order of holy offices as in the case of Uzzah who was struck down for touching the Holy Ark and not following due order. You cannot expect to usurp holy offices and get results."

"Well, where does that leave us?" Sara inquires.

McNair brainstorms for a moment, then his eyes light up. "Of course!" he shouts, and he rushes over to the table. He leafs through the papers, his hands shaking, and comes across the document he was looking for. "Of course!" he says again.

"Get to the point!" Smithe shouts.

McNair has a crazed look in his eye. "Hear me out, okay? I know this will sound a little bonkers, but I may have come up with a solution." He turns to Sara. "This may be hard for you to hear, Sara, but the CCC has preserved your father's heart and brain. What we can do is put your father's heart and brain back into a body."

"What?" Smithe gasps flabbergasted.

Sara's face drops at the thought of her father's heart and brain being put into someone else's body as being something so morbid.

"I know it's bizarre, but do either of you have a better plan?" McNair says. "Our organization has been working with a company that has performed many successful heart transplants, and they just transplanted a monkey's brain in a young boy who was killed in an auto accident. This is new-age technology, and unbelievable things are going on in the medical world. Arms and limbs are being put on people with robotic movements."

"I suppose that in this day and age with stem cells and all, it would be possible to bring my father back in some form," Sara muses.

McNair replies, "We need the royal DNA, but the body needs to have superpowers, which is why it can't be Sara." He turns to Smithe and says, "I know you don't believe in all of this, Detective, but you saw with your very own eyes what Simonides did: he brought the deceased back to the living. We are dealing with something more than magic."

Sara provides an intriguing thought. "What about John's body? His father was also my father, which means he may also have the royal DNA, and he is male, and you said he was a close match."

McNair groans. "Yes," he says. "In theory, John would also be a candidate, though it's unclear if he has any powers."

Sara bites back tears. "I just can't imagine doing that to my brother's body. I know we are getting further in this case, and I know my father would have wanted to be part of this experiment, but I don't know if I can give consent."

Smithe nods his head. It is a very strange request and something he is entirely unfamiliar with. "Well, I guess we'll have to ask Kelly if she is willing to give consent to use John's body," he says.

They sit in silence.

'This keeps getting weirder and weirder,' Smithe thinks.

***

A week later, as Father John's body has returned to England, the heart and brain transplant operation is performed in a staggering fourteen-hour operation. Two

A strange solution

days later, Sara, Smithe, and McNair visit Him, as it has been deemed safe to see him.

Sara holds back tears as she sees her father lying in the bed with tubes and bandages and machines beeping. His face is pale, and a bandage covers his head. Suddenly, he opens his eyes and looks at her.

"Where am I? Sara, is that you? What are you doing at the museum? What happened to me?"

Sara bursts into tears and hugs him as gently as she can. "I love you, Father. You've had an operation," she says, as Smithe and McNair told her to say.

"What kind of an operation?" Dr. Flanders says, confused.

"You had a heart operation, and it is a long story, but for now we want you to just rest and recover." Sara looks into his eyes. "I'm so happy to see you."

"I'm happy to see you too," Dr. Flanders says.

Chapter Thirty-Four

Seven months after Dr. Flanders's operation, he is recuperating faster than expected. He has made a remarkable recovery and is acting as normal after the spectacular operation. It is a warm summer day and he and Sara are out on the back patio reminiscing and laughing about old times and having some tea.

"Would you like some more tea father?" asks Sara.

"No thank you dear, I just want to relax and watch the birds flying about and am enthralled at the yellow warbler drinking out of your birdbath," says Dr. Flanders.

"Yes, God's creatures are truly fascinating," says Sara.

One bright sunny day, Smithe and McNair visit along with Kelly. Everyone is somewhat nervous about how Dr. Flanders will react to seeing a love from long ago. They are even more nervous to tell him about his death.

"Remember Kelly, what you are about to experience is beyond comprehension. You are going to see a man that has the body of your son John and the mind of Dr. Flanders," remarks Smithe in a diplomatic fashion.

"I understand Detective, and I am so happy to have my son John back in some form and can't wait to see my old friend Alex," says Kelly.

"We will come and get you when we're ready," Smithe says as he and McNair get out of the car. Kelly is sitting in the back seat.

"I will wait patiently," she says, but it's obvious that she is nervous.

Once inside, McNair and Smithe take a seat on the couch. Dr. Flanders walks slowly into the living room holding a bottle of water. He looks frail, but well, and he even has a spark in his eye.

Over the last seven months, Smithe has come to terms with the reality of the situation, but it hasn't been easy. In fact, it has haunted him in nightmares. He still can't believe that a person who was dead, could have another person's brain and heart put in them and they could live! He can't wait to talk to Dr. Flanders and ask him some important questions.

"Good morning, Dr. Flanders, it's nice to see you up and about and recovering nicely," McNair says. "Sara and Smithe know all about our involvement with our organization and the royal bloodlines, and the significance of the Stone of Destiny. They know how you have tried to preserve the royal bloodline identity and terminate the imposter bloodline that would produce the antichrist."

"They do?" Dr. Flanders says.

"Yes, I told them everything you told me," McNair responds.

Dr. Flanders bites his lip. Ever since he has been 'brought back,' is how Sara likes to refer to it, she has been overly concerned for his wellbeing. She doesn't want to say or do anything that will upset him, and now she is concerned that they are embarking on this territory.

"Do you know who the antichrist is?" Dr. Flanders says after a moment.

"Yes, we believe he is an individual known as Simonides who is the high priest and Prime Minister of Israel," Smithe responds.

Dr. Flanders's eyes grow wide. "How do you know that?"

Smithe, Sara, and McNair stare at each other, then McNair says, "We saw him resurrect the dead and do exploits consistent with the prophecies of the antichrist."

Dr. Flanders gasps.

"Father," Sara says gently, "I have something to tell you. Remember when you told me that you were in love a long time ago, before Mom, and the woman you were in love with was pregnant with your child? You told me that you didn't know what happened to the child."

Dr. Flanders's eyes grow dark, something Sara has noticed when he is thinking deeply about something. Finally, he says, "Yes, I did tell you that."

"Well, there is someone who came to see you today. She told us all about that time in your life. She worked with you at the museum. Would you like to see her?"

"You mean Katherine is here?" Dr. Flanders says in an exuberant voice.

Smithe nods at McNair who then rushes out of the room and they can hear the front door creak open and shut. A few moments later, the front door creaks open again. Kelly is stymied at what she sees and for the moment forgets who she is looking at.

"Hello, John, I mean Alex," Kelly says as she enters the room. She walks over to Dr. Flanders and clasps his hand ever so gently. For the moment she does not know whether to hug him as her son or kiss him as her old lover.

Dr. Flanders gasps and tears fill his eyes. "Katherine? Is that really you?"

"It's me," she says, crying into his shoulder.

"Well, I never thought I would ever see you again. You're as beautiful as ever."

Kelly blushes and tries to control her emotions. "I'm glad to see you well, Alex," she cries.

Over the next hour, the two reminisce about the past and latest events. Afterwards, Sara, Smithe, and McNair come back into the living room to join in on the conversation.

"You say that Simonides has become this antichrist. I can't believe it! You say he was such a nice boy, but a bit of a puzzle growing up, showing signs of a split personality, maybe even being bi-polar or something," Dr. Flanders says. "I wish you had told me about him Katherine."

Alex and Kelly reunite

"I'm sorry, but this is all just a little overwhelming for me," Kelly responds. "I'm still grieving our son John, and grieving the loss of a son I will never know. And now you, Alex, are sitting before me alive and well. I think I'll take my leave from work now . . . have myself a quiet respite for a while. I will be back in due time."

"Of course," Sara says. "I can't imagine how difficult this is for you, but please know that you can call me at any time if you need anything. There are so many things that feel so much out of our control. You will find peace."

"Thank you, darling," Kelly says, and they hug. She turns to Alex. "I'm so glad that we have reconnected, and I look forward to getting to know you all over again." She smiles.

Alex takes her hands in his and says, "It will be my pleasure, Katherine. There are so many things I want to ask you."

Kelly excuses herself for the moment to freshen up as McNair fills Alex in as to the exploits of his renegade son Simonides as he shows him some of the newspaper headlines. "Look at these articles I've saved for you to see what Simonides has been up to these past few months."

Noahide Laws enforced by Prime Minister Simonides who publicly executes Christians

The Jerusalem Gazette
Updated 5:06 a.m. ET, Fri., July 24, 2025
JERUSALEM—The newly formed Sanhedrin controlled by President Simonides publicly executed 200 Christians last week for distributing the Bible, which is banned by the newly formed Jewish Sanhedrin headed by the president.

It is virtually impossible to verify such reports about secretive executions where the government tightly controls the lives of its citizens and does not allow dissent.

On Thursday, an annual report from an international think tank on human rights said that public executions, though dropping in number in recent weeks, were still carried out for crimes ranging from distributing Christian Bibles to refusing to keep the Jewish Sabbath.

> The newly formed Jewish cabinet headed by Simonides claims to guarantee freedom of religion for its 24 million people but in reality, severely restricts religious observances.
> The U.S. State Department reported last year that "genuine religious freedom does not exist" in Israel.
> Activists claim that such atrocities cannot take place in Israel without Simonides's knowledge or direction as he wields absolute power.
> "Let's file a suit against Simonides to the International Criminal Court," the activists chanted.

Dr. Flanders's eyes dilate as he realizes the truth about his antichrist Son. After years of research and dedicating his entire life to stopping it, he cannot believe it is happening. Part of him is shocked that it is his biological son, as they share the same DNA, but it's still overwhelming.

"I'm still trying to wrap my head around the fact that I had two sons I've never met—one whom I'll never meet," he says sadly and squeezes Kelly's hand. "I still can't believe that our son Simonides is doing these despicable things and has become the antichrist. We need to stop him before he destroys the human race."

"Precisely! Any ideas, Professor?" McNair says.

"Well, yes . . . I know what to do," Dr. Flanders says.

Excited that someone may have a plan, Smithe declares with optimism, "You do?"

"We thought that if anyone would have a solution, you would have the answer and the powers to stop him," McNair chimes in with hope.

Dr. Flanders remarks with caution, "I don't have the supernatural powers to stop him, but I know who does."

"Who is that, Father?" asks Sara.

"God Almighty" Dr. Flanders declares nonchalantly.

Smithe bites his lip and sneers at McNair. The entire reason for bringing Dr. Flanders back from the grave was hinging solely on the fact that he would have the powers to defeat Simonides. This has proved false. Once again, Smithe is annoyed. There are moments like this when he feels duped into this whole thing and wished he had stuck to his guns—there are no such things as superpowers and antichrists. It can be argued that there is some magic in the world, as Dr. Flanders is breathing and speaking, but that is also advancements in medical technology. *'What have they done? Played God in bringing a dead man back?'* he thinks.

"Well, Professor, I'm glad you have the faith that God will stop him, but God is up there, and Simonides is down here, and we need to stop him," Smithe argues, trying not to hide his frustration.

"Oh, I agree, Detective, but what I meant is that God will help us to know what to do," Dr. Flanders says.

Sara sighs. "I think we all believe that, Father, but how is God going to help us?"

"The key is in the Ark of the Covenant," Dr. Flanders says with a big smile.

The trio gasps.

McNair interjects quickly, "Dr. Flanders, because of your directions that you left Sara, we have found the Ark!"

"You found the Ark?" Dr. Flanders declares excitedly. "The Ark has powers to destroy the enemies of God."

McNair concurs, "Yes, Professor, I agree that the Ark the children of Israel were instructed to make by God that held the Ten Commandments has always been able to destroy the enemies of God. But it also had to be in the possession of the rightful hands. Wouldn't you agree?"

"Yes, I agree, but where is the Ark now?"

"My men hid it in Ireland after we found it with the instructions you gave Sara," McNair says.

Dr. Flanders is starting to feel more like himself and demands, "You must tell them to bring it to Jerusalem to fight the antichrist, for only the power of God can destroy the power of the devil!"

Chapter Thirty-Five

Several weeks later, Dr. Flanders's organization, the Christian Crusaders for Christ, has brought the ark from Ireland to Jerusalem and are waiting for further instructions. After a long flight, the troop, including Alex and Katherine, arrive in Jerusalem to put an end to Simonides's powers.

Massive crowds have gathered outside the Temple. Some people are crying, others are holding up signs of protest. Armed guards stand at every corner. It's chaos.

Simonides is performing his daily miracles at the Temple Mount. McNair tells his men to bring the Ark near the Temple to confront the powers of Simonides. "Put the Ark as close to the Temple as you can," he says, and the two men nod and rush off into the crowd.

"Let's hope this works," McNair says.

"What exactly can we expect?" Smithe asks.

"I don't know, but the idea is that the spiritual power contained within the Ark should be enough to defeat anything, even Simonides."

The groups stand impatiently behind a crowd near the Temple steps. Smithe's heart is beating.

Just then, McNair taps Smithe's arm and says, "Look, over there."

Two men dressed in black with black baseball hats carry the Ark, which has a blanket over it to disguise it. They move it as close to where Simonides is performing miracles and place it on the ground. They take a few steps back, never taking their eyes off the most important historical and religious relic.

Smithe provides the answer

Simonides continues to do miraculous things, but nothing so far has happened out of the ordinary.

McNair taps his foot impatiently. "Come on, come on," he says.

"I don't understand," Dr. Flanders muses. "I thought for sure the powers of the Ark would stop him. I thought fire from heaven would rain down on Simonides as it did on the pagan priests of Baal in the days of Elijah.

What can stop Simonides now? I thought it would work, as the person with the DNA genes from the King David lineage is in the presence of the Ark." He shakes his head.

"Maybe it's not enough that the Ark is closed?" Smithe guesses.

As Dr. McNair approaches Dr. Flanders, the two disappointed men discuss their next move. "Tell your men to bring the Ark where I can observe its contents," Says Dr. Flanders with a commanding voice. "I need to look inside the Ark once again to see if anything is missing."

"Inform your men McNair, to bring the Ark to us," Smithe says. McNair nods. The group quickly hurries through the crowd to a back alley and into a garage where they await a white pickup truck.

Twenty minutes later, McNair and his men rush into the garage and unload it from the pickup truck. "Ready?" McNair says. "Just to warn you, only a select few have laid witness to what you're about to see."

Smithe takes a deep breath.

The Ark of the Covenant is one of the most sought-after biblical relics. Over thousands of years, people have searched for the Ark, some claiming to have seen it. Alas, up until present day, its presence and location are unknown . . . that is, until now. According to Scripture, the Ark contains the Ten Commandments, Aaron's rod, and a pot of manna.

McNair removes the cover off the Ark and everyone gasps. Sara and Kelly have tears in their eyes. Dr. Flanders's hands are shaking.

'It all makes sense now,' Smithe thinks, as his heart pounds out of his chest. All this time he questioned and doubted, but to be in the presence of something so powerful, so spiritual, has changed his inner being forever.

"O-okay," Dr. Flanders stumbles, and with shaky hands, he slowly and gently opens the Ark. A scent somewhat familiar wafts up their nostrils, almost like cinnamon and firewood. Carefully he rummages through the items in the Ark.

"I wonder how the High Priest's breastplate got in here," he says in a troubled voice. "I'll bet the prophet Jeremiah put it in here before he fled to Egypt with King Zedekiah's daughters."

"The next item is Aaron's rod that budded and the pot of manna, and on the bottom, there are two ancient stones, and on those two tablets the Ten Commandments are written in Hebrew.

'Hymn' says Dr. Flanders as he pulls out the High Priest's breastplate and gently glides his fingers over it."

"What is it?" McNair asks anxiously.

"They're missing! Of course!" Dr. Flanders shouts.

Smithe is confused. "What's missing?"

"The stones!"

"What stones?" Smithe asks in frustration, wishing the doctor didn't just assume everyone knew what he was referring to.

"The *Urim* and *Thummin*. These are the sacred stones, the two enlighteners in the High Priest's breastplate that gave powers of judgment."

"But where can they be? Who would have taken them?"

"The only person who possibly had the Ark in their possession last and carried the Ark to Ireland was Jeremiah the Prophet. He came there with Queen Teia. He must have taken the stones out of the breastplate and hid them so the enemies of God who might capture the Ark would not be able to use it against God's people."

Smithe provides the answer

"Kind of like taking the bullets out of a gun," Smithe remarks.

"Precisely" McNair says.

"Father, what did these stones look like?" Sara asks.

McNair interjects, "According to the Bible, unlike the twelve colored birthstones for each of the tribes of Israel that were sewn into the breastplate, the *Urim* and *Thummin* stones were black."

"Dr. McNair is right. So where would Jeremiah have hidden them?" Dr. Flanders muses.

It suddenly dawns on Smithe. "Wait a minute. I recall seeing two very curious black stones in the collar of the bushy coon cat that Queen Elizabeth was holding in that painting you showed us Sara."

"Really? I never noticed that," says Sara.

Smithe quickly pulls out his cell phone with a picture he took of the painting Sara showed them of Queen Tea and Queen Elizabeth holding the coon cats. "That's why I'm the detective," he says facetiously. "Look at the two black stones on Queen Elizabeth's coon cat's collar."

McNair pulls out a small magnifying glass to examine the cat's collar more closely. "Indeed, it's plain as day! They're black stones all right!" Then McNair observes the painting of Queen Teia's coon cat; her coon cat's collar is identical but the stones are greenish."

"Your cat Bessy has a very elaborate collar, right, Sara?" Smithe asks.

"Um . . . yes. To be honest, I don't really know where it came from . . ." Sara looks at her father.

"Yes, that collar has been passed down, but I never thought anything of it, to be honest."

"I say let's go back to your place, Sara, and have a better look at your cat's collar," Smithe says.

"Yes, let's do that," Sara complies. "Father, you and Katherine can stay here if you wish. Just hang out in the hotel. I don't want you traveling again."

"That would be nice," Dr. Flanders says.

"Okay, then we will see you soon," Smithe says, "hopefully with answers."

***

After a grueling six-hour flight, Smithe, Sara, and McNair hail a cab to Sara's apartment. They are tired and hungry, but there's an electricity in the air, as they all feel they are zeroing in on the final answers to their questions.

Sara unlocks the front door and calls out to her cat. "Bessy, Bessy!" It takes a few moments before the fluffy animal scurries out into the living room and hops into Sara's lap. "My baby girl," she coos, and pets the cat's chin.

Sara gently takes off the collar and hands it to Smithe who examines it. It's heavy with twelve individual oval-shaped greenish stones and the leather is worn.

"Sara, do you know if this collar is the same one that your great-grandmother Teia had?"

"I don't know for sure. All I know is that when Bessy came into my life, my Father put the collar on. I don't know where he got it from, and I don't even think he knows, but it's clear that it is an heirloom."

Smithe examines the stones. They are dull and lackluster, but something seems off. He turns to McNair. "Can I borrow your magnifying glass?"

"Sure," McNair says as he pulls it out of his bag and hands it to Smithe.

Smithe observes the stones under the magnifying glass with scrutiny and says with confidence, "Uh-huh, just as I suspected!"

"What have you found, Detective?" McNair asks anxiously.

"There are twelve green stones in this collar that look alike, but two stones are of a slightly different shade of green that the naked eye would not detect."

"Can I?" McNair asks and holds out his hands. Smithe hands him the collar and the magnifying glass. After a moment of examination, he jubilantly bursts out, "Bingo! Twelve birthright stones of the children of Israel and two

Smithe provides the answer

Urim and *Thummin* stones that appear to be green, but I'll bet my life that they are black underneath."

McNair turns to Sara and says, "Can I scratch off a little of the stones with my fingernail? I will try not to damage it too much."

"Of course," Sara says.

McNair hesitantly scratches the stone and the finish is starting to come off, but it's still too difficult to tell. "Do you have fingernail polish remover?" he asks.

Sara plops Bessy down on the floor and rushes into the bathroom. There's rustling, and then she sprints back into the room holding the polish remover and a bag of cotton balls.

McNair rubs the stones gently with the polish and the cotton balls as Smithe and Sara watch in silence. And then, before their very eyes, the stones start to reveal their true self: jet-black and shiny!

McNair exclaims, "Well, I'll be a monkey's uncle! Meet *Urim* and *Thummin* everyone."

"Well, I'll be! They were here all along!" Sara says, amazed. "Let's call my father."

In a few moments, Dr. Flanders and Kelly are connected through Facetime. They reveal their findings. Dr. Flanders claps with joy and has tears in his eyes.

"I can't believe it! All this time and it was right under my nose!" he exclaims. "I'll bet Jeremiah colored the stones after that picture of Queen Teia was painted and the coon cat's collar was handed down through the centuries to the King David bloodline stemming from Queen Elizabeth I to our family."

McNair responds in his typical unflappable tone, "Precisely! Good piece of detective work, Smithe. Now that we have all of the stones of the High Priest's breastplate, I think we can stop this renegade antichrist."

"Yes, now I think I can stop Simonides because the breastplate must be worn by the King David lineage as well as having all of the stones. We need to stop this antichrist son of ours even though we brought him into the world," says Dr. Flanders as he looks into Kelly's eyes.

"Don't be so hard on yourselves," Sara says, "What he turned out to be was not your fault."

"I helped bring him into this world, but he is the devil's son and a murderer," Dr. Flanders says.

"My boy John," Kelly whimpers, and she buries her head in her hands.

"We're on the next flight out. Hang tight," Smithe says.

'Finally,' he thinks, *'this will all be over soon.'*

Chapter Thirty-Six

The next morning, Smithe, McNair, and Sara have arrived in Jerusalem with a new sense of purpose. After reuniting with Dr. Flanders and Kelly at the hotel, the troop has a renewed assurance that they can stop Simonides. Together, they head to Jerusalem's Temple Mount. The crowds have grown larger, and it's a bit more difficult to fend their way through.

Eventually, they find a less-crowded spot off to the side and wait. They can't believe their eyes how many people have come to hear this false cleric, but it is just as the prophecies predicted. They believe he is the antichrist based upon the prophecies that predicted the antichrist would perform 'false miracles,' 'martyrs' and desire to be 'worshipped.' They are convinced that they have to stop Simonides before the entire world is duped by his erroneous teachings.

"My followers, please allow me to heal this woman of her crippling arthritis," Simonides says, and the crowd cheers. Behind him, three armed men in camo gear scan the crowd. Additionally, there is a section off to the side where reporters are standing with microphones and cameras in hand.

Simonides places his hands on the woman's head and asks her, "Woman, do you believe that I am the savior that has come to save the world and that I have the power to heal you?"

"Yes, Simonides, I believe," says the woman as she gets up and walks as normal as when she was seventeen. She is ecstatic and runs through the crowd screaming as loud as she can, "Simonides has healed me. Simonides has healed me."

"I think it's time," Smithe whispers.

Dr. Flanders is wearing the High Priest's breastplate under a long robe with Aaron's rod firmly clutched in his hand. Careful not to draw attention to himself, he slowly makes his way to the front of the crowd to Simonides, who is performing fake miracles and deceiving the people into believing he is the Messiah. Dr. Flanders knows the Devil is the real perpetrator behind these miracles just as he was is the days of Moses and Pharaoh's charlatan magicians! He knows the Devil can appear to heal people, although this is not a permanent healing that only God can perform. However, he is not afraid because God is on his side.

Just then, Dr. Flanders and Simonides's eyes meet. Dr. Flanders slowly opens his robe to reveal the breastplate, which is glittering in gold. Those close to him take a step back, confused.

Simonides's eyes widen, and he looks confused, as he looks at an individual approaching him that he thought he had recently strangled. He squints his eyes in anger. He says with venom on his lips, "Who are you? I thought I killed you? What are you doing?"

Dr. Flanders declares with vengeance, "You thought you killed me? You mean you killed your brother just like Cain slew his brother Abel. You surely are the son of the devil! Now I am going to kill you through God's power!"

"Who are you? You can't be my brother!" Simonides shouts and is somewhat scared.

Dr. Flanders reveals himself to Simonides and says, "No, I am not your brother—I am your father, or I should say, I brought you into this world, but you are no son of mine!"

"What you say is true," Simonides sneers. "I am not your son. I am the son of Beelzebub, the god of this world! He alone is to be worshipped! Together we will make a better world, a world that will be one even as we are one!"

The final battle

The crowd is stunned and steps back further. It's quiet now. Dr. Flanders bravely stands his ground. He rips off his robe to reveal the High Priest breastplate in all its glory.

Simonides is quickly blinded by the golden breastplate. Then he turns to anger as he charges toward Dr. Flanders and slams into his stomach, sending him crashing backward onto the concrete surface. Simonides stands above him, smiling.

"You can't defeat me," Simonides sneers.

"We shall see about that . . . *son*," Dr. Flanders shouts. He rises from the ground and grips Aaron's rod tighter in his hand. Just then, the breastplate begins to glow and the stones of *Urim* and *Thummin* flash.

"You and your father of darkness will be one in death!" Dr. Flanders shouts. "Behold, everyone, the antichrist!"

The *Urim* and *Thummin* stones emit lightning bolts and strike Simonides in the chest. He flies backward and slams into the concrete steps. He rolls on the ground, grunting and moaning in pain.

"No, you can't defeat me!" Simonides shouts.

"He in heaven will never be defeated," Dr. Flanders says.

The *Urim* and *Thummin* stones once again pulse and emit bolts that shoot into Simonides's body and his eyeballs begin to pop out. His flesh melts down to the bone, and his bone oozes to and melts to smoke and then vapor. Nothing is left of him except the cloth he was wearing.

People scream and shout in horror. The world has just witnessed the demise of Simonides, the antichrist.

As the guards try to calm the crowds, Smithe, Kelly, Sara, and McNair rush to help Dr. Flanders side and help him up.

"Father, you did it!" Sara says, as she hugs him tightly. Kelly joins in on the embrace.

Sara turns to McNair with a confused look on her face. "I'm still confused about some things," she says.

"What's that, love?"

"My father's understanding was that the antichrist would be from the tribe of Dan, and that his bloodline being from the tribe of Judah would be able to confront the antichrist. Since my father traced his genealogy to the Judah/Pharez/Zareh lineage, how could either of his sons be the antichrist?"

"Remember the story of Abraham, how his two sons Isaac and Ishmael had an entirely different character?"

"Yes, but they had different mothers!"

"That's true, but then there is Cain and Abel, who had different character. And don't forget even the Devil is God's son!"

"So what you're implying is that even though an offspring can have the same parents, they can turn out differently," says Sara.

"Absolutely, and don't forget the mother's genes are also part of their makeup. The lesson we must all learn is that God is sovereign and that He has a master plan that sometimes we just can't fully understand, and so we must have faith."

Sara smiles at McNair and says, "Thank God It is finished."

Reporters swarm Dr. Flanders and everything seems to be in slow motion as Smithe tries to pull out his badge to fend off the madness. Yes, things seemed to have come to a close, but as Smithe knows, it is never truly over until he signs off on the final paperwork. And Lord knows that there are still many things to figure out.

It's been ten years since the new King has been crowned upon the Stone of Destiny. He just celebrated his eighty-second birthday and has been in poor health. The Stone of Destiny awaits the coronation of a new King someday, the Ark is in the possession of the rightful kingly lineage and Dr. Alex Flanders has royal blood in his veins—Who Knows?

The End

Author Ronald Wlodyga
At Westminster Abbey
In September 2018
Photo by Ruth Wlodyga

www.ingramcontent.com/pod-product-compliance
Lightning Source LLC
Chambersburg PA
CBHW070533010526
44118CB00012B/1119